DIGITAL DIPLOMACY

This book analyzes digital diplomacy as a form of change management in international politics.

The recent spread of digital initiatives in foreign ministries is often argued to be nothing less than a revolution in the practice of diplomacy. In some respects this revolution is long overdue. Digital technology has changed the ways firms conduct business, individuals conduct social relations and states conduct governance internally, but states are only just realizing its potential to change the ways all aspects of interstate interactions are conducted. In particular, the adoption of digital diplomacy (i.e. the use of social media for diplomatic purposes) has been implicated in changing practices of how diplomats engage in information management, public diplomacy, strategy planning, international negotiations or even crisis management. Despite these significant changes and the promise that digital diplomacy offers, little is known, from an analytical perspective, about how digital diplomacy works.

This volume, the first of its kind, brings together established scholars and experienced policymakers to bridge this analytical gap. The objective of the book is to theorize what digital diplomacy is, assess its relationship to traditional forms of diplomacy, examine the latent power dynamics inherent in digital diplomacy and assess the conditions under which digital diplomacy informs, regulates or constrains foreign policy. Organized around a common theme of investigating digital diplomacy as a form of change management in the international system, it combines diverse theoretical, empirical and policy-oriented chapters centred on international change.

This book will be of much interest to students of diplomatic studies, public diplomacy, foreign policy, social media and international relations.

Corneliu Bjola is Associate Professor in Diplomatic Studies, University of Oxford, UK, and author or editor of three previous books, including *Understanding International Diplomacy* (with M. Kornprobst, Routledge 2013).

Marcus Holmes is Assistant Professor of Government, College of William & Mary, Williamsburg, Virginia, USA.

Routledge New Diplomacy Studies

Series Editors: Corneliu Bjola, *University of Oxford*, and
Markus Kornprobst, *Diplomatic Academy of Vienna*

This new series publishes theoretically challenging and empirically authoritative studies of the traditions, functions, paradigms and institutions of modern diplomacy. Taking a comparative approach, the New Diplomacy Studies series aims to advance research on international diplomacy, publishing innovative accounts of how 'old' and 'new' diplomats help steer international conduct between anarchy and hegemony, handle demands for international stability vs international justice, facilitate transitions between international orders and address global governance challenges. Dedicated to the exchange of different scholarly perspectives, the series aims to be a forum for interparadigm and interdisciplinary debates, and an opportunity for dialogue between scholars and practitioners.

New Public Diplomacy in the 21st Century
A comparative study of policy and practice
James Pamment

Global Cities, Governance and Diplomacy
The urban link
Michele Acuto

Iran's Nuclear Diplomacy
Power politics and conflict resolution
Bernd Kaussler

Transatlantic Relations and Modern Diplomacy
An interdisciplinary examination
Edited by Sudeshna Roy, Dana Cooper and Brian Murphy

Dismantling the Iraqi Nuclear Programme
The inspections of the International Atomic Energy Agency, 1991–1998
Gudrun Harrer

International Law, New Diplomacy and Counter-Terrorism
An interdisciplinary study of legitimacy
Steven J. Barela

Theory and Practice of Paradiplomacy
Subnational governments in international affairs
Alexander S. Kuznetsov

Digital Diplomacy
Theory and practice
Edited by Corneliu Bjola and Marcus Holmes

'Rapid increases in the availability and power of connection technologies are changing the modes of international relations and the conditions for statecraft in the 21st century. This volume makes an important contribution to our understanding of how. This is a smart read for foreign policy practitioners and those that study them.'

— *Alec Ross, Senior Advisor for Innovation to Secretary of State Hillary Clinton (2009–2013)*

'This unique collection of case studies on digital diplomacy dispenses with technological determinism and concentrates upon the management of change across the core practices of diplomacy. As such, it represents a timely and indispensable intervention in an emerging field of practice and scholarship.'

— *James Pamment, University of Austin, Texas, USA*

'The authors in this book, academics and practitioners, do not only have an interest in everything digital. Crucially, they successfully marry that knowledge to a solid understanding of 21st-century diplomatic practice. That is what makes this book special and so far indeed a unique contribution to the field.'

— *Jan Melissen, Netherlands Institute of International Relations 'Clingendael', and University of Antwerp, Belgium*

DIGITAL DIPLOMACY

Theory and practice

*Edited by Corneliu Bjola and
Marcus Holmes*

LONDON AND NEW YORK

First published 2015
by Routledge
2 Park Square, Milton Park, Abingdon, Oxon OX14 4RN

and by Routledge
711 Third Avenue, New York, NY 10017

Routledge is an imprint of the Taylor & Francis Group, an informa business

© 2015 selection and editorial material, Corneliu Bjola and Marcus Holmes; individual chapters, the contributors

The right of Corneliu Bjola and Marcus Holmes to be identified as the authors of the editorial material, and of the authors for their individual chapters, has been asserted in accordance with sections 77 and 78 of the Copyright, Designs and Patents Act 1988.

All rights reserved. No part of this book may be reprinted or reproduced or utilised in any form or by any electronic, mechanical, or other means, now known or hereafter invented, including photocopying and recording, or in any information storage or retrieval system, without permission in writing from the publishers.

Trademark notice: Product or corporate names may be trademarks or registered trademarks, and are used only for identification and explanation without intent to infringe.

British Library Cataloguing in Publication Data
A catalogue record for this book is available from the British Library

Library of Congress Cataloging-in-Publication Data
Digital diplomacy : theory and practice / edited by Corneliu Bjola, Marcus Holmes.
    pages cm. — (Routledge new diplomacy studies)
  1. Diplomacy. 2. Social media. I. Bjola, Corneliu. II. Holmes, Marcus.
    JZ1305.D54 2015
    327.20285'4678—dc23

ISBN: 978-1-138-84380-6 (hbk)
ISBN: 978-1-138-84382-0 (pbk)
ISBN: 978-1-315-73084-4 (ebk)

Typeset in Bembo
by Apex CoVantage, LLC

CONTENTS

List of figures ix
List of tables x
List of contributors xi
Acknowledgements xiv

    Introduction: making sense of digital diplomacy 1
    Corneliu Bjola

PART I
Digital diplomacy: the policy dimension **11**

1 Digital diplomacy and international change management 13
  Marcus Holmes

2 Digital diplomacy: between promises and reality 33
  Sabrina Sotiriu

3 'Secrecy is for losers': why diplomats should embrace openness to protect national security 52
  Alexis Wichowski

4 Social media and public diplomacy: a comparative analysis of the digital diplomatic strategies of the EU, US and Japan in China 71
  Corneliu Bjola and Lu Jiang

5　America's selfie: how the US portrays itself on its social media accounts　89
Ilan Manor and Elad Segev

PART II
Digital diplomacy: the institutional dimension　**109**

6　Business as usual? An evaluation of British and Canadian digital diplomacy as policy change　111
Amanda Clarke

7　Evolution, not revolution: the digital divide in American and Australian contexts　127
Stuart Murray

8　The International Criminal Court: using technology in network diplomacy　145
Karen L. Corrie

9　When doing becomes the message: the case of the Swedish digital diplomacy　164
Jon Pelling

10　The power of diplomacy: new meanings, and the methods for understanding digital diplomacy　181
J. P. Singh

Conclusion: the future of digital diplomacy　199
Marcus Holmes

Glossary of terms　*207*
Bibliography　*217*
Index　*237*

FIGURES

4.1	Weibo entries of the Japanese embassy	77
4.2	Weibo entries of the EU delegation	78
4.3	Weibo entries of the US embassy	79
4.4	Route of reposting	81
4.5	Layers of reposting	82
4.6	Most reposted and commented on Weibo posts	83
4.7	Analysis of most reposted and commented on Weibo posts	85

TABLES

1.1	Relative levels of usefulness and tools/impediments for change management in diplomacy	24
4.1	Propagation route of G(roup) > 200	80
5.1	Facebook posts and tweets of America's selfie	98
6.1	Tweets published by DFATD, February–June 2012	122
6.2	Tweets published by the FCO, February–June 2012	123

CONTRIBUTORS

Corneliu Bjola is associate professor in diplomatic studies at the University of Oxford. His research interests cover the role of diplomacy in managing international crises, ethical dimensions of diplomatic relations and theories of innovation in international negotiations. In addition to one single authored and three co-edited volumes, Bjola has published articles in *International Negotiation, Hague Journal of Diplomacy, European Journal of International Relations, Review of International Studies, Global Policy* and the *Journal of Global Ethics*. He is currently working on a co-edited volume (with Stuart Murray) on "Secret Diplomacy in the Age of Global Disclosures", which seeks to describe and explain the objectives, methods, agency and ethics of secret diplomacy in the current global political context.

Amanda Clarke is assistant professor at Carleton University's School of Public Policy and Administration. Her research spans public management reform, civic engagement and innovation in public policy, in particular, where these subjects intersect with information communication technologies. Clarke is a 2010 Pierre Elliott Trudeau Scholar and holds a DPhil degree from the University of Oxford.

Karen L. Corrie teaches as an adjunct at Fordham University. From 2005 to 2008, Corrie served as an assistant district attorney in New York County (Manhattan). From 2009 to 2012, Corrie served as an analyst and trial lawyer with the Office of the Prosecutor at the International Criminal Court. She has also worked on international human rights litigation with the Open Society Justice Initiative and served as a consultant to the president of the Assembly of States Parties to the Rome Statute of the International Criminal Court.

Marcus Holmes is assistant professor of government at the College of William & Mary. Holmes is interested in diplomatic theory and practice and is currently writing a book on the role of personal face-to-face diplomacy in the international system. Holmes has published in many journals, including *International Organization, Journal of Theoretical Politics, International Studies Perspectives, Review of Policy Research* and *International Relations of the Asia-Pacific*. He earned his doctorate from the Ohio State University and was previously a faculty member at Fordham University in New York City.

Lu Jiang graduated with distinction with an MSc in global governance and diplomacy from the University of Oxford. She is currently pursuing graduate studies at Beijing Foreign Studies University. Her research interests include public diplomacy and soft power, and the use of social media in diplomacy, in particular.

Ilan Manor is concluding his master's degree studies at the Department of Communications at Tel Aviv University. Manor's thesis examines the manner in which foreign ministries use digital diplomacy in order to portray foreign countries during times of international crises. He blogs on matters relating to digital diplomacy, nation branding and the future of diplomacy (www.digdipblog.com).

Stuart Murray is a senior lecturer at Bond University, Australia, where he teaches diplomatic studies and international relations. He has published with Oxford University Press, *International Studies Perspectives, International Studies Review, Hague Journal of Diplomacy* and *Diplomacy & Statecraft* on international relations, positivist and postpositivist types of diplomacies, sports diplomacy, digital diplomacy and, forthcoming, on the relationship between secrecy and diplomacy.

Jon Pelling started as head of communication at the Swedish embassy in London in 2012. His main task was to develop the Swedish embassy's profile in social media and public diplomacy ahead of the 2012 Summer Olympics. Before starting at the embassy, he worked as a journalist covering politics and society for Swedish media from London, Europe and South America. Pelling has also written a travel guide on London. He has a degree in journalism and multimedia from Södertörn University and an MSc in global politics from Birkbeck, University of London.

Elad Segev is lecturer in media and communications at the Department of Communication, Tel Aviv University. He publishes studies on international news, web mining, network analysis, Americanization and globalization, cultural diversity, digital divide, search engines and search strategies and new applications and methodologies in social and communication research.

J.P. Singh is professor of Global Affairs and Cultural Studies at George Mason University. Singh has authored four monographs, edited two books, and published dozens of scholarly articles. His book *Globalized Arts: The Entertainment Economy and Cultural Identity* (Columbia, 2011) won the American Political Science Association's award for best book in information technology and politics in 2012. He has advised international organizations such as UNESCO, the World Bank, and the World Trade Organization, played a leadership role in several professional organizations, and served as Editor from 2006–2009 and dramatically increased the impact of *Review of Policy Research*, the journal specializing in the politics and policy of science and technology. He holds a Ph.D. in Political Economy and Public Policy from the University of Southern California.

Sabrina Sotiriu is a doctoral candidate with the School of Political Studies at the University of Ottawa. Sotiriu's research interests include nationalist movements and their usage of social media channels to construct and promote national identities and, more broadly, the overall influence of the Web 2.0 revolution on politics and the changing nature of diplomacy. Her past research has covered Western European nationalist parties and their ideological stances and, respectively, their relationship with devolution efforts/campaigns as well as the accommodation of ethnic minorities in federal and unitary states.

Alexis Wichowski is the director of media analysis and strategy at the U.S. Department of State's permanent mission to the United Nations. She is also an adjunct assistant professor at Columbia University's School of International and Public Affairs, where she teaches on technology in government. A former presidential management fellow, she has worked with various State Department offices focused on diplomatic use of technology, including the Office of eDiplomacy and the Secretary's Office of Innovation. Wichowski holds a PhD in information science from the University at Albany, where her research focused on online political communication. She also has BA in Chinese from Connecticut College and was a Fulbright Scholar in China in 1996–97. Recent publication outlets include *Foreign Affairs, The Atlantic, First Monday* and a co-authored book chapter in Wiley's *Handbook of Internet Studies*.

ACKNOWLEDGEMENTS

This project was born out of initial discussions that took place at the 2012 Joint Sessions of the European Consortium for Political Research (ECPR) in Antwerp, Belgium, which then led to an organized panel at the 2013 European Consortium for Political Research General Conference in Bordeaux, France, on the topic of e-Diplomacy and the International System. The overall themes for the book and individual chapters also benefitted greatly from subsequent presentations and workshops at the 2014 International Studies Association (ISA) meeting in Toronto. We would like to thank fellow panelists, discussants and participants in those discussions. Marcus Holmes would also like to thank the students of his 2011 graduate seminar in e-Diplomacy at Georgetown University's Communication, Culture & Technology program who contributed greatly to his thinking about the nature of digital diplomacy in international politics. Corneliu Bjola is particularly grateful to students of the MSc program in Global Governance and Diplomacy at the University of Oxford for their contagious enthusiasm for learning new things and for challenging established wisdom. In addition, we would like to thank Zoltan Buzas, Noe Cornago, Michal Onderco and Alex Wendt for feedback and insightful comments. We would also like to thank the three anonymous reviewers who provided useful criticisms and constructive suggestions, which undoubtedly have resulted in a stronger volume. Last, special thanks to the editorial team at Routledge, including Hannah Ferguson and Andrew Humphrys, who provided superb support and guidance throughout the publication process.

INTRODUCTION

Making sense of digital diplomacy

Corneliu Bjola

Diplomacy as a method of change management

As a time-honoured method of international cooperation, diplomacy has been often besieged by questions regarding the "magic and mystery" of how it works, succeeds or fails (Sharp 2009, 2). Bull's view of diplomacy as "the conduct of relations between states and other entities with standing in world politics by official agents and by peaceful means" (Bull 1997, 156) remains the most commonly used definition among diplomatic scholars, followed closely by Watson's characterization of diplomacy as the process of "negotiation between political entities which acknowledge each other's independence" (Watson 1984, 33). Both definitions have the merit to clearly capture a fundamental feature of diplomacy; that is, its nonviolent approach to reconciling interests among international actors, especially states. At the same time, they arguably fail to remove the veil off the "magic and mystery" by which diplomacy distinctly shapes conflict and cooperation in international politics. Foreshadowing Watson, Richelieu thought "continuous negotiation" was the key ingredient (Berridge 2004, 116). In his advice to a young diplomat, Machiavelli interestingly viewed "sincerity and frankness of great importance" (Berridge 2004, 41). Sir Ernst Satow insisted on "the application of intelligence and tact to the conduct of official relations" (Satow and Bland 1957). More contemporarily, Kissinger spoke about the need to correctly understand the lessons of history (Kissinger 1994, 27), while Hillary Clinton praised the virtue of "blunt talk" in advancing the diplomatic agenda (Raddatz 2009, para. 5).

The key point these scholars and practitioners seek to convey is that diplomacy, at its core, represents a sophisticated method of change management. Certainly, diplomacy involves a certain type of conduct between international actors, as Bull and Watson argued, but the success or failure of these relations is largely contingent upon diplomats' ability to properly recognize evolving power dynamics (hence the relevance of Richelieu's "continuous negotiation"), judiciously interpret one's aspirations in light of contextual circumstances (hence the significance of Kissinger's historical lessons), carefully assess the limits of one's capacity to adjust to change (hence the importance of Satow's esteem for intelligence and tact) and to actively enlist the support of others in promoting or resisting change (hence the insistence on communication clarity and frankness advocated by Clinton). The upshot of this argument is that managing change is a fundamental aspect of diplomatic relations to the extent that it may well inform the magic and mystery behind diplomatic excellence. This observation raises a crucial point. If the functioning of the international society is a matter of ongoing construction, legitimization, and adaptation of shared principles and intersubjective expectations of international conduct (Wendt 1992; Hall 1999), then how exactly do diplomats handle challenges to the status quo?

The theoretical literature on diplomacy has largely overlooked the issue of international change, preferring instead to focus, and often for good reasons, on understanding how diplomats define, orchestrate and uphold the international status quo. A rich body of knowledge has been developed, for instance, to explain the role and relevance for the diplomatic practice of various historical traditions (Berridge 2004; Sharp 2009), legal principles (Bolewski 2007; Chatterjee 2007), negotiation methods (Kremenyuk 2002; Wilkenfeld, Young, Asal and Quinn 2003), power relations (Freeman 1997; Melissen 2005), forums (Mitzen 2013) and norms of professional conduct (Nicolson 1957; Satow and Bland 1957). These studies provide an in-depth picture of the rational and social underpinnings of the diplomatic method, but largely from the perspective of how diplomats can better orient and adapt themselves to the constitutive rules of the international society. Even those studies that examine the more innovative elements of diplomatic practice (Melissen 1999; Kleiner 2010) emphasize the adaptation function of diplomacy rather than its potential role in steering international change. That being said, is there a theoretical difference the examination of international change would make to our understanding of the role of diplomacy in international politics?

After all, the proclivity of diplomatic scholars to structure their research around questions pertaining to the international status quo is, to a certain extent, theoretically defendable. As Headley Bull pointed out, diplomacy is one of the five major institutions of international society, the main role of which is to maintain international order. According to Bull, the latter is "*a fortiori* in world politics" (Bull 1997, 93), and hence diplomacy has a pointed status quo orientation of working towards minimizing frictions and maintaining international consensus, especially among great powers. The pluralistic and presumably conflict-prone nature of international politics, or as Martin Wight put it, "the realm of recurrence and repetition" (Wight 1966, 26), therefore predisposes diplomacy to principally serve as a method of protecting the status quo by anticipating tensions and preventing them from unsettling the international order, an aim that is reflected in our understanding of the origins and modern practice of global governance. Analytical neglect of the question of international change by diplomatic theory may come, though at a high price.

First, it leaves us with ad hoc conceptual tools, largely borrowed from the international relations (IR) literature, for explaining the relationship between diplomacy and international change. Theories of international norm dynamics (Finnemore and Sikkink 1998), institutional political orders (March and Olsen 1998) or foreign policy decision making (Welch 2005) provide, for instance, valuable insights into the topic of international change, but largely from the margins or even from the outside of the densely social and normative milieu of diplomatic engagement, a fact that significantly restricts their analytical value.[1] Most problematically, the dominant methodological individualist orientation of IR approaches by which outcomes are explained through the interaction of socially preconstituted actors, is particularly at odds with an understanding of diplomatic practice as a structure of social relations that emerges, not prior to actors' interactions but through diplomatic engagement.

Second, while change in world politics is driven by fairly complex and rather unpredictable factors, above all military confrontations, technological developments and social learning (Modelski 1990; Tilly 1992; Grübler 1998), the direction of change does not fall completely outside of human control. Diplomacy is particularly suitable for managing international change because at its core it represents a mode of understanding that privileges the plural character of human existence and treats as axiomatic the proposition that relations between groups are different from those within them (Der Derian 1987; Sharp 2009, 10). This condition of insoluble separateness among various groups ontologically anchors diplomacy as a method of institutionalized communication for mediating estrangement and reconciling differences (Bjola and Kornprobst 2013). In fact, all international orders established in the modern period have been the result of conscious and diligent diplomatic efforts to restore international stability and cooperation after periods of systemic upheaval (Ikenberry 2001). Paraphrasing Wendt, diplomacy is probably the only instrument by which we can expect to steer change along certain pathways in order to avoid really bad outcomes and hopefully bring about a few good ones (Wendt 2001, 211).

Third, a closer look at the relationship between diplomacy and international change can also prove theoretically enlightening for understanding who the diplomats are now.[2] The rise of new actors with international standing and the gradual transition towards a polycentric mode of governance (Scholte 2008) is already reshaping traditional diplomatic functions of representation, communication and negotiation and in so doing, the very status of the diplomat (Hocking et al. 2012). This begs the question of whether diplomats will continue to be defined institutionally by their status affiliation to the state or also pragmatically by the way in which they actually affect change in world politics? By altering conventional patterns of diplomatic interaction and introducing new meanings, perspectives and interpretations of what counts as conflict or cooperation in global affairs, this potential transformation of the status of diplomats may have tremendous implications for the constitution and distribution of relations of power in international politics. In sum, the examination of the relationship between diplomacy and change is pregnant with important theoretical and normative implications for the study of international politics.

Digital diplomacy: Harbinger of change, or protector of the status quo?

An excellent opportunity to begin bridging the "change management" gap in diplomatic theory is offered by the recent spread of digital initiatives in foreign ministries, which probably can be described as nothing less than a revolution in the practice of diplomacy. In some respects, this revolution is slightly overdue as digital technology has already changed the ways by which firms manage their business (Weber 2011), individuals conduct social relations (Couldry 2012) and states govern themselves (Mergel 2013). Governments and international organizations are now realizing that social media is also a potential game changer for how international relations can be pursued. In particular, the adoption of digital diplomacy, which we broadly define in this volume as the use of social media for diplomatic purposes, could change practices of how diplomats engage in information management, public diplomacy, strategy planning, international negotiations or even crisis management. Despite the promises that digital diplomacy offers for the conduct of international relations, little is known, however, from an analytical perspective, how digital diplomacy works, with what degree of success and wherein lay its limitations. This volume, the first of its kind on the subject of digital diplomacy, brings together leading scholars and experienced diplomats for the purpose of systematically identifying different strands of research on digital diplomacy and making them speak to one another.

The objective of the volume is to theorize what digital diplomacy is, assess its relationship to traditional forms of diplomacy, examine the latent power dynamics inherent to digital diplomacy, and uncover the conditions under which digital diplomacy informs, regulates or constrains foreign policy. Put differently, we seek to understand the extent to which digital diplomacy represents a critical point of departure from how international actors interact with each other as opposed to a more subtle form of protection of the status quo. As any new field of study, digital diplomacy presents both opportunities and challenges for researchers. On the one hand, it opens up an untapped repertoire of avenues of investigation into how digital technologies shape and potentially reset the practice of diplomacy, for better or for worse. These new areas of research may involve questions about how social media affects the way in which diplomats communicate with each other or with foreign publics, how they take decisions inside their own ministries, embassies and bureaucracies, how they build and maintain relations with other state or nonstate actors or how they handle the normative challenges prompted by this new technological development.

On the other hand, there is also a risk for researchers to be pulled into too many directions at the same time, a fact that may affect the coherence of the overall argument and potentially undercut the significance of the theoretical and empirical findings. Mindful of this tension, this volume is organized around a common theme of investigating digital diplomacy as a form of change management in international politics. Instead of focusing separately on how social media impacts discrete aspects of diplomacy (decision-making, public diplomacy, professional norms and so on), we examine two important themes, *policy innovation* and *institutional adaptation*, by which social media challenges the way in which diplomacy is conducted. At the policy level, we are interested in how social media affects core diplomatic functions of representation, communication and relationship management. At the institutional level, we explore the extent to which foreign ministries are capable and interested in adapting themselves to the social media age. This overarching framework is then used by contributors to explain important aspects of the relationship between digital technologies and diplomacy.

Marcus Holmes starts off the first section of the book on policy innovation with a chapter on digital diplomacy as an international practice. He challenges a common understanding of digital diplomacy as a mere cost-effective form of public diplomacy and instead argues that a more fruitful approach will consist of investigating digital diplomacy's broader role in the management of international change. Drawing from practice theory, Holmes delineates two types of change in the international system – top-down structural exogenous shocks and bottom-up incremental endogenous shifting – and argues that diplomacy is ultimately a way for states to effectively monitor and respond to, thus managing, these two types of change. Psychology and neuroscience findings suggest that states manage these processes differently because each type of change requires different responses. Exogenous shocks require relationship building and intention understanding, activities that are most efficiently conducted in face-to-face personal interactions. Endogenous shifts require the ability to synthesize and analyze large amounts of data in order to determine changing trends, activities that are most efficiently conducted with digital technology. Digital diplomacy represents the latter set of activities – the gathering and analyzing of data from foreign publics that accrues through listening to discourse on the ground. Ultimately, these insights point towards the emergence of a predictive diplomatic theory, where different sources of change predict different types of diplomatic response.

Sabrina Sotiriu notes the similarity between digital diplomacy and the Rorschach inkblot test, the famous psychological technique analyzing the perception of images. As a recent development, digital diplomacy has been interpreted, defined and understood in different yet similar ways by researchers and practitioners alike. She therefore seeks, in her chapter, to take stock of the policy promises and limitations of digital diplomacy by explaining the conceptual genealogy of the concept, describing what has been done thus far on digital diplomacy and outlining how the practice has been presented and promoted by its practitioners. By looking at the policy promises and realities of digital diplomacy, she argues that the latter is not an ephemeral trend in diplomatic practices. Digital diplomacy is here to stay, given the dominance of the latest technological revolutions and the increasing digitization of our every-day lives. She concludes the next wave of digital diplomatic strategies and policies might evolve in a different direction than that set by the current (Anglo American) champions of the practice. While the diplomatic promoters of digital diplomacy may have used an *ad hoc* approach, the "slower" participants of the game have dedicated more time to develop a wholesome digital strategy of communications and to incorporate more mundane uses into their digital approaches.

Drawing on her experience as a media analyst and adviser in the Office of Press and Public Diplomacy at the US Mission to the United Nations, Alexis Wichowski takes issue with the argument that digital diplomacy might compromise national security. She concedes that the digital landscape is a leaky place where unwanted disclosures can happen on a massive, national security-shaking scale. Wikileaks and the Snowden leaks are the most recent examples, but they likely will not be the last. Wichowski argues, however, that governments' temptation to retreat into a culture of secrecy is counterproductive. In her chapter, she makes the case of why more openness would better serve national security interests by detailing the rise of information-sharing culture, analyzing government pressures surrounding information handling, providing a historical examination of leakers and discussing why a culture of secrecy hurts national security. The chapter concludes with three recommendations for diplomats about how to seek greater understanding of digitally redefined threats and allies, how to engage with them like real people and how to take steps to reduce hypocrisy.

Corneliu Bjola and Lu Jiang's chapter focuses on the features that enable social media to play a transformative role in the hands of diplomats. More specifically, they investigate how social media helps advance foreign policy goals via three key aspects of public diplomatic engagement: agenda-setting, presence-expansion and conversation-generating. Empirical analysis of the strategies pursued by the European Union's delegation as well as by the Japanese and the United States' embassies in Beijing on the Chinese microblogging website Weibo reveal that EU, US and Japanese diplomats have creatively used social media to alleviate the suspicion of Chinese authorities, and in so doing they have managed to establish open communication channels with Chinese citizens, especially in terms of agenda-setting and presence-expansion. At the same time, the importance each party attaches to its diplomatic relationship with China largely informs the content and scope of its digital strategy of public diplomacy. The chapter makes two important contributions to the emerging field of digital diplomacy. Theoretically, it develops an original conceptual framework and methodology for assessing the effectiveness of digital diplomacy, both from the angle of the diplomats and of their audience. Empirically, it fills a gap in the existing literature concerning the use of social media in public diplomacy under conditions of digital restrictions.

Building on theories of impression-management, framing and nation-branding, Ilan Manor and Elad Segev seek to identify the recurring themes that define United States' diplomatic self-image. The selfie, a modern day self-portrait, is a prominent example of how individuals craft their image in social networking sites. But what happens when the self is not an individual but rather a country? Nowadays, governments and officials in different countries have warmly embraced social networking sites such as Facebook and Twitter as part of their day-to-day practice. Digital diplomacy channels operated by foreign ministries in particular attract wide and diverse audiences, ranging from private individuals, active citizens, reporters and policymakers, to other foreign ministries and embassies. Thus, official social media accounts are increasingly used as tools for presenting and shaping the images of countries around the world. By searching for recurring themes in Facebook profiles and Twitter channels operated by foreign ministries, one is thus able to gain insight into how countries portray themselves to the outside world in general, and to specific foreign publics, in particular.

In the second section of the book, we turn our attention to the question of institutional adaptation of foreign ministries to digital technologies. Amanda Clarke poses the question of whether digital diplomacy represents the mere digitization of the networking, influencing and intelligence-gathering activities that have long defined the work of foreign ministries, or does it signal the emergence of a more open, networked and collaborative model of international diplomacy? Focusing on Canada's Department of Foreign Affairs, Trade and Development and the United Kingdom's Foreign and Commonwealth Office, and drawing on concepts from the policy-change literature, her chapter responds to this debate. Using data generated through interviews and documentary evidence, Clarke first explores the 'mixed messages' at play in departments' own descriptions of digital diplomacy. On the one hand, officials claim that digital diplomacy signals a more substantive policy change, and the emergence of a more networked, collaborative model of international relations. On the other hand, officials claim that digital diplomacy replicates existing 'ways of working', but with a digital angle. The chapter next tests which of these 'narratives' is evident in these departments' use of Twitter, and concludes that, in practice, use of this medium does not represent a significant policy change. Instead, this component of each country's digital diplomacy strategies follows well-entrenched patterns of top-down, state-centric communications. Clarke concludes her chapter by setting out a series of research avenues to help researchers develop much-needed descriptive and explanatory theories of digital diplomacy.

Building on Amanda's conclusions, Stuart Murray examines the widening gap between foreign offices with advanced vs nascent digital diplomacy operations. By describing and critiquing the respective journeys of a digital diplomacy 'have' – the data-holic United States (US) and its Department of State – and a 'have-not' state – Australia and its Department of Foreign Affairs and Trade (DFAT) – Murray explains the digital divide by reference to a set of key factors: a government that values diplomacy as a key strategic asset and not a marginalized, backwater antique; a pro-digital minister and/or leadership; a history of innovation, reform and openness to new, revolutionary ideas; a realistic budget; the desire to harness technology to enhance flows of information between the Foreign Service and other government departments; and finally, a dedicated office of digital diplomacy staffed by young, entrepreneurial, Web 2.0 tech-heads. This fecund culture, in turn, generates new methods for diplomacy: social media platforms of ministers, ambassadors and diplomats, regularly communicating with thousands upon thousands, or innovative two-way communication processes that allow ordinary people (at home and abroad) to, at last, feel part of a state's once rarefied, elitist and aloof diplomatic machinery. The chapter finishes by offering a number of reflections on digital diplomacy, drawing broad, generalizable lessons from State and DFAT's respective journeys.

While digital diplomacy is being primarily discussed from the perspective of foreign ministries, we have found it important to include a chapter on how digital technologies is affecting the work of international organizations. Karen L. Corrie, a consultant to the president of the Assembly of States Parties at International Criminal Court (ICC), argues that ICC has become a significant force in international diplomacy. Its work has the ability to alter countries' reputations and to affect relationships between senior government officials from different countries. The Court's indictments of Presidents Omar Hassan al-Bashir of the Sudan and Uhuru Kenyatta of Kenya are prime illustrations of this. Because the Court has such influence, it must be sure that its work is as accurate, fair and expeditious as possible. In her chapter, Corrie looks at some of the technological advances that the ICC uses to ensure accuracy and fairness in its work, including rigorous evidence-management systems. She also examines how the Court has embraced new digital tools, including live broadcasts of ICC proceedings as well as YouTube and Twitter accounts, in order to ensure that public information about its work is accurate, widely available and free of suspicion of misinformation or manipulation. As Corrie concludes, these digital tools do make a difference. ICC depends heavily on State cooperation to enforce its decisions and execute arrest warrants, but States' participation in this scheme is voluntary. To encourage such voluntary participation, the Court must be viewed as legitimate, suggesting that is must both be a fair institution, and it must be seen to be a fair institution. Digital technologies can and do help the ICC achieve this goal.

Drawing on his experience as the head of communication at the Swedish embassy in London, Jon Pelling reviews the progress done in recent years by the Swedish Ministry for Foreign Affairs in the field of digital diplomacy. The chapter examines initiatives like the Swedish Initiative for Digital Diplomacy and Diplohack from a practitioner's point of view, and reflects on their role for institutional adaptation. For Pelling, a key question is how diplomats can embrace change in a way that minimizes institutional resistance and helps foster new methods for communication and relationship-building in a global context. He suggests in his contribution that the behaviour of diplomatic institutions and the way in which things are done is increasingly becoming part of the message it wants to convey as this allows for new forms of engagement and communication, thus creating trust, influence and legitimacy. In order to break through the noise, the Swedish Initiative creates content in collaboration with other stakeholders, acting as a platform for ideas and meetings in order to tackle global challenges of shared concern. In order to be successful, digital diplomacy thus needs to be informed by a genuine interest in other people, clear values and a willingness to learn.

In the final chapter, J. P. Singh describes how new meanings arise in diplomacy in highly interactive communication environments and the methods diplomats and scholars can employ to understand these meanings. Singh argues this dynamic can be conceptually captured through the concept of metapower, which speaks to transformations in collective identities of actors and their interests in the context of international interactions. Metapower works at both ends: it specifies actor understandings prior to diplomatic interactions and, more importantly, the understandings are amended as further interactions take place. Singh applies this concept to the case of digital diplomacy and finds that digital technology enables new forms of metapower that fundamentally change the way in which diplomats communicate and engage with each other. As a way of preventing communicational blockage, Singh suggests several methods, including field notes, ethnography, elite interviews and case studies, by which scholars and practitioners can make sense of new meanings in digitally information-rich and mediated environments.

Notes

1 Fore recent attempts to bridge the gap between diplomatic studies and the IR literature, see Bjola (2013) and Sharp (2004).
2 For a good introduction to the topic of the changing status of diplomats, see Langhorne (2004).

PART I
Digital diplomacy
The policy dimension

1
DIGITAL DIPLOMACY AND INTERNATIONAL CHANGE MANAGEMENT

Marcus Holmes

The puzzle of digital diplomacy[1]

Despite the significant changes in communication and transportation that globalization has brought to the world, the structure of international politics and diplomacy has, in many ways, remained unchanged. Today's leaders and diplomats travel the globe to meet personally with friends and adversaries just as their counterparts in the fourteenth and fifteenth centuries did. Indeed the stasis of diplomacy arguably goes back to antiquity and has changed only on the margins.[2] Peculiarly, teleconferencing and Internet communication technologies (ICTs) have fundamentally changed the way that business and other types of social interaction are conducted (Denstadli, Julsrud and Hjoprthol 2012), yet the basic process of negotiating while looking the other in the eye continues to dominate diplomacy efforts, both bilaterally and multilaterally. With the advent of these new communication tools, some have questioned whether these tête-à-têtes are necessary. Consider the recent United Nations Climate Change Conference in Copenhagen. Political pundits astutely observed the irony in negotiators travelling thousands of miles in high-emissions aircraft in order to discuss how best to reduce overall emissions. Similar criticisms have been levied at other multilateral conferences, such as the G-20 Summit. Critics of the 2010 Toronto conference asked whether it was wise for statespeople to engage in costly extravagant meetings at a time of global recession.[3] These concerns are important and go beyond partisan rankle. They are indicative of an important theoretical puzzle: why has diplomacy not been affected by the technological revolution?

One answer is that it actually has. While perhaps not affecting a core aspect of traditional diplomacy – the personal meeting – technology has affected the ways in which foreign ministries and departments of state do business. A survey of OECD countries' foreign ministries, **public diplomacy** scholarship and popular press and media suggest that e-diplomacy is not only a cottage industry of academic study but also a strategy that states take seriously, often at considerable cost and attention. The United States, for instance, as of September 2012, had over 150 full-time staff members "working in twenty-five different ediplomacy nodes at Headquarters," with over 900 individuals using ediplomacy at US missions abroad (Hanson 2012b). Other countries, diverse in terms of power, have followed suit, with the United Kingdom, Russia, Serbia, Montenegro and China all embracing some form of **digital diplomacy** strategy, typically including the use of social media platforms, such as Facebook and Twitter. According to press reports, around two-thirds of the 193 United Nations member states have Twitter accounts (though usage of those accounts varies considerably; Khazan 2012).

While it would be easy to dismiss such activities as a particularly thin version of diplomacy – forms of marketing or epiphenomenal activities to the core processes of international politics – recent political events and scandals, such as the Benghazi embassy attack and Edward Snowden leaks, suggest a more prominent and central role for ICTs in politics. Furthermore, as analysts of digital diplomacy have pointed out, ICTs, if nothing else, have facilitated communication between foreign ministries and diplomats in the field as well as communication between foreign ministries and local populations (Hanson 2012b). One of the insights from the 1998 East Africa US embassies attacks was the lack of effective communication channels within the State department (Hanson 2012b, 10). Similarly 9/11 highlighted the need for the diplomatic and intelligence communities to have access to each other, and pooled data, in order to perform effectively. The benefits of constructing ICTs to aid in this type of information-sharing was seen recently in the Boston marathon bombings. During the attack, the earliest information about the incident was being shared via social media nine minutes before it was reported by major news organizations (Rogers 2013). Today, the State Department maintains over seventy "communities" of information sharing, typically interagency in nature, that are used to provide a platform for analysis for policymakers at home and diplomats on the ground.

The existence of these activities and use of ICTs by foreign ministries raises deep theoretical questions. Are these examples of using ICTs by government tantamount to a new form of diplomacy? Or, alternately, are they simply moving existing processes online, with the fundamental meaning and significance of diplomacy remaining unchanged? Secretary of State John Kerry seems to share this view, having argued in May 2013 that "the term digital diplomacy is almost redundant – it's just diplomacy, period" (Kerry 2013). Nevertheless, even if he is right, what do technologies such as the Facebook, Twitter and secure networking interfaces *mean* for diplomacy, if anything? This chapter will argue that these questions can only be assessed by examining the nature of diplomacy itself. Whether or not the tools and technologies of diplomacy indicate transformation or have the potential to transform diplomacy depends first and foremost on what diplomacy is. What *is* digital diplomacy? Put another way, it is difficult to adjudicate whether Kerry is right or wrong and understand how digital diplomacy differs from traditional diplomacy without first examining what diplomacy, and diplomatic activity, is fundamentally about.

This chapter will build upon recent work that views diplomacy broadly as, among other things, a form of change management in the international system. Change is conceptualized here in two basic forms: top-down exogenous shocks and bottom-up endogenous incremental shifting.[4] Diplomacy helps to manage both sources of change, though there is variation in process and tool effectiveness depending on the type of change that states are actively managing. Digital diplomacy is defined as a strategy of managing change through digital tools and virtual collaboration. I argue that the tools of this collaboration, specifically ICTs and online communities, are most valuable for bottom-up incremental shifting, though under certain conditions they can be helpful for exogenous shocks as well. Contrarily, traditional diplomacy, specifically face-to-face interpersonal meetings, are most valuable for managing change that occurs through exogenous shock, though it can also be helpful for incremental change under certain conditions. I base my argument on insights from social psychology and practice theory, which present conditions for change as well as conditions for when change management will be most successful. In creating this argument, I hope to add to an existing and useful debate on the nature of diplomacy and e-varieties thereof, but from a different angle. As will be discussed below, the existing literature on digital diplomacy has tended to view its activities as the realm of public diplomacy. This is a welcomed move, but it has overshadowed other uses of ICTs in diplomacy. Put simply, to reduce digital diplomacy to public diplomacy is to miss much of the power and capacity that ICTs, such as social media, provide to states and other actors.

In what follows, I briefly review arguments regarding the nature of diplomacy and suggest that digital diplomacy has typically been understood as a form of public diplomacy. I problematize this characterization by turning to practice theory and examining sources of change that occur in the international system. I then develop conditions under which traditional diplomacy, the personal face-to-face meetings that have tended to dominate diplomatic activity through the ages, and digital diplomacy, the use of digital tools and virtual collaboration to further state interests, will be most useful in managing particular types of change. I utilize interviews conducted with current and retired high-level diplomats to intersperse empirical observations of the field with the theoretical argument I construct.[5] I conclude by suggesting what the analysis in this chapter might mean for the study of diplomacy and, in particular, predictive theory.

The renaissance of diplomacy and digital varieties

Diplomacy in practice (and theory)

Diplomacy has traditionally been dismissed in structural accounts of international politics as irrelevant, and as such, "rigorous theoretical and careful empirical work on diplomacy in international relations is extremely sparse" (Rathbun 2014, 22).

Structural theories, at least since Waltz, typically overtly or subtly reduce diplomacy, and its inherent dynamics, to the distribution of power, understood typically as the distribution of capabilities (Waltz 1979). This is the source of leverage for states and is, by and large, outside the scope of agency for any particular diplomat. Stronger states from a power perspective will have the advantage in a bargaining situation, whereas weaker states will typically be in a position where they must compromise. As such, negotiating power and the strategies that diplomats pursue are endogenous to the structure of the system. Diplomats are more or less along for the ride. While states may be able to send costly signals that convey their resolve, this is largely outside the realm of the activities of diplomats (Fearon 1994; Fearon 1995; Schultz 2001). Even worse, because individuals have strong incentives to deceive, or at the very least cloak their true views and intentions, diplomacy is often dismissed as cheap talk at best and potentially quite dangerous. Indeed, one need not look far for examples of diplomacy resulting in suboptimal outcomes for certain states. In addition, the actors of diplomacy, the diplomats, tend not to be imbued with the power of other important actors, such as statespeople. As Iver Neumann has argued, the diplomat is not a hero in international relations (IR) theory (Neumann 2012). Statespeople are understood as participating in the conveyer belt of power in international politics; the diplomat simply plays a supporting, perhaps even nonessential, role.

Further distancing diplomacy from mainstream IR is that the study of diplomacy has typically been undertaken by practitioners of diplomacy or historians of diplomatic practice. As Jönsson and Hall as well as Der Derian have argued, this means that diplomacy has been relatively resistant to theory-building, since practitioners and historians take a different perspective, typically a practice-oriented view, on diplomacy (Der Derian 1987; Jönsson and Hall 2005). IR scholars, on the other hand, have tended to be theory-focused, largely resistant to analyzing the discrete practices of diplomats for reasons mentioned above. The result of this is a relatively strict division, or dualism, between the theory and practice of diplomacy (Bjola 2013). Prediction follows theory in neopositivist models; consequently, it is difficult to make predictions about diplomatic practices.

Recently, however, this dualism and separation has been problematized and reexamined for a number of reasons. First, most generally, there has been growing recognition that structural theories alone have difficulty accounting for change in the international system.[6] The failure of IR to predict the end of the Cold War is often cited as a salient moment of recognition for IR theory (Bjola 2013, 5), which predictably led to reexamination of core assumptions and approaches of extant theory, including advances in neorealism, neoliberalism and constructivism (Cornago 2013). For instance, structure gained an intersubjective/ideational component to complement the existing material conceptualization (Wendt 1999). In addition to looking at structural factors such as diminishing capabilities or a dwindling economy that may have contributed to particular outcomes, such as the end of the Cold War, scholars have complicated the picture by investigating the diplomatic practices that accompanied the change itself. In this particular example, some have suggested that interpersonal meetings between Mikhail Gorbachev and his United

States counterparts, first in Ronald Reagan and then in George H. W. Bush, clarified intentions and made the transition out of the Cold War a smooth one (Hall and Yarhi-Milo 2012; Holmes 2013; Yarhi-Milo 2013). Put another way, there is growing recognition that diplomacy can help to increase empathy, develop trust and ultimately transform conflict (Booth and Wheeler 2008; Wheeler 2008; 2013).

Therefore, in addition to revisiting core concepts such as structure, anarchy and so forth, there has also been a Gestalt shift with respect to the role of individuals in IR, and specifically practices of individuals in world politics. Practice theory, which emerged out of the "practice turn in social theory," including Goffman, Bourdieu, Giddens, Dewey and so forth, seeks to bridge many of the dualist positions that obtained from constructivist approaches. International practices are defined as competent, usually patterned, performances of individuals and collections of individuals (Adler and Pouliot 2011). For example, international practices arguably "close the traditional divide between ideas and matter" (Adler and Pouliot 2011, 13). Practices are material in the sense that they are things that take place in and on the world, engaging the environment and structuring the environment at the same time, thus "changing ideas that individually or collectively people hold about [the world]" (Adler and Pouliot 2011, 14; Holmes 2013). Similarly, practices are both agential and structural at the same time, since practices, either individually or collectively, are an exercise in agency while constrained by structure in the form of standards of competence (Adler and Pouliot 2011, 15).

The link between practice theory and diplomacy has been particularly fruitful in a number of different areas. First, practice theory reorients questions about diplomacy's ontology away from understanding diplomacy through the lens of structural theories. Rather than viewing diplomacy as something epiphenomenal to power politics, examining diplomacy as a discrete practice illustrates its productivity in the international system. One of the important aspects of practice theory is the reemphasis not just of the individual and humanism (Constantinou 2013), but the specific effects of the environment on the individual psychology at the body level.[7] For instance, Ted Hopf combines practice theory with social neuroscience to examine the "logic of habit" at work in the international system (Hopf 2010). Drawing upon the social theorists discussed above, Hopf argues that habit, rather than consequences or appropriateness, drives much of international practice. This is reflected in the brain, articulated by dual process theory, suggesting that much of social life and social interaction is unreflective, automatic, unconscious and habitual (system 1), whereas IR theory has focused on the analytical, conscious, rational, controlled, rule-based processing (system 2); (Kahneman 2011; Holmes 2014). I have similarly argued how these unconscious processes are particularly important in face-to-face social interactions, such as interpersonal diplomacy, where individuals are able to unconsciously share information (even when they do not want to) about their intentions with others (Holmes 2013). Keren Yarhi-Milo and Todd Hall have investigated the emotional cues that are transmitted in interpersonal meetings (Hall and Yarhi-Milo 2012; Yarhi-Milo 2013 2014). These works suggest growing room for social and cognitive psychology in the form of investigating actual international practices of diplomacy, in order to understand outcomes.

Examining diplomacy as practice also highlights the links between diplomacy as knowledge creation and maintenance. While rationalist models of diplomacy tend to look at diplomacy as an act of negotiation, with both sides vying for the better position in a zero-sum game, diplomacy from a practice perspective adopts a broader understanding. As Jovan Kurbalija has argued, diplomatic practice is in some sense *about* knowledge construction: information gathering, automating workflows and routines, information dissemination and cultivating knowledge as a specific institutional resource (Kurbalija 1999). Recent studies of the role of technology in diplomacy have tended to focus on the practice of information dissemination as a type of knowledge management. The conceptualization of knowledge management used here is a broad one, referring to the multidisciplined strategy of capturing, developing and sharing in a way that helps to meet the organization's aims and objectives. From this perspective, knowledge management is not just about collecting, storing and analyzing data but rather controlling strategically what information is shared to the public, creating an important link between knowledge management and public diplomacy, as discussed below. This is viewed as a key benefit of ICTs and other information systems: at least potentially, the efficient handling of vast amounts of information (and subsequently, and arguably, knowledge); (Hanson 2012b). The advent of new web technologies included in the "Web 2.0" (DiNucci 1999, 32), such as Facebook, Twitter and so forth, have spurred much attention in how states are able to disseminate information of their choosing to particular constituencies and groups abroad.

Thus, the digital diplomacy professionals, referenced above, working in state departments and foreign ministries, are ultimately engaged in the practice of politics through engagement with foreign others, understood as a form of "public diplomacy" (Melissen 2007; Snow and Taylor 2008; Hayden 2012; Metzgar 2012; Cull 2013; Hayden 2013; Kremer and Muller 2014; Natarajan 2014). Digital diplomacy as a form of public diplomacy has generated significant attention and criticism, with views ranging from technology allowing "people around the world to obtain ever more information through horizontal peer-to-peer networks rather than through the old vertical process by which information flowed down from the traditional sources of media authority" (Cull 2013, 136), to claiming that efforts in public diplomacy often are understood as little more than top-down dissemination of (counter)-propaganda (Hoffman 2002).

From a public diplomacy perspective, then, the goal of utilizing ICTs, or digital diplomacy strategies, is the production, dissemination and maintenance of knowledge that helps to further state interests. The advent of these technologies has fundamentally changed the ways a state can both engage and inform foreign audiences:

> In the past a competent diplomat might have been able to reach hundreds and possibly thousands of individuals through external engagement. For

a rare few, it might have been possible to occasionally reach hundreds of thousands or millions of people via newspapers, radio and television, but that required going through gatekeepers.

Social media has changed this old dynamic. [The State Department] now effectively operates its own global media empire reaching more than eight million people directly through its 600 plus social media platforms. To provide a sense of the scale of this operation, this reach is as large as the paid subscriber base of the ten largest circulating daily newspapers in the United States, combined (although the impact and influence of the two platforms is likely quite different). This reach is still considerably smaller than Voice of America's estimated 187 million weekly audience, but [the State Department] has no editorial control over its content. After launching State's new Turkish Twitter feed Deputy Assistant Secretary of Public Affairs for Digital Strategy Victoria Esser put it this way: "We are always seeking to expand the ways in which we can inform and engage. . . . Social media offered us a way to do that in real time with much broader reach than we could ever hope for with traditional shoe leather public diplomacy."

(Hanson 2012b, 17)

One need not look far for examples of this type of information penetration. Indeed, any time a state strategically presents information to increase tourism, such as through search-engine optimization or targeted advertising, it is engaging in a form of knowledge management that is linked to public diplomacy initiatives with the specific goal of targeting a particular type of individual – the tourism consumer.[8] Similarly, other types of individuals can be identified and influenced through knowledge management as well. Tom Fletcher, British Ambassador in Lebanon, argues that by carefully monitoring "who to talk to and when to make the most impact," he is able to "[tailor] output on key messages accordingly" and focus on the individuals, or groups of individuals who can influence policy in the Middle East.[9] In 2009, President Obama released a YouTube video message to Persian-speaking people of world to mark the occasion of the Nowruz holiday. While the Iranian government did not necessarily appreciate the gesture, the target of the message, those who Obama sought to influence, everyday Iranians, did; according to Politico, the video had more views in Tehran than San Francisco (Sifry and Rasiej 2009).

This is not to suggest that digital diplomacy as a public diplomacy strategy is immune from critique. Criticisms of the use of social media in politics have included ineffectiveness and danger. For instance, Clay Shirky points out that social media in national politics is often viewed as an example of what Malcolm Gladwell calls **slacktivism** (Shirky 2011). It is much easier to join a cause on Facebook, for example, than to produce more effective **policy change** through costly means. Applied to digital diplomacy as public diplomacy, this is an important critique. It is relatively easy for the United States to produce a video message to be shown to Iranians, and indeed the low cost and ease of production partially explain the strategy's attraction. But real change on the ground in Iran likely would require much more costly activities, and thus YouTube videos could be interpreted as particularly low-cost, low-effectiveness slacktivism. Second, precisely because of the ease of use, social media can often get states into trouble. The infamous Cairo tweet from the US embassy in September 2012 provides a compelling example. After protests occurred outside of the embassy, the staff posted a tweet, saying, "We firmly reject the actions by those who abuse the universal right of free speech to hurt the religious beliefs of others." As Alexis Wichowski, fellow contributor to this edited volume points out, "the tweet made waves":

> The conservative Twitter-watching website Twitchy posted it under the headline "US Embassy in Cairo chooses Sep. 11 to apologize for hurt Muslim feelings." Republicans quickly called the embassy's actions an example of the Obama administration's appeasement of U.S. enemies, and the Romney campaign denounced it as "disgraceful." The White House soon disavowed the statement, saying it "was not cleared by Washington and does not reflect the views of the United States government." @USEmbassyCairo deleted the tweet within hours, and, according to media reports, within weeks the senior public affairs officer on duty in Cairo that night was recalled to Washington.
> (Wichowski 2013, para. 2)

As easily as states can tweet and produce videos, that is, create and disseminate information, they can as quickly find themselves creating problems with the very publics they seek to engage. As Doug Frantz, Assistant Secretary of State for Public Affairs at the US State Department, has recently put it, "I tell people never tweet anything you don't want to see on the front page of the *Washington Post*" (Marks 2014, para. 14).

Nevertheless, the move to investigate diplomacy as a productive and competent practice of international politics is a welcomed one, and delineating precisely what these new technologies allow states to do is important. Practice theory's emphasis on the individual, including the body, and problematization of basic concepts that we take for granted, such as the nature of diplomacy, help to provide a new and important understanding of just what diplomacy is. Yet, as I will argue below, while the emphasis of technology in diplomatic practice on the creation and dissemination of knowledge incorporates an important aspect of practice theory, it belies the more profound contribution practice theory makes to the study of international politics: theorizing change. Put simply, digital diplomacy is not just about dissemination information to foreign publics, it is also about effectively managing a specific type of change in the international system. By reducing digital diplomacy to public diplomacy, we effectively overshadow one of its most important functions.

Diplomacy as change management

In addition to a reemphasis of the individual and underscoring the problematization of knowledge creation and dissemination, practice theory offers a theory of change that is distinct from existing structural accounts. At first blush, change and practice seem to be at odds. If Bourdieu's *habitus* predisposes individuals for particular practices, and unreflective processing – acting on what comes naturally – accounts for much of what occurs in the international system, then *stasis* rather than *change* would seem to dominate. Put simply, a focus on competent performances would seem to reify existing order and structure precisely because "competence is always in relation to existing norms and mores" (Duvall and Chowdhury 2011, 349). Hopf's logic of habit (Hopf 2010) and Pouliot's security practices (Pouliot 2010) are excellent examples: stability and foundations are privileged over instability and change. Nevertheless, habits and ingrained practices *do* change, resulting in fundamental changes in social relations and material underpinnings (often in the form of bodily changes, such as neuroplasticity in the brain); (Doidge 2007; Holmes 2013; Holmes 2014).

In taking up the challenge of how this change occurs through practice, scholars have identified two distinct sources. The first is through the incremental change that occurs through alterations in daily practices over time. Incremental change is represented as a bottom-up process of individuals conducting competent performance of international politics in such as way that through both unreflective and reflective action changes occur in the international system. This is **international change** through quotidian policy-making (Neumann 2012), the everyday decisions of discourse, practice, exchanges, triviality, mistakes, slippage and so forth that at once reifies the existing order while subtly and slowly changes it as the margins. This is the realm of change through everyday life, invoked by social theorists as diverse as Michel de Certeau, Butler, Heidegger, Goffman and Habermas. Importantly, this type of change is endogenous because it results from factors that are internal to the local system; identities, for example, are both created and transformed by system that actors operate in (Wendt 1999). With respect to international politics, incremental change can be found in the day-to-day developments that occur within and between polities, such as public mood, changes in emotion or affective states or even subtle changes in the discourse that surround a particular issue.

De Certeau, for example, finds change potential in the ability for individuals to subvert the "strategies" of organized power structures through "tactics" that allow the subjugated to transcend the rules and transform norms. In everyday life, individuals develop alternatives to objects that may subvert their intended use by a more powerful actor. The city planner, for example, may determine what streets there will be, which direction they will run and so forth, but the individual who lives in and on the streets may creatively determine how they will live, taking advantage of opportunities provided by the system. In this way, people in everyday life have the ability to "poach" or recreate what they need from the system, often in ways that were unintended. While not necessarily a thick version of agency, and perhaps existing only temporarily, this may, through an incremental process, prompt social change. Put more generally, as Hopf argues, "by varying the stylization of our performances/habits, we often subvert, often unintentionally, the cultural norm that is materialized in them" (Hopf 2010, 544). In international politics, the norm lifecycle and discourse that features prominently within processes of norm acceptance and propagation is an excellent example. Norms regarding land mines and debt relief often do not arise through one monumental event that changed minds but rather through incremental, subtle and slow internalization. This involves working with individuals and groups to creatively find opportunities within the given power structure to make changes to social reality.

The second form of change occurs through significant changes to background conditions that make change in practices possible. These background conditions may change through exogenous shock, such as being exposed to "strange (unassimilable) and powerful (instrumentally and/or normatively costly)" events (Hopf 2010, 543). For instance, Berger and Luckmann theorize that liminals, those on the margins or thresholds of societal groups and structures (Douglas 2003), are capable of providing the type of innovation required for change (Berger and Luckmann 1966; Hopf 2010, 543). Bourdieu similarly suggested that *doxa,* that occurring beneath the radar, are only foregrounded "in the face of divergent, novel, or competing discourses and practices" that come through crisis, encounters with unlike others, liminals, and so forth (Bourdieu 1977; Hopf 2010, 543). Part of the reason change requires such powerful exogenous shocks is the material changes that occur in the brain (Adler 1991; Holmes 2013; Holmes 2014). The end of the Cold War may indeed be the type of exogenous shock required cause actors to reflect on current discourse and practice. Similarly, the Ukrainian crisis of 2014, with changing territorial lines and vacillating public policies away from the European Union towards Russia, represent another type of shock to Eastern Europe. These types of events often produce what Emmanuel Adler's has theorized as a "cognitive punch," an event that is so shocking as to cause a fundamental revisiting and change in existing beliefs:

> Dramatic events such as war, depression, acute hunger, or a large environmental accident such as Chernobyl may have the effect of a "cognitive punch," making apparent to political actors that existing institutions and types of political behaviour have become dysfunctional and can no longer deal with the situation in the old ways. A crisis is thus an environmental incentive to hasten the process or re-evaluation and change from one set of collective understandings or "paradigms" to another. It helps to show, in fact, that policies based on old analogies to the past are likely to have deleterious consequences.
>
> (Adler 1991, 55)

Thus, whereas incremental change is represented as a bottom-up process, exogenous shock change, on the other hand, is represented as top-down structural-level shifts that change the conditions and constraints under which individuals conduct those processes. Whereas quotidian change is a slow process, the latter occurs with more alacrity and drama. While difficult to define precisely, exogenous shocks can be conceptualized as events that trigger agents to intersubjectively interpret them as requiring change (Widmaier, Blyth and Seabrook 2007, 748). Critical to this understanding is that the shock is not necessarily just a material change but rather one of intersubjective ideational understanding.

Critically, with respect to international politics and practice theory, both forms of change need to be managed. Recent work suggests that this is precisely the role of diplomacy (Bjola and Kornprobst 2013). Corneliu Bjola, for example, argues that states manage incremental change with respect to the friend/enemy distinction through diplomacy. "Diplomacy offers a specialized form of knowledge for understanding how to draw distinctions between potential allies and rivals, and how to make and unmake relationships of enmity and friendship in world politics" (Bjola 2013, 19). More specifically, traditional diplomacy allows states to develop collective intentionality, which allows diplomats to both create and change relationships. This is incremental change, managed through diplomacy. Similarly diplomats manage change by assessing and reassessing the intentions of others in personal meetings (Holmes 2013). By routinized and regular face-to-face interactions, diplomats are able to understand where others stand and where they might be headed from a policy perspective. Intentions, in this case, provide insight into the incremental change is occurring among allies and enemies alike. Diplomacy allows states to both assess where partners and enemies are on a specific policy and where they are going.

Exogenous shocks, on the other hand, are typically managed through crisis diplomacy and conflict resolution (Kaufmann 1998; Reynolds 2007). Rather than assessing and responding to incremental changes, diplomats involved in exogenous shocks are responding to the changing of significant structural conditions, both material and ideational. When Dennis Ross and other diplomats under the George H. W. Bush administration highlight the significance of personal diplomacy at the end of the Cold War, specifically the question of Germany's reunification, they were referring to the need to manage the most significant exogenous shock to the international system in the twentieth century (Zelikow and Rice 1995; Bush and Scowcroft 1999; Ross 2007; Holmes 2013). While clearly this did not occur overnight, and the degradation of the Soviet economy occurred through incremental steps, the event foregrounded the taken-for-granted relations between actors, understanding of identities of self and other, and forced the major players in the system to reflect on their new position. As Mary Elise Sarotte argues, the fall of the Berlin Wall in 1989 required a new model for European stability and identity moving forward, a new model that would have to respond to the major structural shock of the Cold War coming to an end (Sarotte 2009).

The preceding analysis suggests that, from a practice perspective, at least two sources of change exist in the international system. Both incremental endogenous events and exogenous shocks have the ability to change structure, background conditions, habits, practices and so forth, and thus need to be actively understood and managed by states. This, I have suggested, is the role of diplomacy. Importantly, different sources of change require different diplomatic tools in order to

TABLE 1.1 Relative levels of usefulness and tools/impediments for change management in diplomacy

	Exogenous shocks	*Incremental shifting*
Face-to-face diplomacy	*High*	*Low*
	Relationship management	Cognitive capacity
	Intention understanding	Data asphyxiation
	Identity construction	Opportunity costs
Digital diplomacy	*Low*	*High*
	Relatively impersonal	Data gathering
	Bureaucratic nature	Visual analysis
	Unable to transform relationships	Theorizing correlations

be effectively managed. Incremental change is characterized by subtle and minute variations in quotidian practice that may be difficult to detect due to the vast amounts of data and information generated from daily political life that needs to be analyzed. The difficulty in managing incremental change, then, is on the "supply side": gathering and analyzing the data to supply knowledge creation is difficult. Exogenous shocks are more easily detected, when they occur, but managing them requires a challenge on the "demand side": major changes to the international political structure demands significant attention to reputations, negotiations, shared understandings and relationship construction (see Table 1.1).

These divergent requirements – supplying of information for assessing and responding to incremental change, and demanding relationship care for exogenous shocks – imply that different diplomatic tools will be more or less beneficial depending on the type of change being managed. As scholars in information systems and computer-mediated communication have demonstrated, technologies such as Web 2.0 social media platforms and virtual collaboration excel at data gathering and analysis though they do not fare as well when it comes to understanding and predicting intentions, managing relationships, reducing uncertainty and so forth. Conversely, social psychologists, neuroscientists and political scientists have repeatedly demonstrated that face-to-face human interaction excels that intention-understanding and relationship-building, while cognitive biases and limitations severely reduce our ability to process vast amounts of information effectively.

Digital vs traditional statecraft: A typology of tools and change

The amount of data generated from statecraft is overwhelming (Hanson 2012b, 21). As the recent National Security Agency (NSA) and Edward Snowden events/ debates have highlighted, at least in the case of the United States, information management and data mining are massive undertakings. According to *The Guardian*, during a single month (March 2013) the NSA gathered 14 billion reports from Iran alone. Pakistan created 13.5 billion reports, and Jordan another 12.7 billion.

While the information contained in those reports remain classified, and therefore the usefulness or even epistemological status of the knowledge created from the data cannot be known, the numbers provide insight into the amount of statecraft data that is mined on a day-to-day basis. Much of this data is accumulated efficiently through automated intelligence systems, though much remains collected by diplomats on the ground. The recent **WikiLeaks** publication of US diplomatic records illustrates the scope of these activities. For example, in April 2013 WikiLeaks published over 1.7 million diplomatic reports, covering the period of 1973 to 1976, implying an average of approximately 1,500 reports a day for that period of time. The number of reports forty years later is likely much greater.

This vast array of data is a stark change from previous epochs of history, where information gathering and data collection was a challenge (Bronk and Smith 2012). The availability of data to diplomats provides, as Ali Fisher, Associate Director of Digital Media Research at InterMedia, says, a tremendous opportunity. "From engaging with activists in closed societies to countering the efforts of Jihadist groups; there has never been a better time for diplomats to get into data" (Fisher 2013, para. 1). Today the problem is not too little data, but too much. Cognitive limitations to dealing with "information overload," "data asphyxiation," or "cognitive overload" (Pettigrew 1990), are sufficiently well known and so will not be belaboured here, except to highlight the need for information systems to help transcend those limitations. Effective use of this amount of data requires sophisticated use of visual analytics that help practitioners to transcend human cognitive limitations in processing information (Arias-Hernandez, Green and Fisher 2012; Dill, Earnshaw, Kasik, Vince and Wond 2012). By visually analyzing connections and changes in the data against baselines, through digital technology, diplomats and policymakers are able to, at least theoretically, gain insight into the types of incremental changes identified in practice theory. By moving the analysis outside of the scope of individual psychology, problems of cognitive limitation are overcome, making digital tools an ideal fit for assessing and managing incremental change.

One area where this type of data collection and monitoring that may be particularly promising is detecting changes in the foreign policy preferences, moods and attitudes of distant publics at the population level. As Sheldon Himelfarb argues, the last few years have marked a tremendous increase in U.S. government tracking and analysis of foreign publics:

> Over the last three years, the U.S. Defense Department, the United Nations, and the CIA have all launched programs to parse the masses of public data now available, scraping and analysing details from social media, blogs, market data, and myriad other sources to achieve variations of the same goal: anticipating when and where conflict might arise. The Defense Department's Information Volume and Velocity program is designed to use "pattern recognition to detect trends in a sea of unstructured data" that would point to growing instability. The U.N.'s Global Pulse initiative's stated goal

is to track "human well-being and emerging vulnerabilities in real-time, in order to better protect populations from shocks." The Open Source Indicators program at the CIA's Intelligence Advanced Research Projects Activity aims to anticipate "political crises, disease outbreaks, economic instability, resource shortages, and natural disasters." Each looks to the growing stream of public data to detect significant population-level changes.

(Himelfarb 2014, para. 5)

Traditional methods of measuring foreign opinion on a particular issue have been through sampling, typically in questionnaires and surveys. The advent of programs that can cull social media sites in order to, as in the description of the Volume and Velocity program, "deliver real-time situational awareness"[10] or construct a measure of policy opinion regarding a particular issue at the population level, means that traditional limitations in sampling can be overcome. Researchers are not dependent on *participation* for data, in other words, to analyze how individuals feel about a particular policy or initiative. This is not to say that there are longer selection effects (such as selecting only individuals who engage in social media, for instance), but that theoretically the sample size for researchers is exponentially enlarged.

Difficulties still remain, however. First, for all of the attention given to the ability to analyze this type of data, there have been few empirical results in foreign policy that have been made public, and therefore, little available to analyse. Put simply, we are still in the realm of promise. Second, massive amounts of data, and sophisticated methods to visual linkages within the data, are only as useful as the meaning given to those linkages by individual leaders and policymakers. Put another way, "big data" is ultimately about both the data itself as well as the analysis of that data (Russom 2011). The claims regarding that analysis have been profound: "In the next two decades we will be able to predict huge areas of the future with far greater accuracy than ever before in human history, including events long thought to be beyond the realm of human inference" (Tucker 2014, xiii). Others are less pessimistic. As the Google Flu Trends project illustrates, initial early success stemming from big data predictions may precede disappointment, since "patterns in data collected at one time do not necessarily apply to data collected at another time" (Lazer, Kennedy *et al.* 2014; Marcus and Davis 2014, para. 8). As Gary Marcus points out, the utility of big data relies on the correlations it allows researchers to find, while the usefulness of big data relies on what researchers make of those correlations (Marcus and Davis 2014). Creating relational data from a large unstructured data set is challenging for data specialists (Michelson and Knoblock 2008), let alone diplomats. As Ambassador Laurence Pope recently pointed out, with respect to big data, we will know it is useful when it can help us to answer important political questions: "Are there new ways to measure foreign opinion? What metrics can be extracted from Big Data? What are people in the Crimea thinking this morning, on the eve of a possible confrontation with Russian forces" (Bishop 2014, para. 16)?

In addition to the complex visual analysis of vast amounts of data, diplomats also utilize digital tools to perform less data-intense monitoring of important individuals and themes. Relative to "big data" this is a "small-n" approach. As *The Economist* reports, the US State Department monitors social media in five different languages and attempts to flag potentially important individuals that envoys can befriend online (Economist 2012). This type of thematic monitoring potentially allows diplomats to assess changing conditions, particularly in foreign public opinion, and react quickly to them. Tom Fletcher puts the rhetorical question succinctly: "Would we have been better prepared for the Arab spring if we had discovered the hashtag #tahrir earlier" (*The Economist* 2012)?

Interviews conducted with diplomats in the field suggest that this type of monitoring of social media, looking for possible sources of conflict and change, has replaced public diplomacy as the main value of the technology. As one diplomat put it, the use of Twitter is "more about listening than talking." Diplomats are listening for potential sources of change as well as trying to understand how various constituencies feel about particular issues, who controls information in local publics (i.e. the "information curator"), and who has the potential to influence policy. As Geoffrey R. Pyatt, the United States Ambassador to Ukraine, put it recently in an interview about the use of Twitter, it is a form of aggregation: "I've appreciated it as an aggregator of thinking on foreign policy issue" (Miller 2013). The aggregation comes from using social media as a "two-way street" of talking and listening (Miller 2013). Digital tools thus provide, at the very least, the possibility of assessing and managing incremental change through both sophisticated data mining techniques as well as more mundane monitoring of social media outlets. The difficulty diplomats often encounter when listening through digital tools is that there is a disjuncture between the speed of technology and the speed of the bureaucratic process. As the same diplomat explained, "the speed of Twitter is minutes, the speed of headquarters is still hours or days." As Doug Frantz argues, this inevitable disjuncture means that mistakes will happen, but a certain latitude needs to be given:

> Social media is an interactive platform, so if you wait to come back to the State Department to get clearance on how to respond to a question over Twitter it will take days if not weeks and the conversation will be over . . . So you want people to be engaged. You want them to be willing and able to take responsible risks. . . . Don't take a big crazy risk and try to change our policy on Iran, but if you're behaving responsibly, we can expect small mistakes.
>
> (Marks 2014, para. 12)

Nevertheless, digital tools provide diplomats with the ability to monitor potential sources of change in a real-time environment.

Managing change through exogenous shock is more difficult with digital tools. As suggested above, exogenous shocks do not produce problems of information so much as they produce problems of relationships. Questions emerge regarding how to move forward, not whether we are moving at all. Studies of social media platforms and digital tools when it comes to understanding intentions suggest that trust becomes a major issue to overcome in a digital setting (Wainfan and Davis 2004). Individuals may have difficult reading and trusting the intentions of others they are engaged with in an online environment, prompting serious concerns about the ability to manage exogenous shock change digitally. One reason this may be the case is that social psychologists, cognitive scientists and neuroscientists are increasingly convinced that face-to-face interactions represent a fundamentally different type of interaction modality with respect to a number of salient characteristics. The value of face-to-face interactions is that they provide information about the sincerity of intentions, difficult to obtain through other modalities. Hall and Yarhi-Milo suggest that personal interactions allow leaders to exchange information not only through what they say but also through what they do not say. "Facial expressions, body language, tone of voice, even unconscious movements or reactions" all provide clues to sincerity and intentions (Hall and Yarhi-Milo 2012, 562). This perspective was famously theorized by Erving Goffman, where the individual uses social interactions to derive truth about the interlocutor:

> When an individual enters the presence of others, they commonly seek to acquire information about him or to bring into play information about him already possessed. . . . Information about the individual helps to define the situation, enabling others to know in advance what he will expect of them and what they may expect of him. Informed in these ways, the other will know how to best act in order to call forth a desired response from him.
> (Goffman 1959, 1)

For the present, many sources of information become accessible and many carriers (or "sign-vehicles") become available for conveying this information. If unacquainted with the individual, observers can glean clues from his conduct and appearance which allow them to apply their previous experience with individuals roughly similar to the one before them, or, more important, to apply untested stereotypes to him: "The 'true' or 'real' attitudes, beliefs, and emotions of the individual can be ascertained only indirectly, through his avowals or through what appears to be involuntary expressive behavior" (Goffman 1959, 1).

Robert Jervis concurs:

> When an actor is able to directly observe one of his adversaries he will not only try to understand the other's general outlook, but also scrutinize those presumably uncontrolled aspects of personal behaviour that are indices to the adversary's goals, estimate of the situation, and resolve.
> (Jervis 1989, 33)

"Uncontrolled aspects of personal behaviour" include clues, such as expressional cues and voice timbre (Frank 1988), micro expressions of emotion (Ekman and O'Sullivan 1991; Ekman 2009), generalized facial features (Mondak 2010) and even deception (Ekman and O'Sullivan 1991; Holmes 2013). Precisely because these clues are difficult to control, individuals believe that they can take them at face value; they are "honest" (Heibeck and Pentland 2010).

At least conceivably, digital tools such as virtual collaboration through video conferencing should be able to replicate these processes, yet empirical studies suggest that they fall short. As Wainfan and Davis point out, the literature suggests that while the technology has increased greatly in recent years, there are still distinct and important differences between videoconferencing and face-to-face interaction:

> Although [video conference] image quality has improved since the early [video conference] studies, it is still difficult to maintain eye contact due to image resolution and the distance between the camera and the monitor, and it is challenging to interpret body language and gestures, especially as the number of participants increases. Mediated communication – even [video conference] – limits nonverbal, paraverbal, and status cues and reduces the "richness" of the information communicated. Studies show that [video conference] participants may have difficulty identifying a remote speaker, detecting movements, attaining mutual gaze, and gaining floor control.
> (Wainfan and Davis 2004, 19–20)

Furthermore, when engaged in video conference discussions, researchers find individuals tend to be less social and more task-oriented.

These findings suggest that while virtual collaboration is useful, particularly in the ability to bring disparate actors together to work on tasks independently in a shared responsibility environment (Wainfan and Davis 2004, 1), there is reason to believe that such collaboration is less useful for diplomats managing exogenous shock change than incremental shifting. Typically, virtual collaboration is utilized because face-to-face interaction is not practical, either for geographical dispersion reasons or cost. The preceding analysis suggests that it may also not be utilized in situations where intention-understanding and trust-building is required. On the other hand, for incremental shifting, virtual collaboration may be sufficient. As discussed above, incremental shifting is characterized by less concern regarding intentions, trust-building, and so forth, while more concerned with generating data and knowledge about subtle changes in the environment. In these cases, virtual collaboration may help diplomats to perform the very types of task-oriented fact-finding as which virtual collaboration excels. For example, with respect to the Ukrainian crisis of 2014, it is instructive that the lead policymakers and heads of state convened in Geneva to discuss intentions and craft an agreement. In an age of digital statecraft, traditional diplomacy was required to attempt to "deescalate the situation"[11] and develop trust between the parties.

This is not to say that digital diplomacy tools have no value in exogenous shock situations, though it is often difficult for states to know precisely what is occurring in terms of change. Not all examples of exogenous shocks are as clear as the end of the Cold War. For instance, were the problems encountered in Cairo representative of exogenous shock? Despite the problems that eventually would occur because of a particular tweet, minutes after the September 2012 attacks on US installations in the Middle East, the embassy in Cairo was utilizing Twitter to relay emergency phone numbers for US citizens. The embassy also criticized Egypt's Muslim Brotherhood on their Arabic channels and tweeted condolences after the death of Ambassador Christopher Stevens ("Virtual Relations" 2012). Thus, social media may have a role in managing the change that occurs in intersubjective structures and understanding between actors, though it may be only in retrospect that states realize they were responding to, and managing, top-down structural change.

Conclusion

This chapter has had two broad goals. First, I have sought to define and conceptualize digital diplomacy as a form of international practice that is not only a strategy of public diplomacy but also a mechanism for states to manage international change. The change considered here is rooted in practice theory, which focuses on the competent political performances of different types of actors, including individuals, in the international system. In doing so, I have identified two major sources of change: incremental shifting and exogenous shocks. Second, having argued that diplomacy is, in its essence, about managing both exogenous shocks and incremental shifting, I have developed conditions under which digital diplomacy and traditional face-to-face diplomacy will be most beneficial for change management.

By way of conclusion it is worth considering what the preceding analysis might mean broadly for the study of diplomacy and specifically for predictive theory. One of the interesting developments in diplomacy studies, likely because of the focus on the experience of practitioners and efforts at defining and conceptualizing precisely what diplomacy is, has been the lack of predictive theory. Put simply, we do not, as of yet, have a theory of diplomacy that can predict how it will be practiced or that can answer a number of salient questions. When will diplomacy be favoured over other forms of statecraft? Under what conditions will statesmen attempt personal diplomacy or shuttle diplomacy? When should states be expected to heavily invest in, and utilize, public diplomacy? The preceding analysis suggests some provisional answers.

First, we should expect states to engage in traditional face-to-face diplomacy when there are significant questions about the intentions of the other and concerns about relationship-building abound. We should also expect that face-to-face diplomacy will be less useful, though not useless, in detecting and responding to incremental shifting, and thus states should seek other forms of statecraft to manage that type of change. Most notably, because digital diplomacy is defined as the use of ICTs for information dissemination, collection and analysis, we should expect states with the requisite resources to utilize technology to manage change defined by incremental shifting. Finally, because ICTs and virtual collaboration tools such as social media cannot replicate the traditional face-to-face interaction experience, largely because of the degradation of information richness, we should expect that digital diplomacy will be less useful for relationship management during times of exogenous shock, such as international crises, and thus states will seek other forms of statecraft, such as personal diplomacy, to build and repair relationships with salient others. This is not to suggest that predictive theory should be the only goal in creating a theory of diplomacy, but rather simply that by delineating conditions of possibility, we can begin to point towards a comprehensive predictive theory that includes the conceptualization debates discussed above with testable and falsifiable hypotheses. This may have an ancillary benefit of increasing diplomacy's appeal as a unit of study for neopositivist-oriented political scientists.

Notes

1 There is little consensus on how to refer to the concept of digital diplomacy, or "e-Diplomacy," or even how to spell it. Traditionally the "e-" prefix denoted "electronic" as a way to differentiate traditional forms of communication, such as a letter, from electronic communications. Presumably, however, a cable wire could be classified as "e-Diplomacy" under this conceptualization. In response to this many authors have utilized "digital" to differentiate new forms of Internet-based diplomacy from other forms of electronic communication media. Social media is often included in the umbrella term of digital diplomacy. The two forms, "e-" and "digital" are often be used synonymously, though this volume will utilize digital diplomacy throughout (see also Dizard 2001).
2 There is evidence to suggest that diplomacy and diplomatic practices go back to tribal practices, predating European antiquity as well as ancient Asian civilizations (see Nicolson 1957; Bjola and Kornprobst 2013).
3 See, for example, "The G20 Summit" (2010).
4 The distinction between exogenous shock and incremental shifting will be developed in detail later, though, at the outset, it is important to note that exogenous shocks are characterized by unexpected or unpredictable fundamental changes to the way that politics is currently conducted. They are, to use the words of Markus Kornprobst, events that make "clear that the old ways of doing things have become obsolete and have to be replaced by something new" (Kornprobst 2008, 42) typically involving major structural changes such as revolution, war or natural disasters. Incremental shifting, on the other hand, is often less dramatic, more quotidian in nature and less obvious to the observer, though, as I will argue, possesses no less potential for eventual changing of structures and practices.
5 Interviews conducted with current and ex-diplomats in Washington, DC; New York, NY; and Geneva, Switzerland, in February 2010 and March 2011.
6 However, see Wendt (1999).
7 However, for a more skeptical view, see Ringmar (2014).
8 See the recent edited volume (Egashiru 2013), particularly the chapter by Taudes and Tanaka, comparing e-tourism strategies between Hokkaido and Austria.

9 See Tom Fletcher interview, "Identifying & Engaging with Influencers in the Middle East," at the Foreign & Commonwealth Office: Accessed September 10, 2014. http://blogs.fco.gov.uk/digitaldiplomacy/case-study/identifying-engaging-with-influencers-in-the-middle-east/.
10 See Information Volume & Velocity (IV2), Solicitation Number DTOMC35011_SS_IV2, from Defense Information Systems Agency: www.fbo.gov/index?s=opportunity&mode=form&id=6fda262f46fab5f5273c18b1607e079d&tab=core&_cview=0. Accessed May 2, 2014.
11 President Obama Press Conference, April 17, 2014: www.whitehouse.gov/the-press-office/2014/04/17/press-conference-president-41714.

2
DIGITAL DIPLOMACY
Between promises and reality

Sabrina Sotiriu

In many respects, digital diplomacy is similar to the Rorschach inkblot test, the famous psychological technique analyzing the perception of images. As a recent development, **digital diplomacy** has been interpreted, defined and understood in different yet similar ways by researchers and practitioners alike. As such, there is no widely accepted theoretical framework that covers the concept; instead, digital diplomacy, so far as it is understood currently, has been defined by scholars and journalists independently unfolding their understanding from the ground up from how they perceived digital diplomacy to be implemented in some case studies. Like the subjects and samples of the Rorschach test, there does not seem to be universal agreement on what digital diplomacy stands for, what it represents, its importance and its comprising elements. As such, digital diplomacy has not been adopted and developed after a common blueprint. Given the individual interests of each of the major players and their particular situations, the pioneers of the practice have only followed some of the initial steps undertaken by others, with the final result, not being completed yet and ready for mass distribution. This illustrates the overall theme of the book of **diplomacy as change management**, namely, how the practice has dealt with the changes that it encountered throughout history, be they socio-political or technological, and how these changes have been managed internationally and inter-nationally. In this latter case, as probably in most others, the change has encountered a two-fold reaction, both one of acceptance, and a resilience and fear as to its unknown results and implications.

Unlike the Rorschach test, digital diplomacy is not several decades old, having first been developed in the United States little over a decade ago. Despite this, both have been continually analyzed and questioned despite the differences in their "age". Digital diplomacy has been built on recent diplomatic conceptual and empirical developments such as **public diplomacy** or soft power. These two specifically have often been seen intrinsically connected with digital diplomacy, and analyzed in conjunction with them, given the spill-over of technological innovations into how states carry out their business both inside and outside their borders. This chapter will illustrate the overall theme of the book, of diplomacy as change management, by pointing to digital diplomacy as the latest development to which the practice has been slowly adapting, while at the same time providing an overall perspective on how digital diplomacy has been understood thus far by researchers and practitioners, and how it has been advocated for by its proponents. It is important to understand the reasons why digital diplomacy will remain overall an accepted reality, and as such it will need to be understood in its entirety, both theoretically and empirically.

At the same time, this chapter will also point to the distinction between the promises championed by the supporters of the practice and the realities mirroring these promises, including the instances where it has been deemed by observers to have been successful, or where it has failed. These promises have included a causal link between digital diplomacy and greater interest and participation in policymaking; expanded platforms on which to apply **nation branding**; and an increase in popularity of the diplomat as a national messenger and of his or her home country's policies. In reality, the empirical use of digital diplomacy has brought with it factors and circumstances unaccounted for theoretically. Specifically, while theoretically the emphasis has laid with the public-diplomacy and soft-power aspects of the practice, in reality the spotlight was focused on the security issues and national interests surrounding the digital aspects of diplomacy. Among these factors is the challenge of reliably and impartially measuring the impact of digital diplomacy, both on a short term as well as on a long term, for the governments employing it, beyond the connectivity and tenacity of the social media users. The overall Internet freedom agenda is a distinct example of the discrepancy between an idealistic official rhetoric and the realities of national and international security issues and stakeholders. Despite this, and the fact that it is a new practice, digital diplomacy has been analyzed from the bottom up, and has flourished from trial-run experiments in a wide variety of situations and circumstances, out of which lessons were documented, successes were streamlined and failures quickly curbed and brushed under the rug. That is to say, theoretical and empirical developments have been tightened and improved from the practical use and realities of digital diplomacy, and not the other way around, and this is an important distinction to keep in mind when analyzing and criticizing the approach, especially given the methodological uncertainties surrounding it.

The chapter overview will present a wide variety of perspectives, mostly from secondary sources, since looking at the primary means of digitization employed by the practitioners would not bring much help with the analysis. This is not intended to be an exhaustive analysis of digital diplomacy, given that international developments, as well as technological improvements, have led to perpetually refining foreign digital strategies and ever-evolving scholarly research on the topic. Furthermore, by looking at the promises and realities of digital diplomacy, I will also pinpoint the reasons why digital diplomacy is not an ephemeral trend in diplomatic practices and why it is here to stay, given the inevitability and dominance of the latest technological revolutions and the increasing digitization of our everyday lives. Finally, I must openly acknowledge my own stance with respect to the practice – I stand as a careful supporter of digital diplomacy when it is implemented prudently, based on common strategies widely dispersed amongst a country's practitioners, incorporating lessons learnt from other states. The United States, as the first proponent of the practice, has been seen as initially having had an *ad hoc* approach, given the novelty of the idea and the ways of implementing it since the end of the George W. Bush era. As such, I make no judgement here over how digital diplomacy has come about, or why. Instead, my intention is to expose the lessons to be learnt, and the realities that came about from the promises made by the United States, and other countries, in championing digital diplomacy.

Theoretical beginnings

Conceptually, digital diplomacy has been used interchangeably with other terms that include e-diplomacy, cyber diplomacy or **twiplomacy**,[1] which target its exclusive online dimension and nature. Among some of the definitions proposed so far, digital diplomacy has been presented as the use of the Internet and information communications technology in order to carry out diplomatic objectives (Hanson 2010), or to solve foreign policy problems (Foreign Commonwealth Office 2012), and this will be the definition employed in this discussion. In another chapter in this volume, fellow contributor Marcus Holmes acknowledges digital diplomacy as a "strategy of managing change through digital tools and virtual collaborations" (Holmes, Chapter 1, this volume), adding an emphasis to the inherent collaborative nature of diplomacy both online and offline, which the digital does not affect in any way. Most definitions explicitly avoid linking digital diplomacy with the specific social media platforms with which it has been nonetheless closely associated at times in popular opinion, partially through the mistakenly synonymous use of twiplomacy, or the narrow emphasis of certain social media platforms such as Twitter, given the mundane uses of diplomatic practitioners.[2] As mentioned above, digital diplomacy can, and should, be understood and employed as a novel and practical extension of the soft power and public diplomacy concepts. The rest of this section will focus on these two building blocks of digital diplomacy, with which we can understand how digital diplomacy has been developed, and also why its supporters have made the promises that they made and employed the discourse that they did.

Initially coined by Joseph Nye in 1990, as an effect of the end of the Cold War, he defined soft power to mean the ability to set the agenda in world politics through persuasion, enticing and attracting others through the force of one's beliefs, values and ideas, and not through military or economic coercion (Nye 1990, 176). Two decades later, the concept has been included into the newer diplomatic buzzword **smart power**, which Nye also describes as "the ability to combine hard and soft power resources into effective strategies" and advises that it should be seen mostly as a practice of power conversion, the first step of which is understanding the "full range of power resources and the problems of combining them effectively in various contexts" (Nye 2013, 565). Outside the academic circles, smart power has been particularly seen as "using the full range of new tools to protect U.S. interests and leverage influence abroad – including through public diplomacy and social media sites" (Filiatrault 2012, para. 5) in order to "reach out to both friends and adversaries, to bolster old alliances and forge new ones" (para. 22). As such, its utilitarian nature has benefited the diplomatic circles which have embraced it, more so in industrialized states first, but slowly, to increasing degrees, by countries in the Global South. Given the academic root of the concept, it is of little surprise that the United States has championed it and incorporated it in its diplomatic discourse and digital practices. That being said, while a good part of this chapter will touch upon the Anglo American management of the diplomatic practices and guidelines of engagement, the lessons exposed, promises made and realities uncovered should not be understood as being limited exclusively to these cases, since other middle and small powers have become active players in digital diplomacy too, including Italy, Canada, the Scandinavian countries, Israel and others.

In addition to smart and soft power, digital diplomacy has also evolved from a recent, nontraditional form of the diplomatic practice, public diplomacy. While also not clearly and universally defined, for the purposes of this analysis, public diplomacy will be accepted as an "instrument used by states . . . to understand cultures, attitudes, and behaviour; build and manage relationships; and influence thoughts and mobilize actions to advance their interests and values" (Melissen 2013, 436). The practice of public diplomacy has also gained popularity since its inception because it has signalled a repeated institutional decentralization of expertise and information from the central/national diplomatic headquarters to their local representatives, given their increased abilities for understanding, networking and data gathering on the ground. Bringing the public at large into the diplomatic equation has also increased the number of stakeholders participating in international diplomacy, from state-to-state interactions, to international organizations and international non-governmental organizations. More recently, this has included the everyday people, which diplomats in most cases have relied on for their reinforcing, or diverging, views on a number of issues. Connecting with people under the conceptual umbrella of public diplomacy has somewhat altered the 'old school' perception that diplomats only interact with certain echelons of society. With the general public in play now as an actor, diplomats have become accustomed to listening to them and trying to shape their opinion, while at the same time knowing that this would affect governmental policies in democracies, sooner or later. On the other hand, some countries employed public diplomacy for self-branding purposes, or for strategic purposes, especially the Central and Eastern European states prior to their accession to the EU and NATO. As such, public diplomacy can be understood overall as the strategy by which soft power can be most efficiently maximized. If one throws the Web 2.0 revolution[3] in this mix, meaning the rise in popularity of social media platforms, websites and digital applications, the contour of digital diplomacy starts to appear, tying public diplomacy and soft power together, without yet any of the specific strategies around the practice having been drawn up by individual foreign affairs ministries. As such, one of the main interconnected themes of this chapter will be the public diplomacy aspect/side of digital diplomacy and how closely linked the two are.

A number of the practical goals or factors behind public diplomacy can be distinctively linked with the digital strategies developed by the Foreign and Commonwealth Office (FCO) in the United Kingdom, or the State Department in the United States. As an example, some of the broad steps to be followed in any digital diplomacy activity by the FCO include, in no particular order: *listening* to the angles and tones involved in the discussions of issues; actively *publishing* and pushing the UK's message across the FCO's global web involvement; *engaging* relevant organizations and online groups to encourage debate and foster partnerships; and *evaluating* goals, targets and ways of improvement (Foreign Commonwealth Office 2012, emphasis added). Most of the emphasized verbs do link these goals to public diplomacy directly, while the technological platforms offer the digital medium on which the steps can be achieved. Across the Atlantic, the core of American digital diplomacy efforts have relied on the belief that the Web 2.0 revolution has permeated our everyday lives in ways unthinkable previously, and that it is a permanent technological feature that should be utilized and not avoided. Implementation guidelines at the US State Department are similar to those of the FCO, yet the voracity in their approaches has slightly differed thus far, which has also had an impact on the media and academic attention awarded. As such, the greatest debaters on digital diplomacy have both been American, and in the next section I will briefly present their focal areas of discontent before outlining some of the promises and realities that have emerged so far in parallel to, but not necessarily as a result of, this debate.

Ross v. Morozov

Outside the academic circles, stakeholders have touched upon the role of digital diplomacy with respect to the more 'traditional' (nonpublic) aspects of the practice, whether it is complementary or predominant to the closed-door forms of diplomatic approaches. In other words, the main debate around digital diplomacy has boiled down to issues of change versus continuity with respect to the traditional forms of conducting diplomatic relations, whether bilateral, trilateral, or multilateral. One of the greatest spokespersons of digital diplomacy has been Alec Ross, former senior advisor for innovation at the State Department under Secretary Hillary Clinton, who famously and repeatedly stated that "the twenty first century is a terrible time to be a control freak" (Lichtenstein 2010, para. 28). This is important on two levels: first in that it directs attention to the nature of contemporary societies and states whether they are open and closed with regards to the flow of information and their position on the democratic spectrum, and, second, that there needs to be acceptance of an individual and collective loss of control of public messaging and audiences, given the instant dissemination of knowledge that the Internet has brought with it. Controlling the diplomatic message, or lack thereof, has thus been an unusual issue to deal with by an overall conservative profession adverse to sudden changes. This can be seen in the great length of time that it has taken for technological advances to catch up to diplomatic bureaucrats and become part of their professional lives and duties.[4] If at first the topic of Internet freedom had been one of the staple pillars of public diplomacy, especially under Hillary Clinton at State, this soon backfired against the overall government machinery after both the **WikiLeaks** Cablegate scandal and Edward Snowden's revelations, in light of how the American government dealt with the situation and the discourse and views that emerged from it. (A more in-depth discussion of this can be found in the Realities section of this chapter.)

Ross, among others, accepted that digital diplomacy should, and is meant to, complement, not replace, the traditional practices of diplomacy "behind closed doors along the corridors of power" (Gustin 2011, para. 1). This is understood so since digital diplomacy uses "widely available technologies to reach out to citizens, companies and other non-state actors", while "offline" diplomacy still reflects the "world of communiqués, diplomatic cables and slow government-to-government negotiations, [or] what Ross likes to call 'white guys with white shirts and red ties talking to other white guys with white shirts and red ties, with flags in the background, determining the relationships'" (Lichtenstein 2010, para. 7). The new concept represents for its proponents a shift in form and strategy, in a way to "amplify traditional diplomatic efforts, develop tech-based policy solutions and encourage cyber-activism" (Lichtenstein 2010, para. 8), and builds on traditional diplomacy, to account for the technologies, networks and demographics of today. Moreover, despite the change in the modes and orders of the practice, and to reduce doubts, supporters of digital diplomacy have repeatedly sustained that the communications objectives of international diplomats have arguably not changed, despite the fact that the medium has (Conti 2011). Arguably, this has been emphasized to diminish fears about the importance and effects of digital diplomacy on the core diplomatic practices, pointing to the changes in packaging, but not messaging, and this could be seen in the way through which most social media channels have been used, as extended "tentacles" of a government's message and projection of values and policies. Examples of this can be seen on the official channels of most Western foreign affairs ministries, where they link their news releases, travel updates, latest statements, advisories etc. or emphasize the digital efforts of their missions abroad (either by rotation or circumstantially).

Finally, it is important to point out here the role of the medium and what it represents for digital diplomacy advocates. As the national hub of, and source for, the predominant elements of the Web 2.0 revolution, the recent technological innovations have benefited from considerable attention from US governmental institutions that recognized these would continuously gain traction not just within America's borders. Here the State Department, under Barack Obama and Hillary

Clinton's leadership, was seen as the main force behind the promotion of social media companies, brands and platforms, both internally as well as internationally. Partially the stardom-like status of Secretary Clinton prevailed over the rest of the cabinet, including the hard power departments and agencies that of course were reticent to embrace the new media for non-soft tactics. As such, ignoring these technological developments was also seen as rejecting private sector success from which other states could benefit more. Thus, thanks to the digital channels implemented within foreign services, previously unimaginable audiences (societies at large) have since become targets for the digital diplomats, which otherwise would have remained largely unengaged directly through traditional diplomacy. Here one can only point to the US State Department employees acting as bloggers in Arabic, Urdu and Somali in the Arab blogosphere, in order to counter online extremism while also publicly dismissing false claims and openly disclosing themselves as official voices for the American government (Barton 2012).

Internally as well, digital diplomacy has benefited diplomatic corps and foreign service bureaucrats within their respective institutions, by improving institutional coordination through elevated information sharing as well as information availability/centralization. As such, the US State Department benefits from several tools to improve interagency knowledge management that include Corridor, Communities@State, and Diplopedia (Hanson 2012b, 10). Briefly, Corridor is an "internal professional networking site" similarly looking to Facebook, where meeting minutes and other knowledge and information can be shared both with all State employees as well as smaller, more focused groups; and where colleagues with specific skill sets can be sought for particular projects (Hanson 2012b, 11). Diplopedia, not as new as Corridor, is the internal wiki of the State Department, serving as the "central repository for State Department information, particularly useful when dealing with irregular or unfamiliar issues such as administering the foreign service officer test" (Hanson 2012b, 12). Finally, Communities@State is the oldest tool of the three, and consists of issue-specific blogs that cover a broad range of areas, from policy and management to language and social interests (Hanson 2012b, 13). Communities enable a quick and means of inter/intradepartmental collaboration on any topic (Hanson 2012b, 14); they also facilitate "knowledge retention, by allowing experienced officers who are rotated out of a position to continue to contribute their expertise via the community group" and are more advantageous than Corridor groups because they allow "for more detailed discussions that are more permanent in nature (and are archived and searchable for future reference)" (Hanson 2012b, 14).

The soft rhetoric embracing the digital revolutions within the diplomatic corps has made some observers sceptical not only of the benefits and purposes of digital diplomacy for the diplomatic craft but also for the legitimacy of states' powers, again with respect to the old-school diplomatic practices repeatedly tested throughout the years representing the continuity aspect of the debate. One of the loudest sceptics of digital diplomacy has been Evgheni Morozov, an academic at Georgetown University, whose criticisms have emphasized, among others, that technological developments cannot and would not be able to succeed in opening up the world where offline/traditional efforts fail (in relation to Ross' positions about Internet freedom and open/closed societies; Barton 2012). His concerns have also stressed that diplomacy is, or should be, one element of statecraft that "should not be subject to the demands of 'open government'; [for] whenever it works, it is usually because it is done behind closed doors, but this may be increasingly hard to achieve in the age of Twittering bureaucrats" (Lichtenstein 2010, para. 29). On this specific subject, Morozov has vocally reiterated the weariness of many sceptics, not necessarily over the importance of technology including in the diplomatic practice but more specifically in the perceived role awarded to digital diplomacy compared to the centuries-old, tested, opaque, widely adopted and accepted approaches.

Touching on the close connections between the private sector and the US government with regards to digital diplomacy, Morozov also pointed out that by "aligning themselves with Internet companies and organizations, Clinton's digital diplomats have convinced their enemies abroad that Internet freedom is another Trojan horse for American imperialism" (Barton 2012, para. 19). The implicit danger here for the practice does not lie solely in the renewed sounding board arguments of American imperialism, but that the Web 2.0 revolution, which has permeated people's lives in a variety of ways, may come to be associated too closely with American interests and Western values imposed on reluctant, if often outright unfriendly, countries. Consequently, the marriage between the private sector in Silicon Valley and the US State Department, as it has been referred to, can be seen not only as utilitarian, as Morozov argues, but also as "favouritism or quid pro quo", State Department officials having adopted a "philosophical" stance on the matter, pointing to the distinction between the "governments that control information- or try to- and the governments that do not" with the former having the ability to shut down networks, while the latter do not (Lichtenstein 2010, para. 32). From the private sector end, Morozov warns that repressive regimes now see the US tech companies hosting e-diplomatic efforts as "tentacles of American foreign policy's research, putting all users of those Internet tools under suspicion" (Barton 2012, para. 19). Not just Morozov has drawn on this point, but former US Ambassador to Mexico, Carlos Pascual, also admitted that social media platforms being seen as a tool of the US government would be dangerous for both the companies as well as the people still using the networks, in the eyes of China, Iran or Cuba, for example, indifferent of the actual real connection, or lack thereof (Lichtenstein 2010). These arguments have been based on evidence that, at least in one instance, the State Department has successfully pleaded with social media companies (specifically Twitter in that case) to remain available despite a previously scheduled maintenance during critical moments in sensitive areas, such as the Iranian protests in 2009, which arguably went against President Obama's stated policy of nonintervention in the postelection situation there (Lichtenstein 2010). In light of this, one can clearly see commonalities between the major points of the debate on digital diplomacy, while at the same time the two sides also emphasize distinctive aspects, or impacts of the approach, arguably also providing a more rounded perspective on it from which other practitioners, or states, can take into account when developing and implementing their own strategies. This will be illustrated in the next two sections through some of the promises and realities/limitations of the practice, both with respect to its stakeholders and the public at large.

Promises

Indirectly emerging from the some of the big lines of the debate above, but not necessarily caused by the debate, are several promises that digital diplomats, their supporters and general observers of digital diplomacy make, or see made in the advancement of the practice. These promises theoretically and empirically cover a wide range of topics interconnected with the diplomatic world, both applicable to its more mundane areas (including public diplomacy), as well as to its more sophisticated purposes (entrepreneurial microtargeting, security issues etc.). The following section will break down some of the practical realities that emerged so far given the hope(s) emanating from the widening establishment and dissemination of digital diplomacy. The promises unfolded in this section include a causal link between digital diplomacy and greater interest and participation in policymaking, expanded platforms on which to apply nation branding, and an increase in popularity of the diplomat as a national messenger, and of his or her home country's policies.

Directly related to the public diplomacy norm of the practice, the digitization of diplomacy brought with it a democratic nuance, previously excluded from or ignored by it. The assumption here is that through digital diplomacy, a greater interest and participation into policymaking (diplomatic, but not exclusively) will follow. On the other hand too, some of the functions of digital diplomacy have also been utilized during attempted democratic transitions, such as those during the Arab Spring, to draw awareness beyond a country's borders of what was happening internally, which official governmental sources were denying. From the practitioners' perspective, utilizing digital diplomacy increases the audience of their message, connecting them directly to the people, while bypassing governments and state-controlled media that may distort the initial communications. Admittedly, this is more so important for citizens in "closed societies" as Ross called them, but even outside of these cases, any person anywhere in the world with Internet access and an account on one or more of the major social media platforms (which do not cost anything to set up), can become connected with the official channels and messages of other states (or international organizations), or their own government's.

People as such have become direct recipients of diplomatic messages, which in the past this would have only happened through governmental or journalistic channels. A brief survey of the foreign affairs ministries that have strongly embraced digital diplomacy reveals that from their Twitter accounts (where individual users can be publicly identified, unlike some of the other social media platforms), among the tens and hundreds of thousands of followers, a great number of those are uninvolved, namely not publicly associated with any diplomatic stakeholders (foreign governments, international or regional organizations, NGOs, media etc.). Of course any number of these stakeholders may be following/monitoring the activities of foreign affairs departments, or governments overall, with their personal accounts, or for personal purposes such as background information or a direct line, since users do not have to disclose their professional affiliations and intents. Balancing the total number of followers that these accounts have (specifically with regards to Twitter, where users are clearly publicized) with the overall community of international actors, the former completely overcomes the latter, and leaves considerable space for engaged or curious citizens, to lend an ear to the promoted content online by foreign governments. Given the public and transparent nature of social media channels, users such as diplomatic stakeholders do not have the ability to vastly control their audience (each platform giving its users the ability to block harassing presences and interactions, but not users at random) and as such citizens from any country, as well as stakeholders of all kinds can benefit from this democratic aspect of social media to which most foreign governments have subjected themselves.

In the mundane uses of digital diplomacy, staff at permanent missions, and ambassadors, have developed additional digital channels (on top of their already-established web pages) through personalized accounts on social media platforms, which have seen explosions of users and members of these online communities in the range of millions within recent years. The foreign affairs ministries/departments have even received direct and indirect training and support from some of these companies in preparing bureaucrats for this new added dimension to their job duties. For example, Alec Ross during his tenure at the State Department, along with Jared Cohen, also part of Secretary Clinton's staff, paid numerous visits to Silicon Valley-based companies such as Facebook, Google or Twitter to learn about their services and advantages, and they returned to DC with this knowledge trickling down inside their workplace. Similarly in Canada, at the beginning of 2014, Foreign Affairs Minister John Baird personally paid a visit to Silicon Valley, meeting with executives at Google and Twitter and learning about the effects of the Internet and social media on shaping government and foreign policies. Facebook Canada, in addition to Twitter Canada and Google Canada, also organized training sessions with parliamentary staff in Ottawa pointing to the benefits and uses of their platforms, the companies thus extending their attention beyond the creation and shaping of government policy, and into their political advantages as well. Back to the diplomatic realm, though, we can now also find ambassadors themselves (not just institutional accounts) on some of the existing social media platforms, both connected to the people of the country where they are deployed as well as to other international diplomats, even communicating among themselves and transposing the international diplomatic community to the online universe.

From the perspective of digital diplomats, former US Ambassador Michael McFaul to the Russian Federation claimed to use a multilingual multiplatform social-media strategy as part of his job. One of the first reservations he had involved, of course, blending the personal and the professional and learning where the lines are (Freeland 2012b). This is where, as previously stated, a lot of the lessons have been learnt by practitioners with time and electronic use, and understandably so, given the novelty of the technology and its applicability. Ambassador McFaul specifically used Twitter, blogged when he had a more complicated point to make, and used Facebook when he wanted to converse with a community; he tried to write mostly in Russian, but occasionally used the Latin alphabet and posted in English if he wanted to communicate with his followers outside Russia (Freeland 2012b). In his own words, social media was more than a tool for communication – it was also a well-positioned window into the national debate giving him the tools to reach beyond the sometimes hostile national media and speak to any Russians who cared to listen (Freeland 2012b).

Similarly to Ambassador McFaul, former Israeli Ambassador to the United States, Michael Oren, openly acknowledged the caution he employed with social media, purposefully trying to shy from controversies, while focusing on thanking various US dignitaries for visiting or hosting him, linking to op-eds he had published or speeches he had given, and wishing folks a happy new week on Saturday evenings (Tracy 2012). The impact of his efforts is yet unknown since measurability of digital diplomacy is difficult to be carried out and interpreted. Some of the negative impacts and reactions can be clearer measured as to the attention that they receive (such as the Starbucks incident, mentioned in the next section), while the positive efforts and actions are praised more quietly and/or indirectly (such as with the outreach efforts of Farah Pandith, discussed further in this section). One aspect where it could be strongly agreed that digital diplomacy has considerable success is in raw data/intelligence gathering by practitioners in missions abroad, and this can also be corroborated by some of the diplomats cited in this chapter. Ambassador Oren also admitted that there are now few alternatives as far-reaching and effective, with very wide and young audiences, as Twitter, for example, which enabled him to communicate with other diplomats and journalists while also adding a personal touch (Tracy 2012). Although not directly related to policymaking and negotiations, these exercises on social media platforms have nonetheless facilitated the interaction, or perception of interconnectivity, between the diplomatic elites and the everyday citizens that could find themselves at the receiving end of the diplomatic art. This, of course, while "offline" negotiations and bilateral meetings still took place, which could not always be "tweeted" about. The key perceived benefit for practitioners though as some of them mentioned it, was the ability to personalize (or humanize) themselves via the social media platforms, in a way to sweeten the image that their home countries, far away and removed from their posting places, may have attached to them. After all, increased attention and awareness of the whereabouts of diplomats is sure to soften public opinion up as to the degree of commitment that they have to connecting with their audience and dedicating time out of their busy lives to spend it as every day citizens too – following the timelines and stories of their colleagues/friends, sharing information or photos/videos with those connected with them, thus increasing the transparency and accountability associated with their unelected, power-wielding professions.

From another democratic aspect of digital diplomacy, online tools were also used in various circumstances, to promote democratic practices, or alert other countries of abuses of human rights, and here the most famous cases have so far been the Green Revolution in Iran and the Arab Spring. Even before these though, examples of digital campaigns can be seen in the large-scale protests organized through Facebook, Skype and instant messaging against the Revolutionary Armed Forces in Columbia (FARC) in almost 200 cities around the world, which ended up being the largest protest against a terrorist organization in history (Lichtenstein 2010). The group "responsible" for the mobilization, One million Voices Against FARC, have since also started social networks of people who could talk about how to combat terrorism worldwide, while at the same time effectively replicating online a basic form of civil society that escalated from a single national issue. Similarly and more recently we can find the Israel Loves Iran Facebook campaign, which seeks to bring together Israelis and Iranians and to promote peace between the two countries. Started in 2012, the social media movement now numbers over 120 thousand followers on Facebook, from all over the world, and it has led to other campaigns focused on bringing peace in the Middle East. Elsewhere, the Green Revolution in Iran, which started in June 2009, made use of cell phones and social media to capture and disseminate images and videos of the young Iranian woman Neda Agha-Soltan that sparked it all, drawing peoples' attention from all over the world through the quick replication and sharing of information. In addition, most of the news that reached the West from the Iranian postelection protests came through social networks, proving that in times of crisis "alternative" sources of information and connectivity could now be found. Furthermore, three days into the protests, an online post by the opposition candidate Mir Hussein Moussavi alerted the US State Department that Twitter was scheduled to go down for maintenance, which would have interrupted communication between protesters as well as the flow of information broadcasted. This never ended up happening (Lichtenstein 2010). Similarly, in the Arab Spring movements, social media played a crucial factor in mobilizing forces on the ground while also increasing awareness of the everyday realities on the streets of the urban centres affected by the revolutions.

One final promise that digital diplomacy holds for its practitioners, supporters and audience is the causal link between the time and attention dedicated to connecting and engaging with everyday citizens through online channels and listening directly to their accounts of events/news, and the rise in popularity of the specific diplomat acting as the messenger of his or her home country, or of the government and values that they represent abroad. The clearest example to pinpoint here is that of Farah Pandith, the first US special representative to Muslim communities within the State Department. Digital diplomacy, in this case, proved for Pandith and the Obama administration to be the solution to the problem of trying to engage over 1 billion people in a meaningful way. American diplomacy had Pandith, an articulate Indian-born Muslim woman speaking on behalf of the United States to a large, diverse population that has continued to suspect this country and its government. Her presence was magnified with technology so that her job would "promise more than a Sisyphean series of intercontinental flights" (Lichtenstein 2010, para. 52). Pandith's speaking points and Q&As were broken down, translated into Pashto, Dari, Urdu, Arabic, Swahili etc. and disseminated through previously-identified "influencer" Muslims on social-media platforms, which would act as mediators between Pandith and audiences in Islamic countries not directly attentive to US-specific opinions pertinent to them, or where government-controlled media may distort American stances with respect to Muslim engagement. The results of this commitment can be seen as mixed ones, since under Pandith there seemed to be great attention dedicated to Muslim communities throughout Asia and Africa mostly, but also in Commonwealth countries, though this has not necessarily translated into great shifts in the existing anti-American attitudes to more positive ones. The office has, since the beginning of 2014, a new acting representative, but its online presence has not been greatly increased; on the contrary, post Pandith the activity of the office seems to have winded down considerably (in the first few months of 2014, that is).

Similarly, and with the same targeted audience, Israel opened in 2013 a **virtual embassy** to the Persian Gulf countries (also known as the Gulf Cooperation Council, or GCC),[5] separate from the already-existing communication, commerce and cooperation negotiations that have been held behind closed doors, and far from the public eye. The public engagement of the virtual embassy with its targeted audience on various social media platforms has taken place in Arabic and English, extending appropriate holiday wishes, or promoting Israeli innovation that could benefit the GCC members, and of course staying away from engaging with controversial users and messaging. And this came about in a situation where Israel has no formal physical diplomatic presence in any of the GCC states, but yet the Israeli Ministry of Foreign Affairs managed to employ digital diplomacy to reach out to an overall hostile audience, despite the indirect business interests and transactions between the Jewish state and some of the Persian Gulf countries. Before Israel, the United States first opened a virtual embassy "in" Iran in 2011 in order to enhance dialogue opportunities with Iranian citizens, and for the US to promote its policies, culture and the American people, as well as bringing information and alternative viewpoints to the Iranian people separate from the official governmental sources. Openly, one of the goals of the embassy was declared to be the challenging of the Iranian regime's "efforts to place an electronic curtain of surveillance, satellite jamming and online filtering around its people" (Nuland 2011, para. 3).

The virtual embassy's website includes information on opportunities in the US; examples of famous Americans of Iranian descent; consular information for American citizens; links to other official social media accounts in Farsi; selected stories of Iranians facing unjust imprisonment; and details on American news stories and government policies, as well as what Iran would label as Western propaganda, namely promotional knowledge of open societies, universal human rights, civil societies, the American way of life and Internet freedom. Despite the promises that this virtual presence held for Iranian citizens, within the first twelve hours since its launch, the virtual embassy was shut down by the government in Tehran (Iranians being prevented from accessing it, that is), though the website has been regularly updated ever since its inception, even including greetings from President Obama for Nowruz 2014. Official statistics as to the popularity and/or engagement on this platform, as well as its effects, were not accessible at publication date.

Realities

In opposition to the promises that digital diplomacy holds, the reality is far less clear and predictable as the staunch supporters of the practice would have us believe. That is not to say that all the promises made by digital diplomacy are unfulfilled, merely that there is a discrepancy between some of the rhetoric around the implementation of digital diplomacy and all its benefits, and some of the practical implications and circumstances that are more difficult to transcend. One such example can be seen in the American Internet freedom agenda, which has been a cause, or a result, of the involvement of the State Department with digital diplomacy. Internet freedom has been one of the explicit goals and guidelines of the State Department under Hillary Clinton's leadership, alongside consular communications and response, and information and knowledge management, among others. American diplomats have promoted Internet freedom in authoritarian societies, including announcing multimillion dollar initiatives to support digital activists in these states by training them in employing online tools strategically so they could exercise their universal rights, including the freedoms of expression, association and speech. One such example is of funding panic-button programs or applications for activists spying on corrupt governments, which would erase the incriminating evidence gathered.

At the opposite end of the spectrum, though, we can see the US Central Command, which has been using software to target social media websites used by terrorists. Private companies are not far behind these efforts either, with California-based security firm Ntrepid developing a program that cloaks multiple artificial profiles in the hope of luring out the next Irhabi 007 (a young Moroccan convicted in the UK of using the Internet to incite terrorist attacks; Franke 2011). And while Clinton's bureaucrats emphasized Internet freedom and invested funding into programs promoting it and encouraging online activism in authoritarian states, dissidents in these societies have even been tortured for their online personas and to crackdown the opposition networks that had been established digitally. Regimes in Egypt, Syria, China and Libya had even been spying on their own citizens and their online activities, with similar actions to curb terrorist activities and hubs taking place even in the United States. Finally, the most widely publicized examples of this reality on Internet freedom and the emergence of a new digital era of transparency and accountability, have of course been the WikiLeaks Cablegate scandal and Edward Snowden's revelations on the surveillance programs of the National Security Agency, both which the American government tried in vain to shut down under the pretexts of national security, confidentiality and the sensitivity of the information released, for both allies and enemies to consult at leisure. The word of wisdom here would probably be a relaxation of the idealistically perceived rhetoric of the State Department, and an open admission that digital diplomacy is still an approach in constant evolution, which cannot predict, anticipate or cover all the issues or instances that might arise. And the same stands for the countries developing coherent digital strategies, or improving them, in the discourse employed, guidelines established, and goals aimed at reaching.

Furthermore, on the democratic aspect of digital diplomacy, in the previous section I have also mentioned the perceived causal link expected, or predicted, by foreign bureaucrats in their commitment to engaging with everyday citizens, in addition to their regular "traditional" duties of connecting with the political, cultural, journalistic elites, and others, which now they could also amplify it with the online dimension. First and foremost, there has not been a study yet that could confirm the prediction promised conceptually by digital diplomacy, that engaging online with the wider public of a state will slowly affect the public opinion of that society over the policies of the government the diplomats are representing abroad. Despite the lack of systematic studies, there have been numerous reports by communication firms, such as Burson-Marsteller, looking at world leaders but also at how companies use social media, how they engage with the public, outside of the political and diplomatic realms, for branding purposes. This is partially the case because of the short length of time that digital diplomacy has been implemented as such, and also the novelty of the social media revolution, neither have allowed for any significant analysis to take place that could confirm this hope for change in perceptions and attitudes. In addition, there have been doubts raised over the meaningfulness and depth of this engagement, namely if silently listening to people's online presence has actually any impact on knowledge management, or if engagement represents actual direct interactions, online or offline, with societies at large. Furthermore, while users' data has been mined by specialized companies, and even governments, this has been so far mostly been used to target the availability of information on social media platforms, and for the promotion of some brands/companies over others, without much meaningful diplomatic coverage or benefit.

On the issue of online engagement the jury is still out, as they say, and one way in which this might be proven, or disproven, would be conducting extensive field research through focus groups, questionnaires or surveys in the targeted areas of states' interests. If such research has already been carried out, even by the bigger Anglo American players, the results have not been publicized. I do acknowledge though, the work done by the Burson-Marsteller international communications firms broadly in this area, on the connectivity of world leaders on

Twitter, and their engagement with each other, or their followers. Maybe in the future they might expand their research beyond Twitter to provide bird's eye views of the impact and significance of individual states' digital strategies, but until then, results are inconclusive as to how poignant a state's digital diplomacy strategy is on its target audience. The report itself though looked specifically at the connectivity of politicians and institutions. Amongst its findings, Carl Bildt had the highest number of mutual peer connections, followed by the European External Action Service, the Foreign Ministry of Poland, UK's FCO and the Foreign Ministry of France, with President Barack Obama being the least connected user among those analyzed (Burson-Marsteller 2013). The significance of this lies in the fact that direct private interactions may occur between users reciprocally followed/following.

According to the twiplomacy report released by Burson-Marsteller, over three-quarters of all governments (through world leaders) are on Twitter, with all forty-five European states, and all of the South American countries except for Suriname having official Twitter accounts (Burson-Marsteller 2013). The most followed world leader was found to be, almost predictably, US President Barack Obama, with Pope Francis following in his trail, but with less than three-quarters from the President's statistics (Burson-Marsteller 2013). The study also found that the most active accounts belonged to the Venezuelan presidency (with an average of over forty tweets per day); second, to the presidency of the Dominican Republic (with an average of thirty-five tweets per day) and third, to the Croatian government presence, close enough to the second-spot figures (Burson-Marsteller 2013). In terms of the engagement of some of these users, the prime minister of Uganda was found to have had 96% of replies, followed by the president of Rwanda, Paul Kagame, with 88% and then by Carl Bildt with 86% (Burson-Marsteller 2013). Among the first world leaders who signed up to Twitter in 2007, shortly after the company's emergence, were Barack Obama, Mexico's Enrique Peña Nieto, Belgium's Elio Di Rupo and Canada's Stephen Harper, 2011 seeing the highest rate of creation of Twitter accounts for world leaders, with over 110 being started (Burson-Marsteller 2013).

Outside of the scientific circles (academic or not), general perception can lead to make several observations over the status quo of digital diplomacy in some specific cases. Despite all the human and financial capital invested in rebranding its image in the Arab world, the United States still seems not to have been successful in its efforts online and offline. By far though, the online presence most praised and trusted seems to be that of the Swedish Foreign Minister Carl Bildt, a fact confirmed by multiple sources, including politicians and other foreign diplomats (Sandre 2013). Bildt has had a relatively long involvement with digital technology; going as far back as 1997, as Sweden's Prime Minister, he sent an email to President Bill Clinton directly (Ritter 2012). Partially given this historical connection, but also because of the professionalism he has exhibited (though he was initially sceptical of digital diplomacy), Bildt has gained the reputation of knowing what he's doing in the online world. He has employed social media to build his brand as a politician, while also promoting Sweden as a leader in IT, thus setting a personal example while also becoming a veteran blogger, among others (Ritter 2012). More so, he has become famous for also interacting with other world leaders and diplomats online while staying away from sensitive discussions and not pretending to conduct high-level diplomacy in 140 characters, which has only helped to humanize the diplomatic arena. One such interaction drew the attention of observers when Bildt, unable to reach his Bahraini counterpart, took to Twitter to contact him (Ritter 2012). As former Ambassador McFaul, Bildt also combines the use of his native language, through blog posts, with the contemporary diplomatic lingua franca, tweeting in English, and has managed to integrate social media into his normal routines, blogging during his travels, and having it in the back of his mind all the time, which has made it not very time-consuming (Freeland 2012a).

The nature and effectiveness of connectivity have of course led to another issue, namely, the quality or form of the participation, both of the wider audience but also of the messenger. Multiple diplomats have, out of ignorance or fear of controversies, stayed away from overpersonalizing their presence too much, sticking more to official messaging such as news releases in their "online engagement". And, at the other end of the spectrum, too, online followers have more commonly been divided into passive and active listeners to the diplomatic messaging projected, with unclear numbers as to the difference between the two. For example, is merely following the online presence of an ambassador or a permanent mission considered active listening? The duration of time of online connectivity is also important especially if the messaging is sporadic or abusive in frequency which may lead to changes both in attitudes and numbers. Similar issues have been raised in light of some of the natural disasters that took place within the past decade, namely the deadly earthquakes and tsunamis that ravaged several parts of the world. In these cases, while digital diplomacy has been a quick medium to inform people of consular issues, disaster response and others, it has also given rise to concepts such as *slacktivism*, which has been seen as the limited engagement or passive mobilization in such instances, mostly in the area of fundraising through the online donation campaigns, or through short messaging services (SMS) of mobile phones and networks. This has of course had an impact over the serious reception of the depth (but not breadth) of digital diplomacy strategies in mobilizing large groups of people outside of their own political or natural crises. In the few political crises, too, in which we have seen digital diplomacy at play abroad observers have noted that the public focus has been more on the importance of the medium and slightly less so on the actual events unfolding, or their implications.

Finally, two of the realities that have emerged in light of the promises made by digital diplomacy have to do first with the personalization of the diplomatic online presence, and second with the knowledge and information management acquired from non-official sources. As to the former, I have already mentioned in the previous section that some of the Ambassadors cited praised caution in walking the fine line between personal and professional in their online presence, partially because of several factors, the first being the timing and circumstances of their presence, and of course the nature of the personal detail that they would want to share. One "famous" blunder among the observers of (again) American digital diplomacy occurred during a visit that Alec Ross and other bureaucrats from the State Department paid to Syria in 2010. During this trip, one of the members of the delegation praised his drink acquired at a local Starbucks coffee shop nearby Damascus. This was seen as trivializing their role there, as well as the overall visit and relations of the State Department with the Syrian government. While of course the intent of the praise was not ill-willed, the circumstances of the online message were of such sensitivity that an otherwise harmless tweet became a public embarrassment back in the American capital (and probably was used as a counter example in training future digital diplomats). As for the management of knowledge and information acquired on the ground during times of crisis or peace, there is one huge issue which has not been publicly and directly addressed by the supporters of digital diplomacy – namely, the reliability and legal implications of sharing and receiving information from potentially unnamed sources (to protect their identities, too, if necessary). While this has not become endemic, there is reason to believe that any wrongful information has had to be verified before disseminating it through official channels, which then brings in the issue of risk (or trust depending how this is viewed) in the sources of that information. Technologically it is very straightforward to create online accounts under false identities and this of course needs to be a concern of great importance when relying on informants on the ground, both during times of distress and peace.

Conclusion

Even while exposing so many realities regarding digital diplomacy (whether about the feasibility, or hypocrisy, of Internet freedom, or the ease with which controversies can be started), crafted and well thought-out digital diplomacy, which takes into account these past experiences and try to incorporate them into their specific promises, guidelines and goals, should remain the desirable norm for practitioners. While the diplomatic promoters and practitioners of digital diplomacy may have used an *ad hoc* approach, the "slower" participants to the game have dedicated more time to develop a wholesome (as much as possible) digital strategy of communications. As such, as mentioned previously, we now start seeing the second wave of actors come into play, after the Anglo American champions of the practice. Among these new players we can find Canada, Italy and the Scandinavian countries, which may incorporate more mundane uses into their digital approaches (unlike the more sophisticated targeting employed by the US), separately from their respective intelligence efforts, focusing also more on what Joseph Nye would have called soft power and not so much (not yet, at least) on smart power, given also their hard-power capabilities.

As a brief recapitulation, while the debates over digital diplomacy rest on its complementarity or predominance over the traditional diplomatic approaches, or over the nature of open or closed societies, I have framed the discussion in this chapter alongside the promises and realities surrounding it, both for its practitioners and target audience. Some of the promises that digital diplomacy holds are those of an increased (younger) more mobile audience, and of increased connectivity and popularity, while facilitating knowledge acquisition and distribution. On the other hand though, the promises made by the supporters of the practice do not always manage to mirror the realities created, whether about connectivity, favourableness over a country's policies and values, or the reliability of information acquired from sources on the ground. As such, a prudent and balanced view of both the advantages and disadvantages that digital diplomacy holds for its practitioners as well as the nature and form of the diplomatic art in the twenty-first century and beyond is more advisable than one of the more "extreme" views which wilfully ignore the arguments made by the other side. An overview of both what has worked and what has not until now for larger or smaller states can only be beneficial in developing or improving digital diplomacy strategies, without necessarily having to repeat in practice some of the lessons already learnt. For, as the Rorschach test is meant to show, the outlying views must always be mended towards the more acceptable and reasonable centres of perception, which is also where I think the success and longevity of digital diplomacy will rest.

Notes

1 While several authors talk about digital diplomacy in comparable, synonymous terms, they label it differently depending on their points of focus – the cyber space (Potter 2002), the digital overall (Deruda 2012) or, specifically, a social platform over another, such as Twitter (Sandre 2013).
2 An extensive analysis on the connection between Twitter and diplomats can be found in Sandre (2013).
3 The Web 2.0 revolution has constituted the explosion in popularity of the recently developed social media platforms that led to an increased digital connectivity but also a heavy reliance on electronic applications in many areas of our lives.
4 The inherent benefits of the Web 2.0 revolution for digital diplomats include the assistance and speed (albeit not necessarily reliability) in connecting them with the wider public during their postings, to listen to how policies are perceived or received on the ground; how bilateral relations are understood, if at all; to project and disseminate unmediated information about the values, beliefs and actions of their home countries; and others.
5 The GCC members refers to Saudi Arabia, Kuwait, the United Arab Emirates, Oman, Qatar and Bahrain.

3

'SECRECY IS FOR LOSERS'

Why diplomats should embrace openness to protect national security

Alexis Wichowski[1]

Introduction

> Secrecy is for losers. For people who don't realize how important information really is.... We put [openness] in peril by poking along in a mode of an age now past. It is time to dismantle government secrecy. It is time to begin building the supports for the era of openness that is already upon us.
>
> – Senator Daniel Moynihan, *Secrecy: The American Experience* (1998, 227)

The digital landscape is a leaky place. And in it, government just can't get away with what it used to. While bad behaviour by governments has always been outed eventually, in the digital era it's easier than ever to reveal even peace-making government activities, whole hog and in real time. Exposure in the digital landscape, for good or for ill, is simply much, much easier these days.

This scares the pants off government. Which is understandable – the digital landscape is complicated, and complicated things bring complicated new threats. Some parts of government seem to think the safest thing to do is in the face of this complicated new landscape is to just kind of avoid it. Leave the share-everything social networking to regular folks, and inside government – and in the diplomatic and national security agencies especially – just share less. In a quest to be safe, government is becoming more secret. And **secrecy** is not just a practice, but a culture; an operational mode of being.

This chapter argues that this is a mistake. A culture of secrecy undermines diplomacy by shuttering up windows diplomats need kept open. And in the digital era where information-sharing is an increasingly normal part of daily life, it's not going to work anyway. This chapter will describe in detail why not. But first, some context from recent events:

In June 2013, federal contractor Edward Snowden leaked roughly 200,000 classified documents describing activities of the US government's National Security

Agency, better known as the NSA. Chief among them were papers detailing a digital surveillance program known as PRISM: a massive data collection sweep that scooped up phone records of millions of US citizens – whether they were suspected of crimes or not.

US national security agencies responded to all this with some serious soul-searching. First, they looked at the surveillance practices themselves. The surveillance, they found, may have in fact been illegal.[2] And even if it wasn't, it wasn't all that effective, terrorism prevention-wise.[3] Government investigators also looked at their own workforce – the millions of federal employees like Snowden who have access to classified information.[4] The results of investigation after investigation keep circling the same conclusion: the digital landscape is a new world, with new threats. And old ways of dealing with the threats aren't going to work. As former Assistant Secretary of Defence Paul Stockton wrote, the idea that "if we build a fence around us, we'll be secure . . . is outmoded. It's broken and it needs to be replaced" (Cooper 2014, para. 14).

Diplomacy doesn't deal with physical fences, but the metaphor holds up: the idea that erecting a culture of secrecy around diplomacy will keep a nation secure is outmoded. It's broken. It needs to be replaced.

Note, this chapter does not argue that "secrets" are bad, but rather that "secrecy", as a culture within which to operate, is. This chapter will explore why this is at length, but summed up, it is because the world at large no longer lives in a dominant mode of secrecy. The global population is increasingly tied to a digital landscape where information-sharing, not secrecy, is the norm, both as practice and as principle. Diplomats need to adapt to the digital landscape, and a culture that discourages them from sharing information both within and outside government undermines their ability to do so.

Fifteen years ago, Senator Daniel Moynihan wrote, "Secrecy is for losers. . . . For people who don't realize how important information really is. . . . We put [openness] in peril by poking along in a mode of an age now past" (1998, 227). To secure a nation, governments cannot retreat into an outdated mode of secrecy. They must come to grips with the mode of **openness** that defines the age it's in.

The context

Let's start with a good hard look at the age. On an average day in 2013, 144 billion emails and 19.1 billion text messages were sent (Clark-Dickson 2013). On an average month, 1.19 billion people went on Facebook, 1 billion watched videos on YouTube and 232 million used Twitter via 2.7 billion Internet connections and 6.7 billion mobile phones (Granger 2013; Radicati and Buckley 2012; YouTube 2014). Internet use is up 566.4% in the past decade and a half (Internet World Stats 2014).

These statistics show two things: first, the digital environment creates immense opportunities for people to share; and second, many people are doing just that. They voluntarily share links to things they've read or watched, their opinions about the things they've read or watched, or even original new works for others to read and watch. But they also share information about themselves: run-of-the mill stuff, like professional titles, associations and specializations; but also personal information, from digital versions of kids and spouse pics to self-inflicted Orwellian "check-ins" pinpointing one's own exact location at an exact moment. The digital landscape – both the tools in it and the culture that has risen up around it – make information-sharing of all kinds simply *more*: more possible, more likely, more normal.

It may seem like knowing about general information-cultural norms are all well and good, but the more important issue for diplomacy is isn't the sharing of run-of-the mill information but the sharing of sensitive information: practices and confidences whose public exposure could undermine relationships with allies, embolden enemies and weaken the state. Not so. This chapter argues that information-sharing culture and the preservation of sensitive information are inextricably linked. To understand this link, let us examine who's doing what in the digital landscape, what they're doing and why.

The who

Tools are important. They enable action. But it's necessary to also examine the people who *use* the tools: the agents of action. This involves taking stock of the roles they inhabit and the motivations that drive them. The "who" in this chapter consists of three broad categories: government, leakers and the community of civilians to whom leaks are revealed.

First, to clarify terms. The concept "government" is too broad for in-depth examination. When the term "government" is invoked in this chapter, it means the foreign policy wings of government: diplomatic institutions and defence agencies, the two areas of government most responsible for protecting sensitive information and preventing leaks.

Leakers is a more specific category. They are, simply, people who reveal secrets that they're not supposed to; in this case, government secrets. When public opinion is on their side, they tend to be called "whistle-blowers"; when not, "traitors." This chapter will use the term "leakers" as an intended neutral label, describing this group of individuals by their actions alone.

Leakers, however, are not a distinct, stand-alone group. They're invariably entangled in some way with the first and third groups. They are part of the community of citizens. They're also necessarily part of the government: soldiers, like Chelsea (formerly Bradley) Manning, who initiated "**Wikileaks**[5]"; contractors, like Edward Snowden, who orchestrated the NSA leaks; or analysts, or operatives, or a myriad of other role types which will be explored further on. While to the public leakers may be regarded as just that – He Who Leaked Classified Information – to understand why a culture of secrecy is a bad idea for national security, leakers' roles as citizens and as agents of government must be borne in mind as well.

The third group, as mentioned, is the community of citizens; the broad net of people to whom leakers heave their catch. Here I refer not just to "the public" but rather two fairly distinct subgroups of it: 1. citizens who promote information-sharing as a right; and 2. working-level government officials. This chapter explores these roles in depth.

"Digital" diplomacy

This sums up the "who": government, leakers, and citizens. And the "what" is the secrecy–openness balance whose calibration these groups seek to adjust. The "where" and "how" are tougher to pinpoint, but I suggest that term **digital diplomacy** is a way to get at them. "Digital diplomacy" describes diplomatic activities (the diplomacy) that move along bit-enabled axes (the digital).

At the same time, the "where" and "how" in "digital diplomacy" are a bit of a Schrödinger's cat: these activities are both of and not of a place, referring to diplomatic activities both in countries and not in countries. And it both is and is not of a particular technology: "digital" suggests the *presence* of a connection technology, but this could mean a possible as well as an actual presence. For instance, the awareness that some narrative *could* go "viral" affects a diplomat's decision-making calculus in many contexts, whether a digital tool is actually being used or not.

Thus, digital diplomacy is perhaps best described not as a medium, but a mindset. Marcus Holmes and Corneliu Bjola aptly describe it in this volume as "a way for states to manage change" (Chapter 1, this volume). Sometimes this change is better managed with technology, but not always. Push-pull media can sow a narrative or collect data, but it hasn't replaced the coffee meeting. Like any tool, digital is good for some things and not so good for others. Knowing what tool would work when; that is the art of diplomacy. Knowing how the digital environment influences this art; that's digital diplomacy.

Information-sharing as a cultural value

Information-sharing comes of age

Having established the *whos* and *hows* of the digital information-sharing age, it is now time to take a look at how they got here. People have shared information with each other in some sort of recorded, shareable form – as opposed to spoken, ephemeral form – for thousands of years.[6] Other options didn't really present themselves until long-distance phone service went mainstream after the 1950s. But even after the phone, written correspondence in the form of letters remained most people's primary means for keeping in touch with far-off friends, relatives and colleagues for the next few decades (Schmid 2011).

As the home phone became integrated into American life, people communicated to each other via writing less and less. They could just call – it was easier and got cheaper with each passing year. According the US Postal Service's first annual Household Diary Study designed to study mail patterns, by 2011 the average American household sent or received only one (1) unit of personal correspondence[7] every two weeks (Mazzone and Rehman 2011, 21).

The letter-writing drop off did not mean, however, that Americans en masse just antisocially bowled alone. While communication in the form of mailed letters dwindled, communication in other recorded, shareable form soared. Let's preserve the two-week time frame used in the US Postal Service study for comparison purposes. In an average two-week period in 2011, while Americans only sent or received one unit of correspondence in physical form, they exchanged 4,942 units of correspondence in digital forms[8]: specifically, an average of 812 emails (58/day), 140 texts (10/day) and 3,990 units of social media content (285/day) (Bennett 2013; Smith 2011, 5).

It is worth pausing for a moment to consider what all this says about the culture of communication; not just in the US, but among humans. For the vast majority of history, interpersonal communication was oral, transactional (Fang 1997, 11). And for a really long time, writing remained the sole purview of a teeny slice of educated elites. Letter-writing among the non-super elite began to take hold around the 1840s with the introduction of the postage stamp, making letter-delivery possible for even the personal messenger-deprived masses (Garfield 2013, 239).[9]

We know all this for two reasons: first, because the information was recorded; and second, because it was saved. Now, for all but the last handful of decades, recording was a huge pain. It required either being literate or getting someone else who was to put chisel to stone or quill to parchment. So, as archaeological evidence and good horse sense tell us, ancestral scriveners didn't just record any old thing. To be recorded, information had to be important: from laws of the lands to ledger books. In short, not everyone could make information a physical form, and not every bit of information was deemed form-worthy.

So – and this is the big so-what to this aside – for most of human history, what regular people communicated was simply not recorded; and unrecorded, it couldn't be readily shared. But let's assume for a moment that regular folks' communications might have been recorded and could have been shared: who would read it? Who would want to? The notion that writings of the non-elites might be of interest to masses of anonymous others – not out of sentimental value for sender-receiver but because the information itself had some value as a public good – is difficult to imagine.

It's different now. Thanks to the digital revolution, recorded information's reach has expanded from the elites to the everyman in just a few decades. And sharing that communication virtually effortlessly went from inconceivable to being an every other minute[10] activity since the dawn of social media in the last decade. Given this context, I submit it is reasonable to assert that information-sharing is now, in 2014, a firmly planted new normal for the vast majority of the developed world.[11]

"Information wants to be free"

For some in the developed world, however, information-sharing is not just the new normal. For some, information-sharing is a right. It's something to believe in; a cause to fight for.

It started in the 1980s, and, not surprisingly, with one of the guys from Apple. Company co-founder Steve Wozniak was at a conference with a commune advocate named Stewart Brand. Brand had launched a magazine in 1968 called *The Whole Earth Catalogue*, marketing a whole range of do-it-yourself, back-to-the-land type stuff, including specs on wood-fired stoves and instructions on how to build a yurt (Whole Earth 1969). *Whole Earth*, however, was also one of the first places to advertise the Apple personal computer, regarding it as a tool like any other that could put power back into the hands of the people[12] (Leonard 2014; Morozov 2014).

At the first ever "Hackers Conference" in 1984, Wozniak and Brand casually discussed what would become a paradigm-shifting concept: "Information," Brand said, "wants to be free" (Brand, Kelly and Dyson 2011, para. 16). At the time, Brand was talking about how it would be increasingly difficult to charge money for information once digitized and so easily copied.[13] But as global networked computing became a reality, tech activists adopted the idea and took it as a mantra – a literal one.

The reasoning behind the mantra goes something like this:

- Information, once digitized, is easy to share
- Digitized information is also easy to manipulate and search, from basic quotidian Google queries to sophisticated data mining
- This digital information searching reveals all kinds of valuable things, shockingly fast[14] – from patterns, research material, and regular old knowhow on how to do things
- Since digitized information can be shared with many people simultaneously and since it can reveal so many useful things, many people should be able to benefit from it as a kind of public good
- As such, information, the idea goes, should be free, and freely shared. In other words, information *wants* to be free.

Now, not everyone agrees with this; not least governments, who serve their citizens well by keeping some information secret, like who has what Social Security number or the identities of political asylum seekers. But bureaucrats were not in fact the first opponents of "information wants to be free." Opposition first came from the private sector.

This is perhaps best illustrated with the story of the Pirate Party.

Information-sharing as a movement

The Pirate Party grew out of an online peer-to-peer file-sharing site called The Pirate Bay, or TPB. Launched in 2003, anyone could use TPB to upload any content – mostly videos, games or music – and anyone else could then download any of it for free.

As TPB became popular in the late 2000s, copyright holders of the freely downloadable videos, games and music began to catch wind of what was happening with their works. Much of the publishing and licensing establishments saw peer-to-peer file-sharing as theft, plain and simple. They saw file-sharing sites like TPB as not only abetting theft, but doing so aggressively and on a massive scale.

In 2009, the Motion Picture Association of America (MPAA) and the Recording Industry Association of America (RIAA) lobbied hard for a crackdown on the TPB. It worked. That year, the four founders of The Pirate Bay – Rick Falkvinge, Peter Sunde, Gottfrid Svartholm and Marcin de Kaminski – were tried in their home country of Sweden and convicted of copyright infringement (Pfanner 2009; Swartz 2009).

The MIAA and RIAA may have seen TPB as just a landing pad for thieving, but to the TPB organizers, file-sharing was more than a practice; it was a belief. They believed "information wants to be free", and believed others did too. So when the four founded TPB in 2003, they also established the Piratbyrån, translated as "The Bureau of Piracy". This is perhaps best described as a "loose collective." In the words of the founders, it's "not an organization," per se, but rather, "an ongoing conversation . . . reflecting over questions regarding copying, information infrastructure and digital culture" (Andersson 2009, 1). TPB associates were among the first quasi-political digital groups to take up the "loose collective" mantle; others, like the hacker collective Anonymous, came later.

If TPB were just a website, jailing the four founders and shuttering the Piratbyrån should have spelled the end of the story. But both the site and the movement are very much alive. Fans have kept the site going over the last five years through a vast underground network, changing its domain name six times in 2013 alone to evade shutdown by the authorities. The Pirate Bay is still the most widely used file-sharing site in the world. At last count, it had 18,911,877 users (RT News 2013; Pfanner 2009).

While TPB's collective, Piratbyrån, officially shut down in 2010, its affiliated political party, The Pirate Party, grew. Under the umbrella "Pirate Parties International", PPI has active chapters in sixty-two countries at the time of this writing. Their electoral record is still thin, but gaining ground: PPI won 7.1% of votes – 2 seats – in the European Parliament in 2009, 8.9 % of votes in the Berlin state election in 2011, a senator seat in the Czech national parliament in 2012 and 5.1% of votes – 3 out of 63 seats – in the Icelandic parliament in 2013 (Beyer 2014, 144).

This story matters to national security because it helps to explain why retreating into a culture of secrecy isn't going to work. The fight to share information is not just a consumer preference; it's a worldview. And it's spreading.

Who leaks, and why it doesn't happen more often

To understand why diplomacy lists, siren-called, towards a culture of secrecy from an age long past, we have to talk about leaks. The digital landscape doesn't make leaks happen, but it enables them to happen on a cosmological scale. Like Big Bang-expelled particles in the physical universe, leaked information in the digital universe expands, accelerates and is almost immediately nonretractable. Once the information is out, it's not possible to just burn some files and make the leak go away. Leaked information races to the far corners of digital space, irretrievable and order-altering.

This makes the digital landscape, as mentioned at the outset, scary for governments. And it's eminently understandable why that's so. In addition to the speed and scale of their spread, leaks of all kinds – big and small – can do damage; not just gargantuan ones like Wikileaks or the NSA leaks. Tiny sensitive tidbits, if leaked, are just as irretrievable as the big ones.

To prevent any leaks, then, national security institutions within governments logically take steps to self-fortify. As discussed earlier, this might include more physical defences – fences – and more cyber defences – firewalls. And it's not hard to imagine that it wouldn't seem like a bad idea to have some more psychological defences, too; a healthy dose of pants-scaring for everyone who works with sensitive information with a subtle but palpable culture of secrecy.

It's not necessary, though. Because let's be honest: nobody loves government. That said, most officials in most countries aren't doing anything to undermine their own government. Fear of reprisals might account for the bulk of why not. Or it might just be too much work to bother trying. But as unfashionably uncynical as this may sound, I submit that the reason most officials don't try to undermine their own government is because they believe that it would be wrong to do so. A heavy-handed hatch-battening culture that stifles information-sharing simply isn't necessary.

Perhaps the culture of secrecy isn't aimed at most officials, though; it may just be to deter would-be **leakers**. Before we get to the leakers, though, let's take a closer look at government officials in general and the information-handling culture in which they work.

The government and its information

Information, in national security, is not just currency; it's current. Information is the force that powers decisions. Without information – data, analysis, chatter, chatting – diplomatic and defence agencies couldn't do much. Information enables identification of threats and allies, the confirmation of context and history; it makes possible the deliberation on and delivery of plans. Information is a governments' most valuable inorganic foreign policy asset.

The most valuable *organic* foreign policy asset is, of course, the people who use the information: government officials. Here, I temporarily muddy the taxonomic waters by collapsing "government" and "working-level government officials." For a moment, let's step back and consider a huge overgeneralization of government, lumping together defence secretaries and ambassadors with the legions of officials whose work orbits theirs. Doing so is necessary to make the following point: in democratic countries, such as the United States, the same information-handling rules apply to everyone in government. Everyone. Anyone with a security clearance – that is to say, absolutely everyone in government from the ambassadors to interns – is required by law to protect diplomatic information according to a very specific set of rules.

"Classified" describes one set of rules. For people who work in government, figuring out which information is classified is pretty easy – it's literally got the word "Classified" stamped all over it. But assuming for a moment it didn't, it'd be worth perusing the rulebook. In the US, the rules governing classified information appear in the form of Executive Order 12958.

According to Executive Order 12958, potentially classifiable information includes: military plans, weapons systems, or operations; foreign government information; intelligence activities; foreign relations or foreign activities of the US; scientific, technological and economic matters related to national security; nuclear materials- or facilities-related information; infrastructure vulnerabilities; weapons of mass destruction (White House 1995).

Some of this is straightforward: weapons stuff, secret; nuclear materials info, secret. But some of the categories are a bit vague. For instance, "foreign government information" and "foreign relations of the United States": this could include just about anything the State Department or Department of Defence works on. Fortunately, "classified" and "unclassified" are not the only tiers of information-handling rules. The most important of the other tiers for this argument is information known as "Sensitive But Unclassified" (SBU).[15]

Introduced by President Jimmy Carter in 1977 and expanded considerably after 9/11, SBU-category information covers what it sounds like it would cover: information that's not a state secret, but shouldn't be broadcast willy-nilly. This includes a wide range of categories, the most obvious being personal citizen information, like Social Security numbers, medical records, passport details or visa info. But it also includes a fair bit of nonobvious information.

For instance, consider two aspects of SBU described in the US Department of State's rulebook – the "Foreign Affairs Manual," aka, the FAM (12 FAM 540 "Sensitive But Unclassified Information [SBU]") (US Department of State 2013):

1 "Inter or intra-agency communications, including emails, that form part of the internal deliberative processes of the U.S. Government, the disclosure of which could harm such processes" as SBU information (12 FAM section 541 "Sensitive But Unclassified Information [SBU]" 2013, point b subpoint 9)

In other words: Work emails? Those could be SBU.

2 "Before distributing any SBU information, employees must be sure that such distribution is permissible and, when required, specifically authorized" (12 FAM section 543 "Access, Dissemination, and Release", point b) US Department of State 2013)

In other words: Who's supposed to know if info is SBU? You. And you; and you.

No sharing is safe sharing

This is the crux: emails with other officials can be considered "sensitive"; and figuring out if they are or not is up to each individual official. Or put more simply, even with nonclassified information, there are restrictions.

Herein rests the great dilemma of the government official. No one *likes* hoarding information or being excessively secret-like. But it's maddeningly easy to accidently share something that turns out to be a no-no. And the penalty for sharing something that's not supposed to be shared can be pretty stiff.

Here is a hypothetical example of an entirely plausible diplomatic information-sharing fail:

An intern helpfully offers to post something on Twitter on behalf of the perennially busy ambassador. Assume the ambassador did in fact compose the tweet, but his punishingly packed schedule prevents him from getting to a desktop to complete the tweet process himself. Oh, and there are no cell phones allowed in the buildings (for security purposes), so blackberry-tweeting under the desk isn't an option.

The intern posts the tweet. It's the coolest thing he's ever done. The intern then brags about it on his own Twitter account.

Almost immediately, a reporter notices. A story appears within the hour: "Ambassador X, famous for his 'Twitter diplomacy,' gets interns to tweet for him."

The ambassador's credibility takes a hit. The intern is mortified. And officials who hear about the story may laugh or shake their heads, but also just tweet a little bit less after that.

I picked on an intern, but variations on these things happen to veteran officials, too. Here's an actual example (which, I remind my clear-ers, was already cleared once for my *Foreign Affairs* article, "Social Diplomacy, or how diplomats learned to Stop Worrying and Love the Tweet" (Wichowski, 2013a)):

> On September 11th, 2012, protests erupted across the Arab world in response to an American-made anti-Islamic video posted YouTube. Someone in the Cairo embassy defied recommendations from headquarters in DC and posted a tweet that read: "We firmly reject the actions by those who abuse the universal right of free speech to hurt the religious beliefs of others."
>
> It was an election year. Mitt Romney, attempting to unseat incumbent president Barack Obama, leapt on the tweet, denouncing it as "disgraceful." A popular political blog ran the headline, "US Embassy in Cairo chooses Sep. 11 to apologize for hurt Muslim feelings." Within weeks, the senior official on duty at the embassy that night was removed from his post and recalled to Washington.

I chose Twitter examples because this is a book about digital diplomacy. But the phenomenon of seemingly benign and well-intended words sparking a diplomatic outrage is as old as the modern nation state. Yet for diplomats dealing with the digital landscape in particular – an environment in which information-sharing, information-consuming, information-recording are simply more – the work of knowing what information should be shared and what information should be kept secret is much, much trickier than it used to be.

This chapter focuses on culture. In my 2013 article in *The Atlantic* (Wichowski 2013b), I focused on how the structure of government contributes to that culture. Rather than holding onto the structure of government from an age long past – the legacy of hierarchical "cathedral" like command structure – government would be better served by adopting a flatter, more "bazaar" like structure, similar to the one adopted by the open source programming community.

But whether information-sharing is discouraged because of government's structure or culture, the effects are the same: failure to share information is bad for national security. Kneejerk secrecy scares off officials from sharing information with one another – 9/11, Benghazi and the Boston Marathon bombing are just a few examples of terrorist attacks that were found to be potentially preventable if government agencies had shared more information with one another. A culture of secrecy is also expensive. According to a May 2013 report by the Congressional Public Interest Declassification Board, each intelligence agency classifies a petabyte of information every 18 months, the storing of which costs over $11 billion dollars (Cox 2013).

The billboard-sized message here is that the vast majority of diplomatic government officials are already – without any additional secrecy-culture pressures – really, really careful with information. Diplomats are profoundly imbued with information-handling awareness and generally exceedingly careful with whether or not to make information public. Ramping up a culture of secrecy doesn't prevent the occasional ill-advised publicizing of sensitive information. It just adds another layer of pressure onto an already highly-pressured work culture. And it exacts a heavy toll. One of the unfortunate side effects of that pressure is that is teaches officials that the safest thing to do is to share as little information as possible; with the public, one's own colleagues; with anyone.

Leakers and their communities

Leakers are government officials. But they also step outside of that role. Once they take the step to leak government secrets, they become something different. The leaker is a highly feared kind of government official, and thus worth spending some time on.

Who leaks? Technically, to qualify as a leaker you have to be a. one of the 1.4 million federal workers with a security clearance, and b. release information you're not supposed to.[16] Can leakers be reduced to job type? Perhaps contractors, like Edward Snowden or the other 485,000 security-cleared contractors,[17] are less loyal than career officials? Or is there some other unifying characteristic that connects them?

'Secrecy is for losers' **63**

If there is a leaker profile, perhaps it's possible to see it by comparing some of the most prominent leakers from the past few decades[18] (Currier 2013):

Daniel Ellsberg

Senior military analyst. Employed at RAND. PhD, Harvard University. US Marines, '54–57. Leaked documents that showed the US government knew the Vietnam War was unwinnable. They became known as "The Pentagon Papers".

Why he did it

"I felt that as an American citizen, as a responsible citizen, I could no longer cooperate in concealing this information from the American public. I did this clearly at my own jeopardy and I am prepared to answer to all the consequences of this decision." (UPI 1971, para. 10)

Samuel Loring Morison

Intelligence analyst. Grandson of Pulitzer-prize winning naval historian Samuel Eliot Morison. Described as a "quiet and scholarly analyst" (Stanley 1984). Leaked photographs of Soviet ship-building facilities.

Why he did it

He's quoted as saying the "public should be aware of what was going on on the other side" (Sunlight Foundation 2013, para. 15).

Lawrence Franklin

Senior Middle East analyst for the Defence Department. Father of five. PhD in Asian Studies. Fluent in seven languages. Gave classified information about Iran to pro-Israel lobbyists working for AIPAC (Johnston 2006).

Why he did it

According to 2009 interview with *The Forward*, Franklin said he had warned superiors that American soldiers "would return in body bags" from Iraq if policy stayed the way it was. He wanted to "shock [people at the NSC] into pausing and giving another consideration" to current policy (Guttman 2009, para. 19).

Chelsea (formerly Bradley) Manning

23-year-old soldier stationed in Iraq. Downloaded 1.6 gigabytes of classified diplomatic cables onto a Lady Gaga CD, then transferred the files to a single thumb drive.

Why she did it

"I realized that (in) our efforts to meet the risk posed to us by the enemy, we have forgotten our humanity. . . . When I chose to disclose classified information, I did so out of a love for my country and a sense of duty to others" (Drury 2013, para. 5).

Edward Snowden

Computer specialist formerly employed by the CIA and NSA. Dropped out of high school; completed GED certificate; dropped out of community college.

Revealed NSA surveillance practices including PRISM, which involved collecting troves of data on US citizens who were not under any investigation.

Why he did it

"My sole motive is to inform the public as to that which is done in their name and that which is done against them" (Leger 2013, para. 10).

There are other leak cases that have gone to trial and many more still under investigation. But even just looking at this small subset, one pattern in particular emerges in sharp relief: why they did it. Regardless of their rank – from senior executive to temporary contractor – , educational background – from Harvard PhD to high school dropout – , family ties – from father of five to bachelor – every one of them said they did it because they believed they were right to do it. And with the exception of Edward Snowden, they remained in country to endure punishment for their actions.[19]

Now we get to the point where all that background on information-sharing and information-culture matters. That point is this: leaks don't just happen. Anyone with a security clearance can leak; almost nobody does. The handful of officials who leaked didn't do it because they thought they'd get away with it. They didn't do it because security was too lax. They didn't do it because government culture encouraged wanton information-sharing behaviour.

They did it because they believed their information needed to be shared. They believed it needed to be given to the public. They themselves may not put it in the words of the Brandians or the Pirate Partiers, but through their actions they become advocates for it: they believed the information they had should be free; perhaps even that that information wanted to be free.

~~Soft~~ difficult power

So far, this chapter has sketched a portrait of the digital landscape. It's explored how nerve-racking the digital landscape can be for national security agencies. It's discussed information-sharing trends in the broader culture, information-sharing influences in government culture and information-sharing motivations of leakers. There's one other information-sharing element that demands attention: information-sharing as part of diplomatic power.

A good place to start is the academic battle over "hard" versus "soft" sciences.

In 1987, Pulitzer-Prize winning author Jared Diamond wrote an op-ed in *Discover* magazine, commenting on what he called an "intellectual dogfight" over the distinction between "hard science" – the fields of cleanly measureable phenomena such as physics, chemistry, biology etc. – and "soft science" – the domain of squishier, more nebulous social sciences like psychology, sociology, anthropology and the like (Diamond 1987). He argued that "hard scientists" often looked to their "soft" counterparts derisively because the latter's research subjects seemed so damned fuzzy, and, as such, easy.

Wrong, he said. Soft sciences are actually harder than the "hard sciences". "A revolution in the Third World doesn't fit into a test tube," Diamond wrote. "You can't start it and stop it whenever you choose. You can't control all the variables; perhaps you can't control any variable" (1987, 35). As such, he argued that the soft sciences would be more aptly called "difficult science." The "hard sciences" would then become "easy science," as in easy to measure, control, quantify, test, and replicate.

National security isn't so different. We call diplomacy "soft power",[20] military might "hard power". Diplomacy is, like the social sciences, difficult. It's hard to measure, it's hard to control – it's just plain tricky.

Fortunately, good diplomats know how to master this murk. They're a nation's resident traders of tricky terrain. Yet to do their job well, they need information. A culture of secrecy makes it harder for diplomats to get information, and harder for diplomats to share information. It makes it harder for diplomats to exchange information with those outside government, and it discourages information-sharing even inside government.

In this way, a culture of secrecy disables not just diplomats, but it disables soft power. It ignores that soft power is actually difficult power. It's complicated power. Like the digital landscape in which it now must operate, diplomatic power is often muddy, fuzzy and squishy. It defies category and certainty. And since the digital landscape will only continue to expand, since dissent and disaffection will spread there before and while and after it erupts in the physical world, and because as more of the world's population finds its way online potential threats tied to the digital landscape will only increase, governments need powerful and empowered diplomats more than ever.

The diplomat's how-to: Three steps towards openness

There are actual, tangible, non-job-threatening steps available to diplomats and other officials to protect national security *and* loosen the reins on secrecy. The final section will explore a few of them.

Step 1: Broaden definitions

Know your audience, and expand your understanding of it. In national security circles, the "audience" includes anyone and everyone who might pose a threat, and anyone and everyone who might be counted as an ally. To find out who's who involves talking to people in government and outside government.

This is perhaps the most important of the three steps. This is because the nation state's not the only game in town anymore. This chapter argues that the "anyone and everyone" may sort themselves by nation, religion, or ethnic group. But it also includes digital associations where people identify borderlessly with like others. They may do so for lofty purposes, like beliefs, or very humdrum ones, like shared TV show preferences.

While threats to a nation's physical security may still involve in-person action, like the Boston Marathon bombers dropping off an explosives-filled backpack at the finish line, threats to physical security may also involve a whole lot of behind-the-digital-scene activity. Diplomats must be aware of who's out there, regardless of whether they identify by nation or beliefs like information-wants-to-be-free.

An example, featuring the activist group Anonymous, illustrates this. On July 3, 2011, in San Francisco, California, 45-year old Charles Blair Hill, a homeless man, drunk and reportedly making threatening gestures, was shot and killed by police officers working for San Francisco's Bay Area Transit System, better known as BART. Immediately after the killing, angry citizens used social media to coordinate mass protests in real-time, forcing the transit system to a halt (Fagan 2011).

After the protest in San Francisco, the activist group Anonymous stepped in online. Anonymous self-describes as an "Internet gathering" that "operates on ideas rather than directives." They're totally decentralized. No one really knows how big they are, but they're a force of some magnitude: they've been linked with WikiLeaks, the Occupy movement, and the Arab Spring. In 2012, *TIME* magazine listed Anonymous on its "World's 100 Most Influential People" list (Norton 2012).

Anonymous orchestrated a second protest: OpBART, a flash mob that would assemble via on-the-fly cell phone coordination. But authorities at BART got tipped off about it before the protest had a chance to take place. To prevent the real-time flash mob, authorities shut down cell service throughout the stations (Fagan, 2011).

Citizens did not like this.[21] News stories about the service shutdown spread through social media networks around the country, prompting nation-wide outrage. The ACLU sent a letter to the BART chief of police, denouncing BART as the "first known government agency in the United States to block cell service in order to disrupt a political protest" (Soltani and Schlosser 2011, para. 1). The Federal Communications Commission launched an investigation to determine the legality of BART's actions.[22]

It might seem like the scenario described here is a bad example for a chapter for foreign policy professionals – this happened on US soil. But Anonymous, and movements like it, are not domestic; they're international. As Internet and cell phone reach expands and the rest of the global population get online, borderless associations will only grow.

This example also shows that the same categories of person can be both a threat to national security or act as ally in protecting it. For instance, citizens who physically disrupted subway service may be seen as a threat to public safety, but those who protested against the cell phone shutdown may be seen as advocates for defending freedom of speech. The authorities could also be seen as both and threat and ally: police officers who use excessive force are threats to citizens, but police officers who halt transportation-disrupting protests are allies in protecting them.

Diplomacy is trickier than ever; let's not pretend otherwise. Expand your awareness of who's out there. To do so, diplomats must resist retreating into the comfort of secrecy. Talk to people. Know what's going on online, as well as in country.

Step 2: Engagement

Diplomats can't avoid social media. They must stake a flag in the public online domain. Most diplomats get this by now – official Twitter and Facebook accounts are by 2014 accepted practice. But while lots of diplomats use social media, only a handful of them use it really well.

To use it well, you have to post more than anodyne press releases. People don't care about policy guidance; they care about other people – especially powerful people who say something interesting and real. So say something real. Be careful, but don't let care keep you from saying anything. Reflexive secrecy prevents realness.

In an article I wrote for *Foreign Affairs* (Wichowski 2013a), I describe some of good diplomatic Twitter practices in detail. To summarize here, I argue that 140 characters at a time, diplomats can make statements; condemn, call out, exhort, urge, shine a light. One tweet may not seem to matter; but a record of tweets – and their retweets and their retweets – can add up quickly.

The US ambassador to the United Nations and diplomatic Twitter devotee Samantha Power often says that when approaching foreign policy problems to "look at every tool in the toolbox" (Gerstein, 2013, para 7).[23] When she wrote this in *A Problem from Hell* she was talking about preventing genocide. Twitter didn't exist then; "digital diplomacy" wasn't one of the tools. But the spirit of the message applies. Social media is a powerful tool. Thousands of ambassadors, foreign ministers, presidents and kings are starting to get that. Diplomats can help them by showing foreign policy leadership how to not just use social media tools, but how to use them well.

Step 3: Reduce hypocrisy

Assume everything – everything – will be found out. It won't, but assume it will. Align what you do with what you say you do. Some people won't like some policy, but no people like hypocrisy.

In the intriguing essay, "The End of Hypocrisy: American Foreign Policy in the Age of Leaks," political scientists Henry Farrell and Martha Finnemore (2014, para. 4) suggest that damage from leaks comes not so much from any specific revelation, but because they "undermine Washington's ability to act hypocritically and get away with it." They argue that hypocrisy has been especially damaging to America's soft power precisely because it's America: a nation that repeatedly seeks legitimacy through its ideals, like rule of law, democracy and free trade. If government actions undermine the law, democracy or free trade, the nation's legitimacy is undermined too.

In other words, hypocrisy damages national security, because it calls into question whether the ideals on which a nation is built actually matter. And if people online are indeed increasingly allying themselves with borderless collectives centered on beliefs, then bolstering the ideals of a country as something to believe *in* is more important than ever.

Closing thoughts

Digital information expands the reach of human capacity – to connect, to ally, to inform others and be informed by – and it does it at an accelerating pace. Like outer space, the digital universe expands.

To step back and consider this expanding, accelerating plane can be overwhelming, and terrifying, and awesome; it's a little like space in this way too. Thus, it feels only fitting to conclude the chapter with a quotation from someone who's been there.

Describing what it was like to see the earth from the moon, Apollo 13 astronaut Edgar Mitchell said:

> "You develop an instant global consciousness, a people orientation, an intense dissatisfaction with the state of the world, and a compulsion to do something about it.
>
> From out there on the moon, international politics look so petty. You want to grab a politician by the scruff of the neck and drag him a quarter of a million miles out and say, 'Look at that, you son of a bitch'."
>
> (People magazine 1974, para. 1)

A people orientation, an intense dissatisfaction with the state of the world, and a compulsion to do something about it: sounds a lot like diplomacy.

Notes

1 Alexis Wichowski is an employee of the US Department of State and an adjunct assistant professor at Columbia University's School of International and Public Affairs. The views expressed here are her own.
2 In December 2013, a federal judge presiding over Klayman v. Obama ruled that the PRISM data collection practices may have violated citizens' constitutional rights

(Jamieson, 2013, para 8). On January 3, 2014, the government filed an appeal (USCA Case #14–5004).
3 The White House report on PRISM, prepared by a task force handpicked to assess the pros and cons of the surveillance program, concluded: "There has been no instance in which NSA could say with confidence that the outcome [of a terror investigation] would have been any different" without the surveillance. See "Liberty and security in a changing world: report and recommendations of the President's Review Group on Intelligence and Communications Technologies" (White House 2013).
4 This was a long time coming; Snowden wasn't exactly unique in using his security clearance for nonapproved purposes. Three years prior to the NSA leaks, Chelsea (then Bradley) Manning, a private in the US Army, used her active security clearance to download hundreds of thousands of classified diplomatic cables. And three months after the NSA leaks, in a far grislier manifestation of abusing a security clearance, Aaron Alexis, an honorably discharged Naval reservist, used his still valid security clearance to gain access to a Navy yard in downtown Washington, DC, where, after being approved to walk through the front gates, he shot and killed twelve people.
5 "Wikileaks" refers here to the November 2010 event in which 251,287 classified diplomatic cables were made public, not the activist organization who assisted Manning in doing so
6 Admittedly, predigital-era folks wouldn't likely have characterized their written communication as "shareable", but for context-setting purposes of this chapter it must be pointed out that, technically, it was.
7 "Personal correspondence" is defined in the study as "household to household mail" (Mazzone 2011, 21) that includes "personal letters, holiday greeting cards, nonholiday greeting cards, invitations/announcements, other personal" (24).
8 The comparison is not precise: it is not possible to determine that the emails, texts and social media content conform to exactly the same definition of "personal correspondence" that was used in the USPS study. However, I argue that these digital correspondence statistics are a fair fit for comparison purposes, for two reasons: 1. the email statistics represent individualized human correspondence, excluding spam and marketing newsletters; 2. in 2010 it was still illegal to text someone's phone without their permission, making texts also a form of personal correspondence. Social media correspondence statistics are less clear, but many social media networks, such as Facebook, suggest a personal relationship between the users. It should be notes that, others, like Twitter and YouTube, do not.
9 Apparently some elites bemoaned the postage stamp for contributing to the "cheapening of an art form." As Simon Garfield (2013) notes the 1919 Yale Review lament on the dying art of letter-writing, blame was also laid on the telephone, the typewriter, the telegraph and even the train (for delivering letters too quickly) (271).
10 Literally: derived by assuming 16 waking hours in an average day, divided by 353 units of communication per day, totaling 22 per hour.
11 With only about 35% of the world's population online, it must be acknowledged that those in developing nations may not yet experience information-sharing in the same way as those in developed ones. However, there are signs the gap will shrink quickly: in 2014, around 70% of people in developing nations have basic cell phones, and some marketers estimate that within five years about 60% of the developing world will have access to smart phones (Internet World Stats, 2014; Fitchard 2013).
12 Evgeny Morozov wrote a critical but intriguing *New Yorker* piece on Brand, *Whole Earth* and the "Maker Movement," the 2013 outgrowth of World Earth's DIY activism. *Salon's* Andrew Leonard laments Morozov's takedown in an enlightening rebuttal. Both are worth the read.
13 Brand's full quote reads: "On the one hand, information wants to be expensive because it's so valuable. The right information in the right place just changes your life. On the other hand, information wants to be free, because the cost of getting it out is lower and lower all the time. So you have these two things fighting against each other."

14 Fun fact: Google alone was queried 5,922,000,000 per day in 2013 (Google Annual Search Statistics, 2014); 15% of its daily queries – 500,000 million of them – had never before been asked (Farber 2013).
15 Variations on SBU abound, such as "For Official Use Only" (FOUO) and "Controlled Unclassified Information".
16 A caveat: this is an unnuanced, oversimplified definition. Far more government officials leak than ever get caught. Reporters have suggested that even presidents leak information to the press on occasion (Van Buren 2012).
17 In truth, no one knows exactly how many federal contractors have security clearances. Former Secretary of Defense Robert Gates admitted in an article in the exhaustive *Washington Post* investigation "Top Secret America," "This is a terrible confession. I can't get a number on how many contractors work for the Office of the Secretary of Defense." (Priest and Arkin 2010, para. 20)
18 With gratitude to ProPublica and the Sunlight Foundation for their thorough spade work on which I expanded here.
19 A month after Snowden fled the US, Daniel Ellsberg (the Pentagon Papers leaker) wrote an op-ed in *The Washington Post* supporting Snowden's decision to leave the country. He wrote, "The country I stayed in was a different America, a long time ago . . . for the whole two years I was under indictment, I was free to speak to the media. . . . There is no chance that experience could be reproduced today" (*Ellsberg 2013, para. 1*)
20 There was an attempt to re-valorize diplomacy by introducing it as "smart power" – defined as enlisting other nations to achieve one's own national security goals (Nossel 2004); but in practice most foreign policy professionals still retain a fairly binary view on state power: diplomacy or defense; soft or hard.
21 Citizens didn't like it in the Ukraine, either, when in 2014 now-ousted President Yanukovich forced cell phone providers in Kiev to tag protestors, sending the text: "Dear subscriber, you are registered as a participant in a mass disturbance" (Murphy 2014, para. 1).
22 Under Standard Operating Procedure 303 (SOP 303) the government is permitted to shut down cell phone service in certain circumstances. The SOP 303 (Emergency Wireless Protocols) detail shutdown and restoration procedures in the event of a "national crisis." The FCC investigation was to determine if BART was operating under such conditions. As of April 2013, the FCC inquiry was still open (EPIC 2013). To force a decision, internet advocacy group the Electronic Privacy Information Center (EPIC) sued the Department of Homeland Security (DHS) under the Freedom of Information Act. According to EPIC, "How do we know that DHS is following the First Amendment or considering these important interests adequately? DHS has said nothing about its deactivation policy apart from a single paragraph in an old report." On November 12, 2013, the federal judge presiding over EPIC's case ordered DHS to disclose the details of their deactivation policy (http://epic.org/foia/EPICvDHS-SOP303-Order.pdf). At the time of this writing, the DHS had not yet done so, as they were within their sixty-day window to appeal.
23 Disclaimer: I work in her press office. I feel reflexively compelled to note her Twitter handle is @AmbassadorPower.

4

SOCIAL MEDIA AND PUBLIC DIPLOMACY

A comparative analysis of the digital diplomatic strategies of the EU, US and Japan in China

Corneliu Bjola and Lu Jiang

Introduction

The application of social media to the field of diplomacy has been hailed as a transformative development of international politics (Stein 2011; Seib 2012). Not only is social media able to transcend hierarchical chains of diplomatic communication, but by bringing ordinary people into the spotlight of political life and making their voice heard, it also allows diplomats to directly engage foreign publics in a sustained dialogue. These critical changes and their consequences largely explain why social media has become such a powerful symbol of the '**new public diplomacy**'. Diplomats now have the possibility not only to promote a message unidirectionally, but also to carry on enlightening conversations with a broad segment of the population of the country in which they operate. Similar to other contributions in this volume, this chapter seeks to explore the potential for policy innovation of social media and its ability to reshape the conduct of **public diplomacy**. At the same time, this chapter focuses on a less understood aspect of this relationship, namely, the features that enable social media to play such a transformative role in the hands of diplomats.

More specifically, we are interested in examining *how effective is social media for public diplomatic purposes?* What type of information diplomats can best deliver through social media, how deep their message can reach into the target audience, and what forms of communication are most suitable for engaging the foreign public? To address these questions, this chapter will compare strategies of **digital diplomacy** pursued by the European Union's Delegation and the embassies of Japan and the United States (US) in Beijing on the Chinese microblogging website Sina Weibo. While Twitter, Facebook and YouTube, along with some other social media networks, are blocked in China ("China Blocks Skype" 2010), a widely used Chinese-version microblogging website called Weibo enables Chinese netizens to catch up with world trends. Sina.com began its Weibo service in April 2011 and has enjoyed rapid growth ever since, not least because of its occasional success in promoting governmental transparency and accountability.[1] It is now the most visited site among all other competitors,[2] turning it into an ideal venue for conducting public diplomacy. By the end of 2012, there have been 165 authenticated official accounts of foreign institutions, of which 95 were set up in Sina Weibo. As of April 2014, the embassies of the US and Japan and the EU Delegation have attracted 868,780; 271,195 and 140,617 followers, respectively (Sina 2012).

To probe the relevance of digital diplomacy at the embassy level, this chapter investigates the conditions under which social media is able to perform three key aspects of public diplomatic engagement: **digital agenda-setting, digital presence-expansion** and **digital conversation-generating**. Each dimension speaks to an important aspect of exerting influence: message content, informational reach and mode of engagement with the audience. Our empirical analysis reveals that the threat of digital censure by the Chinese government is hardly effective. Weibo users do face the threat of cancellation of their account if they violate certain rules, such as opposing the basic principles of China's constitution, revealing national secrets, or threatening China's honour (BBC 2012). However, EU, US and Japanese diplomats have creatively used social media to alleviate the suspicion of Chinese authorities and in so doing they have managed to establish open communication channels with Chinese citizens, especially in terms of agenda-setting and presence-expansion. At the same time, the importance the EU, US and Japan attach to their diplomatic relationship with China largely informs the content and scope of their digital strategies.

The chapter aims to make two important contributions to the emerging field of digital diplomacy. Theoretically, it develops an original conceptual framework and methodology for assessing the effectiveness of digital diplomacy, both from the angle of diplomats and of their audience. Empirically, it fills a gap in the existing literature concerning the use of social media in public diplomacy under conditions of digital restrictions. The chapter is structured in three parts. The first section reviews existing research on the application of social media to diplomacy, the second part introduces the conceptual framework for assessing the effectiveness of digital diplomacy and the third part comparatively examines the digital strategies of the EU Delegation as well as of the US and Japan's embassies in Beijing on Weibo. Drawing on these findings, the chapter concludes with a set of recommendations for diplomats about how to make better use of social media in support of their diplomatic aims and functions.

Diplomacy and social media

Social media began to be taken more seriously academically in the aftermath of the revolutions, uprisings and the ensuing political unrest in the Middle East in 2011. Largely because of this historical event, many studies called attention to the untapped potential of social media in mobilizing social and political activism against repressive regimes (Burns and Eltham 2009; Li and Wang 2010; Seib 2012; Ghannam 2011; Shirky and Gladwell 2011). However, the use of social media in diplomacy precedes the revolutionary upheavals of the Arab Spring and relates to an important conceptual innovation. As Sabrina Sotiru explains in more detail in her chapter, digital diplomacy represents a novel and practical extension of the concepts of soft power and public diplomacy. It builds on the first concept by expanding platforms on which governments launch campaigns of nation branding (Aronczyk 2013). It boosts the latter by enabling multidirectional communication between diplomats and foreign publics. In short, digital diplomacy was married from the very beginning to the credo of the "new" public diplomacy of maximizing engagement with increasingly interconnected foreign publics and moving away from one-way information flows towards dialogue and engagement (Melissen 2005).

The global reputational decline suffered by the United States during President's George W. Bush's "war on terror" (Kohut 2010) created the opportunity for these ideas to be translated into practice. During her tenure as the US Secretary of State, Condoleezza Rice pressed her department to engage in what she called "transformational diplomacy". What she meant by that was to make the State Department 'smarter' by transforming old diplomatic institutions to serve new diplomatic purposes (Wilson 2008). Her successor, Hillary Clinton took the "art of smart power" to a new level by seeking "to reach beyond traditional government-to-government relations and engage directly with people around the world" (Clinton 2012, 117). Her 21st Century Statecraft platform sought to complement traditional foreign policy tools with newly innovated and adapted instruments of statecraft that fully leveraged the informational technologies made available by our interconnected world (US Department of State 2014). By reaching audiences in strategically important parts of the world for US foreign policy which traditionally were more difficult to engage, Rice and Clinton thus sought to restore the US reputation and diplomatic clout around the world.

As Stuart Murray comments in his chapter, these policy changes have transformed the US State Department into the world's leading innovator and user of digital diplomacy.[3] Thus, it comes as no surprise that many academic studies have focused on the US experience with digital diplomacy. In some cases, scholars have explored the social media tactics the US government has adopted for winning the "war on terror" and whether digital diplomacy has proved successful in creating a favourable policy environment towards the US, especially in the Middle East (Zaharna 2010; Khatib et al. 2011). Some others, borrowing from communication studies, have examined the particular mechanisms by which social media shapes public diplomacy. For example, Zhong and Lu (2013) argued that blogging and microblogging platforms could prove highly effective tools for improving US public diplomatic communication. Zhang (2013) proposed that social media use in US public diplomacy should first be a strategic issue management process. Wichowski (2013a, para. 20) went as far to argue that diplomats' refusal to use social media "would amount to professional malpractice."

Building on research on the "new" public diplomacy (Leonard 2002, Melissen 2005, Cowan and Arsenault 2008, Pamment 2013), a second body of literature has focused on examining how digital diplomacy has diffused to other regions and countries. Social media platforms have been found, for instance, to be instrumental in attracting public engagement in South Korea and Japan (Park and Lim 2014), or in fostering positive change in Nagorno Karabakh via two track diplomatic initiatives (Geybullayeva 2012). An (2011) conducted a textual analysis of the Weibo feeds of the President of the European Council, Herman Van Rompuy, and discovered that the special feature of Weibo as a platform for dialogue was not fully taken advantage of. A similar conclusion was reached by Uysal *et al.* (2012) about the Turkish government's twitter accounts: social media was used only for image cultivation through one-way information communication.

In light of the recent integration of social media into diplomatic practice, it is safe to assume that current studies have only begun to scratch the surface of what digital diplomacy means and how it works. This explains the absence in the current literature of a reliable conceptual framework for assessing the effectiveness of social media for public diplomatic purposes. More specifically, little is understood about how social media can help diplomats articulate an effective message to a foreign public, how to get it across and how to keep the target audience engaged. This chapter seeks to fill this gap by developing a conceptual framework for assessing social media effectiveness in public diplomacy by taking into account the perspective of the message senders as well as of the audience. It will be thus argued that key to understanding the effectiveness of a particular strategy of digital diplomacy rests with its capacity to move beyond information dissemination and to create conditions for a two-way conversation between diplomats and the foreign public at large.

Assessing social media impact

This chapter will advance a three-dimensional framework for examining the effectiveness of social media in public diplomacy. The first dimension relates to *agenda-setting* and the extent to which social media platforms enable diplomats to set the agenda of discussion with their target audience. Information-dissemination has always been a central task in public diplomacy. For the new public diplomacy, informing is the prerequisite for interaction because real dialogue must be based on topic familiarity, shared understandings and common interests. McCombs and Reynolds define agenda-setting as the "ability [of the new media] to influence the salience of topics on public agenda" (McCombs and Reynolds 2002, 1). Public diplomacy helps build a certain image of the country for foreign audiences by directing the latter's attention to certain topics while downplaying others through well-selected news. Diplomats can thus construct an issue as salient and worthy of attention for their audience by repeatedly providing relevant information on that issue. Compared with traditional mass media, social media boasts a great advantage in "grabbing headlines" due to its reach, frequency, usability, immediacy and permanence (Agichtein *et al.* 2008, 188). At the same time, the ease and speed of information dissemination may lead to situations in which audiences are being flooded with massive flows of data, which in turn could undermine the effectiveness of digital efforts of public diplomacy.

The second dimension of social media's impact is *presence-expansion*. If a government aims to develop a good relationship with a foreign audience, it first needs to be "out there" in the relevant public sphere. Diplomatic presence does not directly lead to a better image or favourable opinion, but without enough exposure, the public diplomatic strategy will ultimately fail. Traditionally, "presence" is realized mainly through mass communication, cultural exchanges or educational programs. The emergence of social media extends the scope of diplomatic presence over space and time. For example, the Digital Outreach Team of the State Department has directly engaged citizens in the Middle East through posting of messages about US foreign policy on popular Arabic, Urdu and Persian language Internet forums (Khatib *et al.* 2011). In the digital age, presence-expansion becomes an even more critical condition for diplomats to make their voice heard. As Wichowski points out above, the credibility and authority of diplomats would likely suffer if they fail to stay abreast with the constantly changing digital technologies. Not only would their message not be heard, but they also would lose out to competing information campaigns.

The third and final dimension is *conversation-generating*. One of the most appreciated feature of the new public diplomacy is its engagement with the audience (Pamment 2013). Good public diplomacy can no longer be monologue-based but must be dialogue-based. It has to facilitate a two-way or multidirectional communication between parties and to stimulate collaboration initiatives (Cowan and Arsenault 2008). Social media, with its interactive feature, has much to offer in this regard as it can generate a quasi-continuous dialogue between diplomats and foreign publics. Two-way conversations allow diplomats to readjust the focus of their agenda, reduce misinformation and enhance mutual understanding. It is this particular feature that enables social media to realize the goal of public diplomacy in a different way from traditional methods. At the same time, in spite of all the convenience it provides, social media is not necessarily easy to use as a tool of public diplomacy. In fact, it might involve even more human resources and financial investment than traditional media-based tools as its objectives, methods and operations require a complex digital infrastructure and well-trained staff to carry out the missions.

These mutually exclusive dimensions of social media impact offer a comprehensive and reliable framework for assessing the effectiveness of digital diplomacy. Thus, as one of the main purposes of the latter is to advance foreign policy goals by influencing public opinion in the host country, is it then important to understand what kind of information is being used to inform and influence the public (agenda-setting)? How far can this influence reach (presence-expansion)? And finally, through what kind of mechanism is influence exerted (one-way information dissemination vs two-way conversation)? This way, we can not only showcase how social media assists public diplomacy but we can also explain the mechanisms by which social media makes or does not make a difference in public diplomacy. The last point is particularly important as it goes at the heart of the argument about the transformative role of social media in foreign policy in general and in public diplomacy in particular.

This chapter will use these three dimensions to compare the effectiveness of the digital diplomatic strategies of the Japanese embassy, the EU Delegation and US embassy on Weibo. The selection of the case studies and of the medium is justified on two grounds. First, against the backdrop of the public debate regarding the rise of China, it is important to understand how other key regional or global powers, such as Japan, US or EU, react to this geopolitical development from a public diplomatic perspective. The cultural, political and ideological differences between these three countries have also important implications for how social media is used for public diplomatic purposes, both in terms of objectives and styles. Second, conducting digital diplomacy in China could be challenging given the constant threat of censorship by Chinese authorities. Unlike Twitter, Weibo is not a public landscape. Simply copying and pasting the same content from Twitter to Weibo is not enough. Foreign embassies in China must bear in mind the limits of what they can publicly communicate, otherwise they may face consequences.[4] Making sense of how diplomats can use social media under conditions of digital restrictions leads us to an important practical conundrum that deserves closer scrutiny.

Digital diplomacy at work

The data set used to probe empirically the effectiveness of social media as a tool of public diplomacy consists of Weibo entries of three units of analysis (EU Delegation, US and Japan embassies in Beijing) collected during a fifty-day period, between February 5, 2013, and March 26, 2013. This period was marked by two important events: one nonpolitical, the Spring Festival[5] and the other one heavily political, the end of the transition period for the leadership of the Communist party.[6] We first investigate what kind of information was offered by the EU, US and Japanese diplomats on Weibo, and with what strategic purpose. The response of the audience is then examined to see whether and how the three agencies expanded their presence among Weibo users. In the final part, we take a look at the interaction between the three official accounts and their followers.

Agenda-setting

To understand how the EU delegation and the US and Japanese embassies used Weibo as an agenda-setting platform, we categorize all posts sent during the selected timeframe based on the original topic of discussion (see Figures 4.1–4.3). A close look at the three Weibo accounts reveals important patterns and regularities. First, the frequency of daily posts, all written in Chinese, is surprisingly stable. The number of embassy posts totalled 81, 201 and 257 for Japan, the EU

Social media and public diplomacy   77

and the US, respectively, and these posts were evenly spread throughout the fifty-day period (around two, four and five posts per day, respectively). Clearly, posting on Weibo has become a regular activity for the delegation and the two embassies, which suggests that dedicated staff must be in charge of carrying out this task. Second, the design of Weibo feeds shows a crafty combination of informative texts, lively pictures and hyperlinks to policy papers. A balance is actually struck between the effort to stimulate the interest of Weibo users in an entertaining manner and the need to maintain an authoritative stance and provide official messages. Third, each Weibo diplomatic account follows a specific content pattern. Consider, for instance, the Weibo feed of the EU account, which starts each morning with famous European paintings or quotes from renowned writers, followed by more elaborate and policy-oriented content. The same holds true for the other two embassies, which offer daily or weekly information on fixed topics. However, the focus of each account is slightly different, a fact that reflects the different agenda-setting strategies and styles pursued by the three diplomatic actors.

For example, Japan exerts a strict control over its agenda, as suggested by the topics it chooses to post about but equally important by those it chooses *not* to post about on Weibo (see Figure 4.1). First, there is an explicit and active classification of posts according to their content. Each post falls into one of about ten topics (Japanese cuisine, Japan news, Japan-China cooperation, Japanese society, Japanese tradition, activities, language learning etc.), the name of which is usually highlighted in square brackets before each post. In this way, the embassy actually frames the topic in the way it wants the audience to understand. Second, there is a strong focus on nonpolitical topics. As can be seen from these posts, the Japanese account provides information on a wide range of topics such as food, travelling and traditions, while there are hardly any posts on trade, economy or other politically related topics. Of all Japanese posts, 75% are covered by nonpolitical news falling into one of three categories: 'Japan society', 'Japan news' (mainly technology and entertainment news) and 'offline activity'. Consistent with the 'nonsensitive topic' approach, the Japanese ambassador to China conveyed his greetings

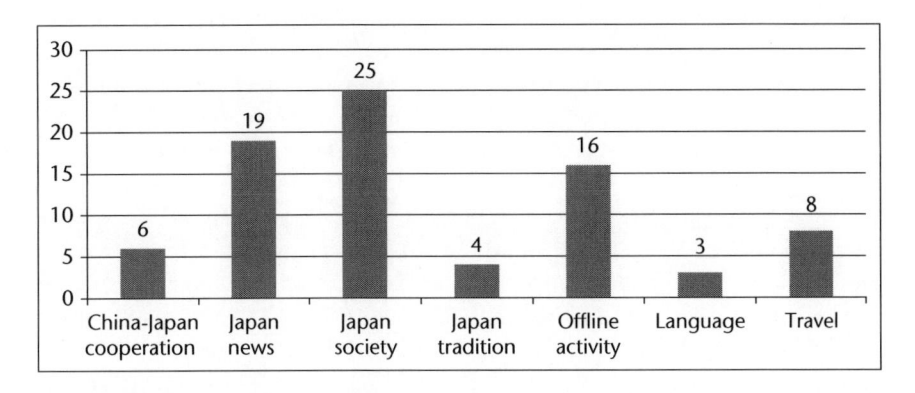

Category	Count
China-Japan cooperation	6
Japan news	19
Japan society	25
Japan tradition	4
Offline activity	16
Language	3
Travel	8

FIGURE 4.1 Weibo entries of the Japanese embassy

78 Corneliu Bjola and Lu Jiang

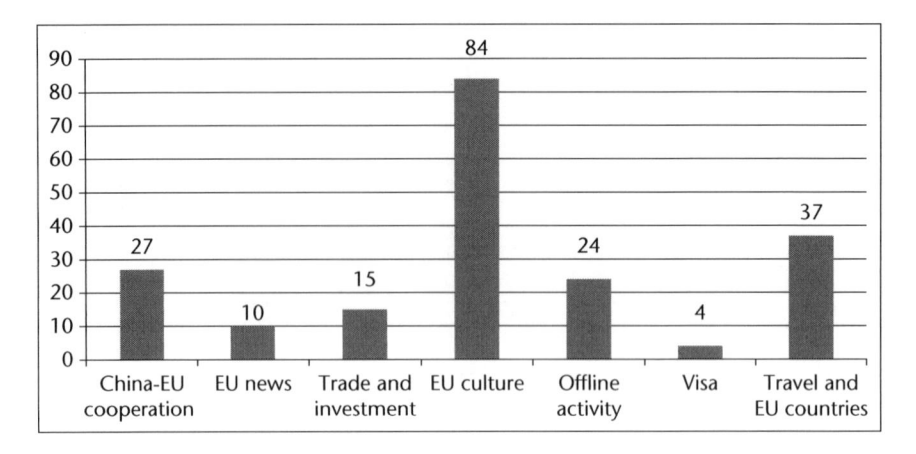

```
90 ┤           84
80 ┤           ■
70 ┤           ■
60 ┤           ■
50 ┤           ■                              37
40 ┤     27    ■          24                  ■
30 ┤     ■          15    ■                   ■
20 ┤     ■    10    ■     ■                   ■
10 ┤     ■    ■     ■     ■           4       ■
 0 ┴────────────────────────────────────────────
    China-EU  EU news Trade and EU culture Offline  Visa  Travel and
   cooperation       investment          activity        EU countries
```

FIGURE 4.2 Weibo entries of the EU delegation

during the Chinese New Year on Weibo, but stayed silent when Xi Jinping was elected as the new president of China.

The Weibo account of the EU Delegation has adopted a systematic approach with a clear focus on culture. EU posts are being also classified under different topics, but in a more casual manner than the Japanese account. For example, the contents of 'European information' and 'travelling' might overlap, while some others are posted without being clearly defined under a specific topic. However, daily posts on EU culture (famous paintings or quotes) are a must-do and amount to more than one-third of all posts. The other two common topics are 'travel and EU countries' and 'China-EU cooperation'. For example, a post falling under 'travel and EU countries' talked about St. Patrick Day in Ireland; another one on 'China-EU cooperation' regarded the Confucius Institute in Europe as an example of bilateral cooperation. These efforts aim to showcase the "unity in diversity" of the European Union, the richness of European cultures as well as the lifestyle of Europeans. On February 9–10, 2013, the EU Delegation launched an offline activity to celebrate the Spring Festival and to introduce European food to the Chinese audience. Soft political messages were also present. A timely congratulatory message on behalf of the EU president Van Rompuy was posted by the EU embassy upon Xi being elected president of China. The post also expressed EU's willingness to deepen cooperation with China in areas like security, economy and trade, rule of law and people-to-people exchanges.

Compared with Japan and the EU, the posts of the US embassy are much more engaged in delivering "hard" political messages, especially those with potentially high social impact for the Chinese people. The embassy generally avoids topics that might be construed as a direct criticism of Chinese authorities, and its posts usually cover aspects of US history, landscape, culture, tradition or domestic policy. Around one-third of them fall, for instance, under the rubric of 'US news', which, quite differently from 'Japan news', mainly talks about US policies,

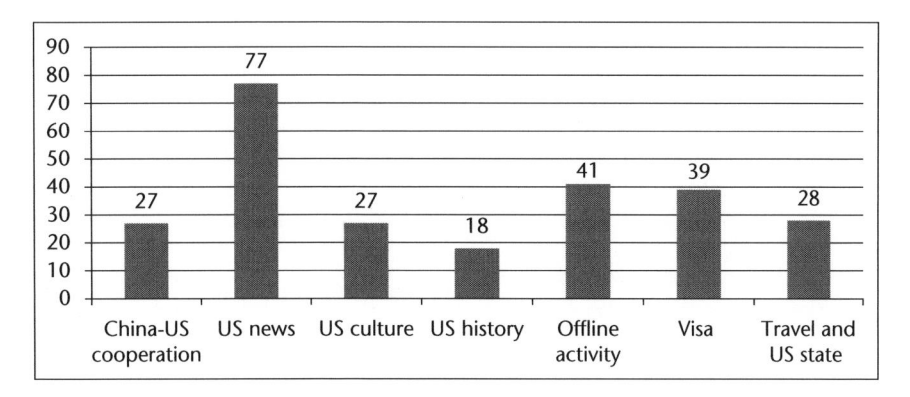

FIGURE 4.3 Weibo entries of the US embassy

bilateral ties and high-level exchanges. At the same time, the embassy does not shy away from commenting on some controversial issues. For example, when Chinese people expressed frustration about the level of air pollution in China, a post about the level of air pollution in Salt Lake City (PM 2.5) appeared on the US embassy's Weibo homepage.[7] This post was commented on and reposted more than 4,000 times.

In a similar fashion, responding to public concerns about soaring housing prices in Chinese large cities, the US account posted several messages talking about how much it would cost to buy a house in America. Another third of US Weibo posts were mainly service-oriented or offline-activity promotion, targeting a broader community. The importance that US attaches to its relationship with China is illustrated by the embassy's posts on two occasions: four greeting messages from President Obama, Ambassador Locke, State Secretary Kerry and the embassy during the Lunar New Year, and one post on the prospects of a bilateral relationship after Xi was elected president of China. A survey of the reposts and comments written in reaction to these entries indicates these messages were well received by Chinese Weibo users.

Presence-expansion

While agenda-setting helps measure influence from the perspective of message senders, presence-expansion looks at the same issue from the perspective of message receivers. Due to privacy and technical constraints, it is rather difficult to know precisely how many times each post has been viewed by other users. Weibo statistics allow us, however, to accurately capture two important channels of presence-expansion: reposting (how many times a post is circulated among users) and commenting (whether a post generates discussion or not). For reasons of statistical relevance, we have decided to select only Weibo feeds with more than 200 reposts or comments (see Table 4.1). The propagation route of G(roup) > 200 feeds is first examined to find out how presence is expanded. Fifteen of the

TABLE 4.1 Propagation route of G(roup) > 200

	Number of posts	G > 200	Ratio	Number of followers
Japan	81	40	49%	209,049
EU	201	2	1%	90,278
US	257	57	22%	671,293

most reposted or commented feeds are then chosen from each Weibo account and reclassified according to their core messages. In so doing, we seek to find out how successful presence-expansion was, that is, whether the interest of the audience converged with the agenda-setting strategy of the message senders.

For the Japanese embassy account, forty posts out of the total of eighty-one received over 200 reposts or comments. This translates into a 49% ratio, the highest in our sample. The ratio for the US embassy stood at 22%. In striking contrast, only two of the 201 posts of the EU Delegation received in excess of 200 reposts or comments. A closer look at the three ratios reveals that Japanese Weibo feeds generated wider discussion among followers, with a spread of about 70–500 comments or reposts. EU feeds received about thirty–forty reposts or comments for each feed. In comparison, there were two extremes in the US case. The post about Salt Lake City was, for instance, very influential, witnessing over 4,000 reposts or comments. It should be noted that even if these comments and reposts did not always reflect favourable sentiments from the audience, they did help provoke discussions, and in so doing they enhanced the visibility of the message sender.

Propagation routes

In order to track the propagation routes of the US, EU and Japanese posts, we randomly pick two posts from each G > 200 cluster representative of the three agencies and then apply the Weibo analytical tool 'Weiboreach'[8] to examine how the message is spread (by whom, via how many layers of repost and how many times).[9] The results uncover a diversified pattern of propagation. Figure 4.4 shows, for instance, how a single message gets around. The cluster in the centre represents the original information source. Each dot in Figure 4.4 represents a node in the propagation route, and the curves connecting each repost refer to the direct relationship between a user and his or her follower who reposts the message from him/her. Denser dots mean more reposts, and larger clusters signify greater influence.

Figure 4.5, on the other hand, shows the repost layers of these six messages. As it can be seen from the figure, if a Weibo post has more than 200 reposts or comments, reposting usually happens at about four levels. The stronger the impact of a message, the greater the number of repost layers. Two or more repost layers suggest the influence of the message reaches beyond the immediate group of followers to a wider range. It is in this way that public diplomacy is able to expand its presence

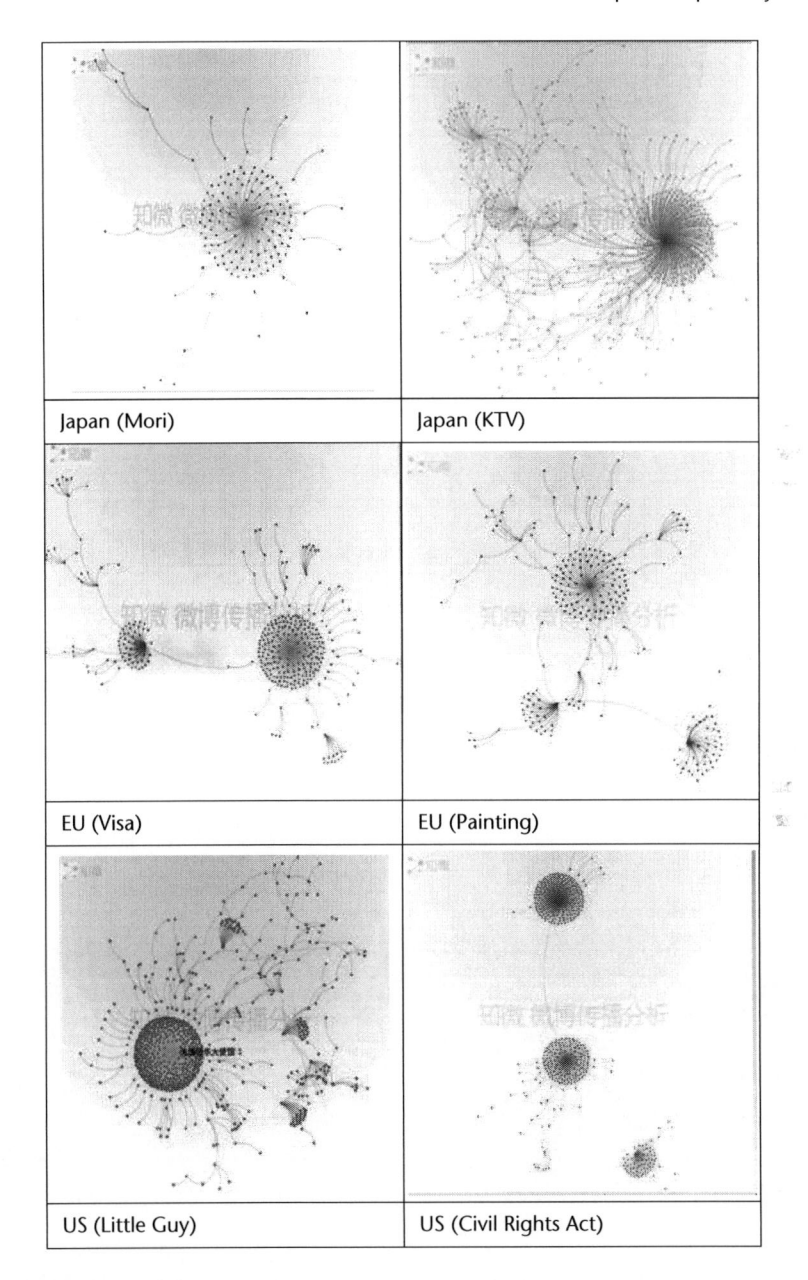

Japan (Mori)	Japan (KTV)
EU (Visa)	EU (Painting)
US (Little Guy)	US (Civil Rights Act)

FIGURE 4.4 Route of reposting

on social media. Two Japanese posts reflect the most typical reposting pattern, that is, at the first layer. This kind of reposting is created by direct followers of the embassy, usually ordinary (as opposed to authenticated[10]) and individual (as opposed to organizational[11]) users who are personally interested in the topic but do not have an extensive recommunication capability.

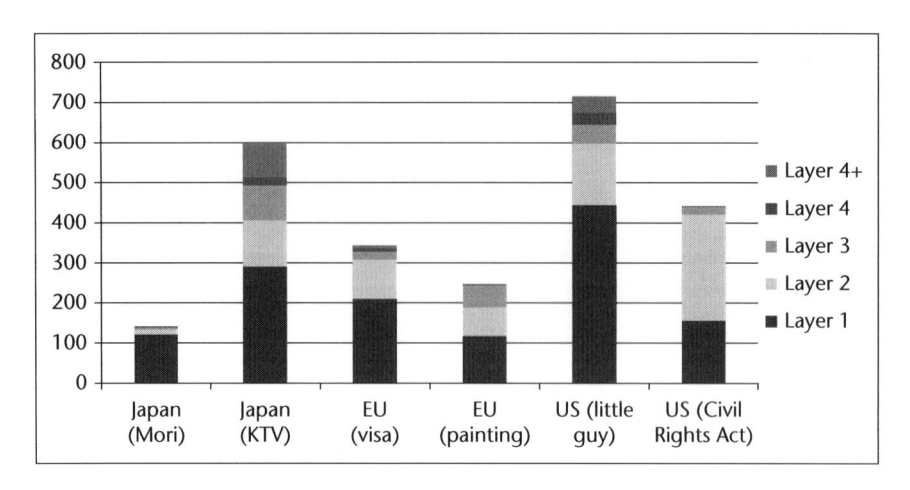

FIGURE 4.5 Layers of reposting

Another pattern, reflected in two EU posts, is featured by small clusters of second-and-higher-layer reposts. The nodes of second-time and third-time reposting, with no exception, are authenticated users, who have a considerable number of followers. The same holds true for the US post about the 'little guy'. Three repost clusters can be seen on the right side of the central cluster. According to Weiboreach, these reposts were generated by two authenticated individual users (lawyer Liu Xiaoyuan and civil law scholar Li Jianmin) and one organizational user (Renmin University Weibo Group). Finally, a very atypical pattern is discovered in the second example of US posts, where much more reposts take place at the second layer than at the first. The corresponding diagram in Figure 4.4 illustrates this more vividly. There is a larger cluster at the top, whose centre represents a follower of the US embassy who reposted the feed on the Civil Rights Act. According to Weiboreach, this user is Xue Manzi, a famous Chinese philanthropist and entrepreneur whose Weibo account has more than 11 million followers. The conclusion to be drawn from this example is that a popular follower can serve as an "influence-multiplier" and substantially increase the spread and impact of a post.

Agenda-setting effectiveness

The final step in evaluating the influence of public diplomacy on Weibo consists of comparing the topics that have attracted the most attention among Weibo-users on the one hand, and the agenda-setting goals of the message senders on the other hand. In other words, how effective really was presence-expansion? To address this question, we selected fifteen most-reposted or commented posts of each official account and reclassified them into five general categories: science/culture/traveling, economy, politics, society (of Japan, the EU and the US, respectively) and services (visa etc.).

Social media and public diplomacy 83

As shown in Figure 4.6, six out of fifteen (40%) most-reposted or commented feeds from the Japanese embassy talked about the Japanese society, while five other posts (33%) were about science, culture or travelling to Japan. Specifically, these posts referred to concerns of ordinary Japanese people, the underground water treatment in Japan, Japanese festivals and so on. The remaining four posts were more service and cooperation-oriented. In general, Chinese Weibo users appear to be quite interested in Japanese traditions and Japanese society, a fact that can be partially explained by the cultural similarity between the two nations. At the same time, the topics also reflect the public diplomatic priorities of the Japanese embassy.

For the EU Delegation, a majority (nine) of the top fifteen posts belonged to the 'science/culture/travelling' category, among which seven were culturally related. Weibo users appear to be relatively indifferent to economic and political topics in the EU case, which also happen to be areas of potential diplomatic friction between the two sides. According to these research findings, Chinese citizens are fond of the diversity of European cultures, including paintings, literature, architecture and religion. Culture seems to be the most attractive and effective way of getting to know this rather unknown region for most Chinese people. The interest of the Chinese audience here coincides with the sender's message and EU's strategic focus on cultural promotion.

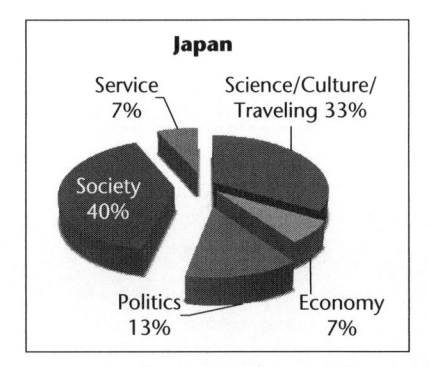

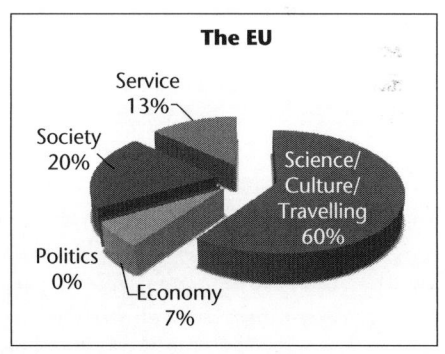

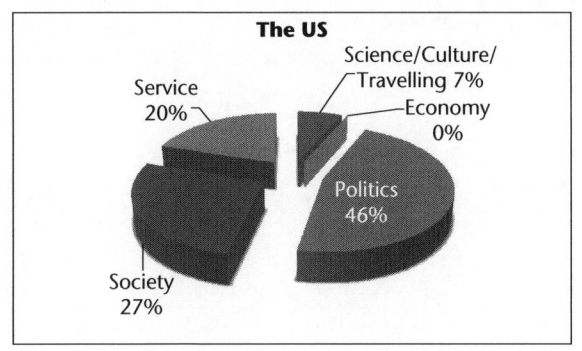

FIGURE 4.6 Most reposted and commented on Weibo posts

As for the US embassy case, Weibo posts covering political issues and societal differences received a great deal of attention. Politically related posts (e.g. about the legal system or high-level exchanges) represented 46% of the Top 15 posts. American values such as freedom, human rights or the rule of law run through almost all political- and society-themed posts, with a combined account of around 75% of the Top 15. When one post talked about entrepreneurship in the US society, one could sense the calling of the "American Dream". When another post discussed whether the US president and senators could afford to buy a house from their salary, it touched upon the tender sensibility of the Chinese public on corruption issues and housing prices. These topics received much attention because they exposed some deep-seated anxieties of the Chinese public regarding the development strategy of their country. Tellingly, these social problems were given a voice through 'US news', the main focus of the US agenda-setting on Weibo.

By comparing the pattern of the messages sent by the three diplomatic actors (Figures 4.1–4.3) and that of the fifteen most reposted or commented messages (Figure 4.6), we find the two categories to largely overlap with each other. This demonstrates the effectiveness of the agenda-setting and presence-expansion strategy in each case.

Conversation-generating

While the capacity of social media to facilitate interaction between the message sender and the audience is well recognized, the mechanism that enables this interaction is not fully understood. This is a gap this section seeks to bridge. First, what distinguishes new public diplomacy from the old one is *listening*. On Weibo, the users you follow indicate whom you are listening to. The number of users followed by the embassy of Japan, the EU Delegation and the US embassy has reached 104, 69 and 245, respectively (as of April 2014). The US embassy tends to follow public opinion leaders in China, the Japanese embassy chooses to follow current-affair commentators on Japanese issues (Qin *et al.* 2011), while the EU Delegation primarily follows the official account of European countries. In general, the three accounts rarely follow ordinary Weibo users and prefer instead to listen to authenticated or organizational users.

Second, the conversation process involves a repetitive circuit (see Figure 4.7) of information providing (I_t), receiving comments and reposts (II_t), providing feedback, readjusting information (III_t & I_{t+1}) and making new comments (II_{t+1}). I, II, III represent different actions taken by EU, US and Japanese diplomats, whereas t and t+1 refer to successive stages of repetition of this cycle. Agenda-setting and presence-expansion have been discussed above as I_t (I_{t+1}) and II_t (II_{t+1}). In this section, we focus on III_t: providing feedback to the audience. This constitutes a pivotal step in the conversation process because without it, the repetitive process will likely stop after a one-shot conversation. The three agencies provide feedbacks to other Weibo users in two major forms: by reposting on commenting on tagged feeds (using the @ function[12]), or by commenting on Weibo users' responses to their original Weibo feeds.

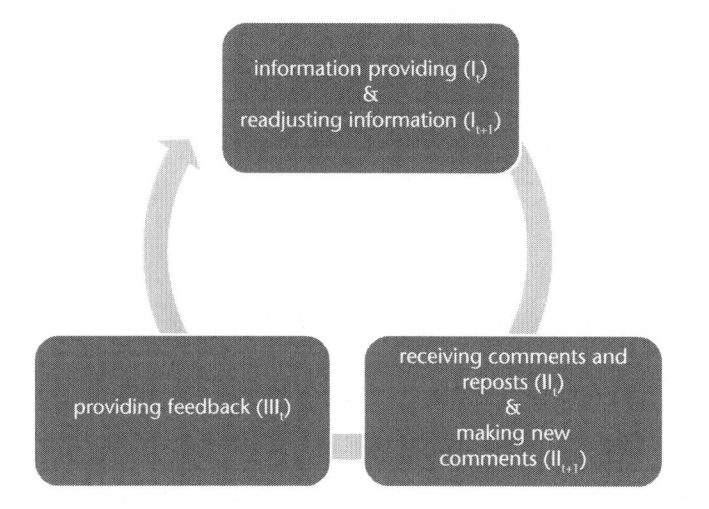

FIGURE 4.7 Analysis of most reposted and commented on Weibo posts

With respect to the first mode of feedback, we found that none of the three diplomatic accounts reposted or commented on Weibo feeds that tagged them within the chosen timeframe (February 5–Mar 26, 2013). We also found no solid evidence of official responses to Weibo users' queries. For instance, when one post from the EU Delegation introduced the Belgian chocolate stamps, one interested user asked where he or she could buy the stamps, but no response was provided. These findings may be disappointing to those defending the transformative role of social media in public diplomacy, as they raise doubts about the extent to which foreign publics are able to engage diplomats in two-way conversations. However, our research also reveals that the interactive dimension of social media has a broader scope of application, with additional diplomatic implications.

First, some of the Japanese and US posts triggered a variety of attitudes and emotions among Chinese Weibo users. Consider, for instance, the festival greetings sent by the Japanese embassy. The users' comments can be divided into three groups: one group expressed thanks to the ambassador and wished him back. Another group took the opportunity to express hope in a peaceful bilateral relationship. While the third group behaved quite extreme: users ignored the greeting, blamed the Japanese side for raising tensions in the "Diaoyu/Senkaku Islands" controversy and even threw insults at the ambassador. A similar situation happened when one post from the US embassy told the history of the Civil Rights Act. Most users expressed admiration for the democratic values and equality enshrined in the Act, but others criticized the perceived US double standard and gamesmanship with China. In contrast, most comments to EU posts stuck to topics under discussion. The reason, as one Weibo user pointed out, could be that "EU feeds are distinctive for that they always talk about European arts".

Second, although the message senders rarely engaged directly the audience, exchanges nevertheless took place between the members of the audience. When one user asked "how do Japanese young people cope with pressure", but failed to get any official response from the Japanese embassy, another Weibo user replied. In a different case, in September 2012, almost all comments on the Japanese embassy's website were highly critical of Japan for its position on the "Diaoyu/Senkaku Islands" issue. However, some Weibo users began to reflect upon whether such reactions were appropriate and appealed to the other Weibo users to calm down. Therefore, conversations between audiences could serve as a barometer of the mood of the public opinion on issues of particular importance for the relevant parties.

Another way by which to evaluate the level of interaction between message senders and the audience is by checking whether the feeds of the former are original or reposted from other Weibo users. The results show that all 85 posts of the Japanese embassy were original. 30 out of 201 posts of the EU Delegation were reposted from other users and 171 were original. Among the reposted ones, three were from ordinary Weibo users who took part in activities organized by the Delegation. The other 27 were from organizational users such as embassies of European countries, the Lufthansa Airline and various travelling websites. For the US Embassy, out of 257 posts, 201 were original and 46 were reposted. 32 posts came from ordinary users asking questions about visa policy. The other 14 reposts were from "Education USA in China" and US Consulates in Guangzhou, Shanghai, Chengdu and Shenyang, and served mainly to introduce the events convened by these agencies. These results indicate that the main function of reposting in the case of EU and the US is to disseminate information and clarify policies rather than to engage the audience in a two way conversation.

To conclude, the use of social media by the EU Delegation and the embassies of the US and Japan for public diplomatic purposes was not particularly conducive to generating genuine conversations with the target audience. As our analysis shows, digital diplomacy is being primarily used as an instrument of information dissemination. At the same time, there are important differences in the way in which the three diplomatic actors set the agenda of discussion and disseminate their message. The nature of the bilateral relationships between China and the three countries largely explains these differences. Due to painful historical memories of World War II, Japan has traditionally had a difficult relationship with China. It therefore prefers a cautious agenda-setting strategy free of political or controversial topics. Its attempt to win the Chinese public opinion appears to pay off thus far as it can be seen from the rate of positive reposts and comments. Aware of the soft power of its traditions and cultures, EU has focused its digital diplomatic efforts on cultural aspects. The objective is to increase the visibility of the EU among the Chinese public, which arguably does not yet have a clear understanding of the region. To some extent, this strategy explains why EU public diplomacy is more focused on information providing than conversation-generating. The US digital diplomacy, on the other hand, reflects the long term strategic objective of the US to facilitate a peaceful rise of China. By focusing on messages reflective of its core values and institutions, the US digital diplomacy strategy aims to provide ideological support to those seeking to steer the Chinese political system into a more democratic direction.

Conclusion

In comparison with more conventional means of communication, social media presents three key advantages for conducting public diplomacy. It offers a highly effective instrument for delivering information, it makes possible for the intended message to reach deep into the target audience, and it enables a two way conversation between diplomats and the foreign public. Our analysis of the diplomatic strategies of the EU Delegation and the US and Japan's embassies in China indicates however, that digital diplomacy is being primarily used as an instrument of information dissemination and much less for engaging the audience in a two-way dialogue. To be sure, certain interactive features of social media are still present, such as the feedback mechanism (e.g. the audience's comments and reposts), which enables embassies to learn about the opinions of their audience and readjust their tactics and strategies accordingly. The nature of the bilateral relationship between countries also influences the way in which social media is being used for diplomatic purposes. The more estranged the relationship between the two parties, the more cautious the digital diplomatic strategy and the less controversial the message.

The self-feeding influence of digital diplomacy creates a couple of challenges for diplomats. Due to the fast-changing nature of social media, digital diplomacy requires diplomats to constantly update their digital skills and strategies in order to stay relevant in cyberspace. For example, before Weibo became so influential, Renren.com (a Chinese version of Facebook) used to be a more popular platform. Weibo itself is currently slightly out of fashion as Chinese people are spending now more time on Wechat, a Chinese mobile voice and text messaging communication service. It should be also noted that once diplomats have decided to conduct digital diplomacy, they should bear in mind that a piecemeal approach might not enough. A holistic perspective that combines social media with more traditional forms of diplomatic interaction is more likely to yield good results. Social media can help deliver a strong message in a highly effective manner, but it cannot act as a substitute for good strategy planning, relationship-building and crisis managing, the well-established marks of professional diplomatic conduct.

Notes

1 For example, the 'Li Gang incident' and the 'Wenzhou train collision' were first uncovered on Weibo (Hassett 2011; MacLeod 2011).
2 By the end of 2013, the number of monthly active user and daily active user of Sina Weibo has reached 129 million and 61 million, respectively (Sina 2014).
3 After starting modestly with a few people in 2002, the digital diplomacy office has developed into a 150 strong unit by 2012, working in 25 different digital nodes and providing services for more than 900 people at US missions abroad. A single US diplomat can now

communicate directly with a million people every day through one of the State Department's 600 social media platforms (Hanson 2012b).
4   For example, after the US consulate-general in China published on Weibo their independent monitoring data of air pollution in 2012, their account was immediately deleted without being given any reason.
5   The Spring Festival, also known as the Chinese New Year, is the most important celebration in the Chinese calendar (BBC Home 2014).
6   China completed the power transition at the end of the annual session of China's top legislature with Xi Jinping as the incoming president. The once-in-a-decade handover marks the third generational power transfer in China ("China Completes Leadership Transition" 2013).
7   PM 2.5 is an airborne particle of roughly 2.5 micrometers in diameter, which has been used as an indicator for China's air pollution (http://aqicn.org/city/beijing/). The US Weibo post simply stated that air pollution in Salt Lake City had exceeded the 69 level (on the PM2.5. index) several times in the past, and even topped 125 in 2013. However, the two benchmarks (69 and 125) were officially considered good air conditions in Beijing or Shanghai, and hence the US post could be construed as a veiled critique of the level of air pollution in China.
8   Weiboreach (www.weiboreach.com/) is a social media information intelligence website in China. Established in 2010, it provides services in propagation analysis, information monitoring, event analysis and information collection.
9   In the case of the Japanese embassy, one post introduced a famous Japanese politician called Mori-Motonari (repost: 144; comment: 179), while the second post was about Japanese Karaoke (repost: 605; comment: 131). In the case of the EU Delegation, one post was about the Schengen visa policy (repost: 348; comment: 234) and the other presented a painting of a beautiful girl on Women's Day (repost: 247; comment 30). In the case of the US embassy, one post was about the speech given by Ambassador Locke, where he talked about the "little guy" in the US (repost: 725; comment: 262), while the other introduced the history of the Civil Rights Act in 1964 (repost: 448; comment: 100).
10 Authenticated users are usually celebrities, scholars or officials whose identities have been confirmed by Sina Weibo. Authenticated users are held accountable for their remarks on Weibo, but at the same time their accounts are protected against counterfeiting.
11 Including businesses, NGOs and governmental agency accounts.
12 Similar to Facebook, Weibo users can tag other users in posts or comments using the @ key, followed by a link to the user's profile.

5

AMERICA'S SELFIE

How the US portrays itself on its social media accounts

Ilan Manor and Elad Segev

Introduction

In recent years, nations throughout the world have incorporated the use of social networking sites (SNS), such as Twitter and Facebook, in their diplomatic efforts. **Digital diplomacy** is seen by researchers as an important tool in furthering a nation's foreign policy as it enables direct interaction and engagement with foreign publics (Metzgar 2012; Cowan and Arsenault 2008; Hayden 2012). Yet digital diplomacy may also prove a useful tool in **nation-branding** activities. While the existing scholarly work on nation branding is extensive, few studies to date have evaluated the manner in which nations use digital diplomacy to proactively manage their image. This could be a result of the fact that until recently, nation-branding activities focused primarily on traditional media, such as advertising campaigns in television, radio and print. Moreover, as the practice of digital diplomacy is still evolving, the use of SNS in order to manage the national image and reputation is a novel practice. Investigating the manner in which foreign ministries employ social media in their nation-branding activities is warranted as it may represent a shift in the conceptualization, practice and assessment of nation branding.

This study attempts to fill this apparent gap. In the first part of this chapter we explore the current literature on nation branding and illustrate the manner in which digital diplomacy can further nation-branding activities by altering an image of a nation that has taken root in the minds of international audiences. As nation branding is an attempt by a nation to draw its own portrait, we refer to the use of digital diplomacy in nation-branding activities as **selfie diplomacy**. In the second part of the chapter we analyze America's selfie by searching for recurring themes in all social media content published by the US State Department over the duration of one month. By so doing we demonstrate the manner in which nations use digital diplomacy to manage their image and offer scholars the means by which to investigate such images.

Our study aims to expand the reach of nation branding research to SNS, and offer a conceptual model for the relationship between digital diplomacy and nation branding. While SNS is increasingly employed by foreign ministries, our study shows that digital diplomacy is particularly useful in altering the prevalent image of a nation among foreign audiences and mending national images following times of crisis. It also demonstrates that analyzing digital diplomacy content enables one to identify the new national image being promoted. We therefore believe that this chapter may be beneficial to both scholars and practitioners of digital diplomacy.

Nation branding

The body of scholarly work on nation branding has grown substantially over the last decade. However, researchers, practitioners and policymakers remain divided over the question of whether nations can, or should, be branded like commercial products or financial corporations. Gudjonsson (2005) identified three separate groups of researchers within this debate. Absolutists are those who believe that nations share the same qualities and obey the same rules as brand products and can therefore be branded. Absolutists believe that like brands, nations attempt to differentiate themselves from other nations and even reinvent themselves from time to time. Following this logic, the motto "Liberté, Égalité, Fraternité" was an attempt by France to differentiate itself from the old system of government, and by so doing reinvent the French brand (Gudjonsson 2005). Moderates believe that nations differ from products as they consist of individuals with varying needs and characteristics (e.g. gender, education, social class). Thus, unlike a brand, the nation is not one monolithic unit and cannot be branded as such. However, moderates also believe that the government's main goal is to ensure the prosperity of its citizens. Thus, they suggest that branding techniques may be used by a government in order to shape the nation's image, and strengthen its industries and brands. The third group, referred to by Gudjonsson as royalists, believe that changes that occur within a nation are far more profound than changes that influence a product. Such changes and reforms are based on a higher philosophical ground, and have greater significance than changes that occur to a product. Royalists view the nation as holistic and even divine, and therefore believe that the nation cannot, and should not be branded like a bottle of Coca-Cola (Gudjonsson 2005).

While settling the aforementioned debate is beyond the scope of this chapter, we are drawn to the middle ground accepting the notion that nations differ from products but that branding techniques may be used to shape a nation's image and reputation. We therefore adopt the definition of nation branding as "a process by which a nation's images can be created, monitored, evaluated and proactively managed in order to improve or enhance the country's reputation among a target international audience" (Fan 2010, p.6). In this case the "image" of a nation is what its people recognize and maintain as most central, enduring and distinctive about their nation. Reputation, on the other hand, is a form of feedback received from the outside world concerning the credibility of the nation's identity claims.

Thus, nation branding is understood to be a tool for both image and reputation management (Kaneva 2011).

Aronczyk (2013) further suggests that nation branding is an integral part of national identity. A nation has to be imagined before it can exist and be branded. Branding techniques constantly communicate the national identity, using tools and expertise from the world of corporate brand management. Aronczyk also identifies three dimensions of nation branding. First, nation branding is a strategy of capital generation achieved by using national resources to obtain fiscal advantages over other nations. Second, nation branding is used to generate an image of legitimacy and authority thereby enabling the nation to find a seat at the tables of trans-national institutions and organizations. Third, by creating a unique national identity leaders hope to generate positive foreign public opinion which may "boomerang" and foster domestic consensus and pride (Aronczyk 2013, p.116).

Rooted in marketing research, nation branding first emerged from studies examining the Country of Origin Effect (COO), which states that consumers use country of origin information (i.e. made in America label) as an indicator of product quality (Kotler & Gertner 2002). While the definitions, methods, concepts and principles of nation branding have all been addressed by researchers, it is the varied origins of such scholars (e.g. marketing, international studies, public relations, public diplomacy) that have created a research body that is as comprehensive as it is diverse. However, a review of the existing literature has enabled us to identify common arguments that resonate across the research corpus with regard to nation branding.

The financial aspect

Although it attracts scholarly work from numerous fields, nation branding is still seen as an inherently economic imperative. In the globalized marketplace, nations aggressively compete over investments from multinational corporations, direct foreign investments and tourism (van Ham 2001, 2008; Papadopoulos and Heslop 2002; Anholt and Hilderth 2005; Rawson 2007; Kaneva 2011; Wang 2006). The globalized marketplace necessitates that nations differentiate themselves one from the other in order to successfully compete with a growing number of competitors over a shrinking pool of available resources (Aronczyk 2008, 42). Such differentiation is achieved by developing a unique national image. Poland, for instance, uses its official Facebook page (www.facebook.com/polandgovpl) to promote all things distinctly Polish, ranging from Polish artists and culture to Polish foods and its national space agency.

The cognitive aspect

Researchers seem to agree that countries have images whether they proactively manage them or not (Papadopoulos and Heslop 2002; Kotler and Gertner 2002; Anholt and Hilderth 2005; Kaneva 2011; Aronczyk 2008; Fan 2010; Jain & Winner 2013). Moreover, a nation's image is believed to be a cognitive mechanism similar to stereotypes (Papadopoulos and Heslop 2002; Kotler and Gertner 2002; Gudjonsson 2005) and, as such, they enable people to make sense of the world around them. However, viewing a nation's image as a cognitive device suggests that altering a nation's image and reputation is a complex and long-term process (Fan 2010; Kotler and Gertner 2002; Papadopoulos and Heslop 2002), involving an intricate interaction between governments, media and people. In an attempt to alter and perhaps "soften" its national image, which is associated with the Israeli–Palestinian conflict, Israel's foreign ministry now operates a twitter account (@Israel), which deals solely with Israeli technological innovation, culture, lifestyle and tourism.

The personal aspect

People's perceptions of nations are often shaped by personal experience, be it when someone arrives at a foreign destination as a tourist or when one encounters citizens of a foreign country (Papadopoulos and Heslop 2002; Fan 2010; Jain and Winner 2013). Therefore, marketing scholars often call on citizens of nations to "live the brand" and manifest the nation's image in their own personal behaviour (Aronczyk 2008; Gudjonsson 2005; Anholt and Hilderth 2005; Rawson 2007; Anholt 2005). Yet, the personal aspect of nation branding also calls on nations to engage directly with foreign audiences in order to promote their image and reputation and build long-lasting relationships that may facilitate brand loyalty (Szondi 2008; Lodge 2002; Fan 2010; Skuba 2002). The US State Department, for instances, engages with global audiences through live Q&A sessions with US officials hosted on the State Department's English Facebook page (www.facebook.com/usdos).

Implementation

Successfully branding a nation calls for close cooperation between all stakeholders taking part in the process. These can include policymakers, governmental agencies, governmental ministries, marketing agencies and financial corporations who believe that the nation's image has an impact on their own brands (Kotler and Gertner 2002; Papadopoulos and Heslop 2002; Fan 2010; Skuba 2002). Some world leaders (i.e. US president, chancellor of Germany) are seen as influential components of nations' brands, given their high media visibility (Rawson 2007). While these leaders are but a part of the national brand, they also have the ability to affect the brand in its entirety, an effect referred to as a "halo effect" (Papadopoulos and Heslop 2002). The influential status of some world leaders in the age of social media is best exemplified by US President Barack Obama, who is followed on Twitter (@BarackObama) by more than 43 million people throughout the world (Twiplomacy 2014).

Limitations

In order to be effective, a nation's brand and image must hold true to reality (Kotler and Gertner 2002; Fan 2010; Skuba 2002). A nation torn by civil war, for example, will not be able to brand itself as an attractive tourist destination. Yet, unlike consumer products, a country's image and brand are not always under the control of marketers. World events, and nations' reactions to these events, often shape the nation's image, reputation and brand (Kotler and Gertner 2002; Papadopoulos and Heslop 2002; Anholt and Hilderth 2005; Fan 2010). Such was the case with brand "America" following the 9/11 terrorist attacks.

Between nation branding and public diplomacy

Szondi (2008) attempts to explore the relationship between nation branding and public diplomacy. Szondi states that recent definitions of public diplomacy no longer place an emphasis on influencing foreign governments but rather on influencing foreign publics in order to create a receptive environment for foreign policy goals and the promotion of national interest. Such definitions reflect certain similarities between public diplomacy and nation branding, as both target foreign audiences, both focus on facilitating dialogue with foreign publics and both aim to promote national interests, such as a nation's image. Szondi's extensive literature review reveals that there are four distinct models with which one can interpret the relationship between the two concepts. The first views public diplomacy and nation branding as distinct spheres, since branding deals more with economic goals and public diplomacy with foreign policy goals in general (Szondi 2008, 15). The second holds that public diplomacy is part of nation branding, as some believe that foreign policy initiatives can also be branded (Szondi 2008, 19). The third model states the exact opposite, that is, that nation branding is part of public diplomacy as nation branding is understood to be an instrument through which foreign publics and nations can be reached (Szondi 2008, 22). The fourth and final model, which we adopt for the purpose of this chapter, is that these are two distinct yet overlapping concepts. Elements shared by the two concepts are image creation (as positive images of a nation are by-products of both activities), promotion of a national identity, culture and the promotion of national values, which are important facets of the nation's image and brand (Szondi 2008, 26). Szondi adds that relationship building and two-way communication should be the ultimate goal of both public diplomacy and nation branding, and can serve as yet another element that integrates the two concepts.

By contrast, Pamment (2013) does not believe that two-way communication *should* be the goal of public diplomacy but rather that two-way communication is the very essence of the **new public diplomacy**. According to Pamment, the old twentieth-century public diplomacy was characterized by a one-way flow of information, in which there was limited interaction between communicator and recipient and which relied on persuasion models that were deterministic in their interpretation of the effects of political communication on audiences. However, the emergence of a new media landscape, characterized by a continuous global flow of information, challenged the position of foreign ministries as the sole communicators of foreign policy. These changes necessitated new tools for communicating public diplomacy to non-governmental international audiences. Thus, the new public diplomacy is characterized by dialogue, collaboration and inclusiveness. It represents a clear break from the one-way broadcasting model of public diplomacy and takes advantage of social media to establish two-way engagements with publics (Szondi 2008, 3). It is this two-way engagement that enables social media to serve as a very useful tool for **change management**.

Digital diplomacy as a tool for change management

Our main proposition is that nation branding practiced through digital diplomacy channels (e.g. Facebook, Twitter) can serve as an effective tool for image and reputation management and as such may help nations alter their status quo images. By digital diplomacy we refer mainly to the growing use of social media platforms by a country in order to achieve its foreign policy goals and proactively manage its image and reputation.

Digital diplomacy exists at two levels: that of the foreign ministry and that of embassies located around the world. By operating on these two levels, nations can tailor foreign-policy and nation-branding messages to the unique characteristics of local audiences with regard to history, culture, values and traditions, thereby facilitating the acceptance of their foreign policy and the image they aim to promote. Digital diplomacy can also overcome many of the obstacles of nation branding. Foreign ministries can oversee cooperation between all stakeholders in the branding process as they may work horizontally with other governmental branches and agencies and vertically with local embassies and diplomats. Digital diplomacy could help ensure that the image a nation promotes is linked with reality as content shared on social media accounts deals both with foreign policy goals as well as the concrete actions taken by a nation in the global arena. Moreover, social media enables two-way interaction and engagement between foreign ministries and their followers, thus facilitating the creation of long-lasting relationships and brand loyalty. Finally, digital diplomacy is an important tool for image management as people who visit a nation's social media accounts often seek interaction and are therefore willing to open channels of dialogue. As Yoram Morad, director of the digital diplomacy unit at the Israeli foreign ministry told the authors in an interview on March 30, 2014, when people ask questions on Facebook pages or Twitter they indicate a willingness to listen, and to open channels of dialogue which may pave the way to understanding and even persuasion.

The crisis in brand "America"

Studies on nation branding have shown that intervening events may have immediate effects on a nation's image. Such was the case with the 1988 Olympic Games in South Korea and the 1989 Tiananmen Square protests (Papadopoulos and Heslop 2002). With regard to the US, some scholars view the 9/11 terrorist attacks as a watershed event that dramatically impacted brand "America". These researchers believe that as it emerged victorious from the Cold War, the US was judged favourably by nations and citizens throughout the world on three dimensions: military, moral and economic (Quelch and Jocz 2009). America symbolized values such as democracy, freedom, prosperity and human rights. Yet the 9/11 terrorist attacks, and the US's response to these attacks, altered the manner in which the US was perceived and altered the values that comprised brand "America". The global war on terror and military invasions of Iraq and Afghanistan lad many to view the US as arrogant, imperialistic and a threat to world peace (Silver and Hill 2002; Rawson 2007; Quelch and Jocz 2009). The new perception of the US, and its transition from a beacon of democracy to a militaristic empire, led to a crisis in brand "America". It is this crisis, and the US's desire to regain its standing in the world, that demonstrates the relevance of the US case study with regard to the exploration of nation branding practiced through digital diplomacy.

The crisis in brand "America" was made evident in a Gallup Poll conducted in nine Muslim countries during January 2002. The poll revealed that most of the respondents viewed the US as having a corrupting influence on their societies and as being anti-Muslim and, specifically, anti-Palestinian (Skuba 2002). The Pew Research Center's Global Attitude Project documented the decline in America's image during the Bush years. Surveys taken between 2002 and 2004 showed that America's image, following the invasions of Afghanistan and Iraq, became unfavourable even in the eyes of its closest allies (e.g. UK and Spain) and friendly Muslim countries, such as Indonesia and Pakistan (Fullerton et al. 2007). During this period, America's favourability suffered from double digit drops in many countries, including Germany, France and Turkey (Pew Research Global Attitudes Project, 2013), and hatred towards the US intensified in Muslim countries (Fullerton et al. 2007). A BBC World Service poll from 2007 found that across all countries polled one in two respondents saw the US as playing mainly a negative role in the world (BBC World Service 2007).

Some believe that President Bush personified the values that came to define brand "America" following 9/11 and may have had a "halo effect" on the brand in its entirety (Quelch and Jocz 2009). Studies from 2005 and 2007 demonstrated that the anti-American sentiment was tied to America's foreign policy and its leaders, but not to the American people or American culture (Rawson 2007; Fullerton et al. 2007). Given the negative views associated with President Bush, the election of Barack Obama in 2008 was seen as an opportunity to "wipe the slate clean" in the hope that Brand Obama would save brand "America" (Quelch and Jocz 2009).

Pew's latest global survey from 2013 indicates that Obama's election in 2008 did in fact aid brand "America". America's image and reputation is now more positive than it was during the Bush years. Amongst its allies in Europe and Asia, America's image is now more favourable than unfavourable. However, the 2013 survey also indicates that brand "America" has yet to be restored to its former glory. The majority of respondents still believe that America acts mostly in its own self-interest, while ignoring the interests of other countries. Notably, the image of the US in the Middle East is overwhelmingly negative, with less than one in five

Palestinians, Jordanians and Egyptians holding a positive view of the US. While President Obama is still rated higher than President Bush, his global image has sharply declined since 2008, with confidence in the US president plummeting double digits in ten of the twenty-two countries surveyed (Pew Research Global Attitudes Project 2013). A BBC World Service poll from May 2013 revealed that positive views of America had declined yet again throughout 2012 and 2013 in European and Middle Eastern countries such as UK, France, Germany and Egypt (BBC World Service 2013).

The most recent findings of the BBC World Service Poll and Pew's 2013 Global Attitude survey indicate that the crisis in brand "America" has yet to be resolved. This could be explained by the fact that nations' images are stereotypes and therefore take a long time to change. As Kotler and Gertner (2002) explain, people are more likely to process information that corresponds with their stereotype and disregard information that contradicts it. Moreover, people tend to avoid the effort necessary to reconstruct cognitive constructs, such as nations' images (Kotler and Gertner 2002). Therefore, we propose that America's negative image and reputation, which has endured for more than a decade, can be viewed as a form of status quo. We further propose that nation branding, practiced through digital diplomacy, is a powerful tool which may enable the US to alter its global image and reputation and, subsequently, revitalize brand "America". Thus, we view digital diplomacy to be a tool for change management amongst foreign policymakers.

However, nation branding cannot be regarded as a magical wand, able to alter the US's image with one stroke. As Papadopoulos and Heslop (2002) state, nations attempting to brand themselves often face an uphill struggle. For instance, countries often fail to attract foreign direct investments, given a lack of understating of corporate mentality and corporate decision-making processes. Moreover, nations often have more than one product that requires branding (e.g. Swiss scenery, Swiss banking) thus requiring a distinct branding strategy of each product. In his analysis of two nation-branding campaigns, one for New Zealand and the other for Ontario, Lodge (2002) emphasizes the need for a long-term commitment to a branding strategy which is often unattainable, given domestic political transitions. Finally, countries engaging in nation branding walk a tightrope between image-management and propaganda. Once nation branding turns into propaganda, it becomes more of a double-edged sword than a magical wand. Illustrating the manner in which digital diplomacy can help reshape America's image first necessitates an understanding of the relationship between nation branding and public diplomacy.

Selfie diplomacy

Nation branding may be viewed as an attempt by a nation to draw its self-portrait. In the age of social media, such self-portraits are known as "selfies". Thus, the art of nation branding practiced via social media may be referred to as "selfie diplomacy". As world nations attempt to proactively manage their image and reputation, analyzing a nation's digital diplomacy channels may enable researchers to characterize a nation's selfie and illustrate the image it attempts to promote around the world. Since selfie diplomacy is practiced through SNS, it may, when used properly, enable nations to overcome some of the challenges of nation branding. SNS such as Facebook or Twitter offer specific tools and interfaces, enabling engagement with foreign audiences in the form of dialogue between foreign ministries and their online followers. By engaging with their followers in *meaningful* dialogues, foreign ministries may alter the perception of their countries, given the fact that people's perception of a certain nation is influenced by their personal experience with that nation. Selfie diplomacy is powerful as it reaches users wherever they are. It may thus be more effective in tackling stereotypes that have taken root in people's mind. This could be achieved by publishing attractive content, which reveals a country's multifaceted nature. Countries perceived to be dull may highlight their dramatic landscape, while countries associated with armed conflict may emphasize their cultural heritage, democratic tradition or diplomatic efforts to promote global peace.

Aronczyk argues that when used in the diplomatic arena, nation branding may serve as a proactive tool, enabling the nation to repair reputations damaged by political legacies or avoid unfavourable international attention following unpopular domestic decisions (Aronczyk 2013, 16). In so doing, she may also view nation branding as a tool for change management. By drawing a new self-portrait, nations may be able to distance themselves from their past and reinvent their brand. One method of creating the nation's new selfie on digital diplomacy channels is launching a social media campaign, which focuses on a global issue. Such is the case with the UK's campaign to end sexual violence in conflict, which has been aggressively promoted on the Foreign Office's Twitter and Facebook channels, using the hashtag #Timetoact. By targeting the issue of gender-based violence during times of conflict, the UK may be attempting to associate its brand with humanistic values and distance itself from the legacies of the invasions of Iraq and Afghanistan. Thus, the term "selfie diplomacy" refers not only to the actual use of social media by nations to promote their desired image but also to the entire SNS language that is required in order to achieve their goals.

Like the UK, the US has also used SNS in order to promote its new selfie in various means. In the following section we analyze America's selfie by evaluating two of its social media accounts: the State Department's English Facebook page and English Twitter account. We chose to analyze America's selfie for several reasons. First, given its negative image and the crisis in brand "America", it is fair to assume that the US State Department is currently attempting to reshape America's image through nation branding. Second, America has eagerly adopted digital diplomacy and the US State Department is one of the most active and developed foreign ministries on social networking sites. Finally, the US State Department is one of the most popular foreign ministries on SNS, attracting a large global audience. We employ here a qualitative thematic analysis. This form of analysis seeks to find overlying themes, which stem from the research corpus itself. The data

TABLE 5.1 Facebook posts and tweets of America's selfie

Themes identified in America's selfie	Number of Facebook posts	Number of tweets
Mending relations with the Arab and Muslim world	11%	18%
America's moral leadership	57%	58%
America's military might	17%	11%
America's economic leadership	14%	11%
Total	63	112

analyzed included tweets and Facebook posts published by the State Department on its English social media accounts between December 1 and December 31, 2013. We chose this time period as December saw intensive US diplomatic efforts on a global scale, be it in leading negotiations between Israel and Palestine, halting violence in the Central African Republic and promoting a diplomatic solution to Iran's nuclear ambitions. A total of 147 tweets and eighty-four Facebook posts were published by the US State Department during the sampling period. Out of these, sixty-three Facebook posts and 112 tweets were analyzed and arranged in four overlying themes: mending relations with the Arab/Muslim world, America's moral leadership, America's military might and America's economic leadership. Facebook posts and tweets that were not part of the analysis had various subject matters that could not be categorized (e.g. picture of Secretary Kerry and his dog, invitation to hear remarks by President Obama on the passing of Nelson Mandela, diplomatic trivia questions).

The Table 5.1 presents the number of Facebook posts and tweets comprising each of the four themes identified as part of America's selfie.

America's selfie

Mending relations with the Arab and Muslim world

Following his election in 2008, US President Barack Obama sought to mend America's relationship with the Arab and Muslim world (Quelch and Jocz 2009). In a major foreign policy address delivered at Cairo University in June of 2009, Obama stated, "I've come here to Cairo to seek a new beginning between the US and Muslims around the world, one based on mutual interest and mutual respect, and one based upon the truth that America and Islam are not exclusive and need not be in competition" (White House 2009, para. 5). In his speech, Obama addressed America's military presence in Iraq, its desire to enter into dialogue with Iran and the need to reach a peaceful solution to the Israeli–Palestinian conflict.

Four years after the "New Beginning" speech, mending America's relationship with the Arab and Muslim world seems to have remained a major foreign policy goal for the US. During the sampling period, the Middle East was the most frequently mentioned region on the US State Department's Twitter account, far ahead of Europe, Africa and Asia/Pacific. Of all tweets analyzed, 18% dealt with Middle Eastern countries, including Iran, Iraq, Egypt, Lebanon, Yemen and Israel, which was mentioned mostly in relation to the Middle East peace process. The high visibility of Arab and Muslim countries on its Twitter account may represent an attempt by the US to portray its commitment to creating new relationships with these countries. During December 2013, America demonstrated its new policies towards Arab and Muslim countries. An example of these new policies is a tweet published by the State Department on December 23, which stated that the "U.S. deeply concerned about jail sentences for peaceful demonstrators, worsening climate for free assembly in #Egypt".[1] In this tweet, America seems to be distancing itself from military and totalitarian regimes in the Middle East, with whom it is so often identified. By openly criticizing the Egyptian military regime, America may be signalling that it has altered its foreign policy, and that it is now committed to aiding Egyptians to realize their democratic aspirations. Such aspirations were made evident during the Arab Spring that swept through the Middle East during the summer of 2011.

Facebook posts dealing with the Middle East accounted for 11% of all posts analyzed. As was the case with its Twitter account, the Middle East was also the most frequently mentioned region on the State Department's Facebook page. Arab and Muslim countries mentioned on Facebook included Palestine, Syria, Iran, Iraq and Israel. Two posts published during the sampling period capture an important facet of the new image America is promoting via its social media channels. The first, published on December 8, included a remark by Secretary Kerry, according to which diplomacy, backed by the credible threat of military force, enabled the world to tackle the menace of Syria's chemical weapons, and it may also enable the world to face the menace of nuclear weapons in Iran. The second post published three days later included Secretary Kerry's opening remarks when testifying in front of the House Foreign Affairs Committee on the issue of the interim agreement reached between the world powers and Iran. Kerry stated that "this is a very delicate diplomatic moment, and we have a chance to address peacefully one of the most pressing national security concerns that the world faces today". In our opinion, these posts illustrate America's new commitment to settling differences with the Arab and Muslim world by means of diplomacy as opposed to military conflict. Thus, America's new image is that of a nation, which treats Arab and Muslim countries with respect, and is committed to dialogue with them on the basis of shared respect. This new image of America was best demonstrated by Secretary Kerry, who was quoted in a post from December 12, saying "It has never been more clear that diplomacy can be a transformational tool that shapes the world according to our values."[2]

As the 2002 Gallup Poll suggested (Skuba 2002), the Israeli–Palestinian conflict is a major source of tension between America and the Arab and Muslim world. During the month of December, the peace negotiations between Israel and Palestine were in full swing, and Secretary Kerry frequently visited the region in order to seek an interim agreement between Israel and Palestine. From analyzing tweets and Facebook posts dealing with these negotiations, it becomes evident that the US went to great lengths to depict itself as a fair mediator between the two sides, who is also committed to realizing the aspirations of both sides. This attempt is best demonstrated by the fact that, except for one instance, Israel and Palestine were always mentioned in unison, as were their leaders. If a State Department tweet mentioned Israel or Prime Minister Netanyahu, a second tweet soon followed mentioning Palestine and President Abbas. This symmetry was even more evident on Facebook. On December 5, the State Department published an image of Secretary Kerry meeting with President Abbas opposite of a picture of Kerry meeting with PM Netanyahu.[3]

On December 12, the US State Department published a Facebook post that included an image of snow falling on the Palestinian president's compound in Ramallah, where Secretary Kerry was meeting with President Abbas. The following day, a post featuring an image of Secretary Kerry meeting with Prime Minister Netanyahu in a snow-covered Jerusalem was also published. We assert that this symmetry is not coincidental but rather an active effort by the US to alter its image among the Arab and Muslim world as being too pro-Israel. Of all Facebook posts published during the sampling period, 6% of all posts, and 8% of all tweets, dealt with the Israeli Palestinian negotiations. The high visibility of these negotiations is an important element of America's selfie and represents a proactive attempt to alter its image as being pro-Israeli while neglecting to promote the cause of Palestinian statehood.

America's moral leadership

The second theme identified in our analysis dealt with the US attempt to rebrand itself as the world's moral leader. Tweets dealing with moral issues accounted for 58% of all tweets analyzed, while Facebook posts dealing with such issues accounted for 50% of all posts analyzed. The most visible moral issue identified in this theme was that of America as a beacon of democracy that promotes democratic reforms, supports democratic transitions in foreign countries and calls on world leaders to uphold the democratic process during times of civil unrest. A prime example of America's promotion of democracy can be found in tweets dealing with the mounting tensions in Ukraine. During the month of December, violent clashes erupted between pro-EU protestors in Kiev's Maidan Square and Ukrainian police forces. In a tweet from December 4 Secretary Kerry urged the Ukrainian government to "listen to the people who want to live in freedom, opportunity, prosperity".[4] Following additional violent clashes on December 10, Kerry tweeted, "Ukrainian authorities' response to Maidan Square protests is not acceptable, does not befit a democracy".[5] In a Facebook post published the same day, the US "expressed disgust with the decision of Ukrainian authorities to meet peaceful protest . . . with riot police, bulldozers and batons rather than with respect for democratic rights and human dignity".[6]

US support of democratic transitions and reforms throughout the world can be demonstrated by a tweet that congratulated Honduras on an "election that was generally transparent, peaceful, and respected the will of the Honduran people" and a tweet from December 9 stating that the "U.S. strongly supports democratic institutions and the democratic process in #Thailand, a long-time friend and ally".[7]

On December 10, which marks the UN's Human Rights Day, the State Department published tweets dealing with America's promotion of the rights of LGBT (Lesbian, Gay, Bi-sexual and Transgender), and a statement by President Obama regarding the US's "unwavering support of the principles enshrined in the Universal Declaration of Human Rights".[8] The US observance of this day on its social media channels represents another instance, in which the US is portrayed as a member of the international league of nations. Additional tweets and posts dealing with human rights included a call on the Chinese government to release Nobel laureate Liu Xiaobo, concern expressed over antihomosexuality legislation in Uganda, a call on Russia to carry out judiciary reforms and a statement by Vice President Biden during a visit to Japan in which he called for the integration of women in the national workforce and leadership.

Finally, America's moral leadership was also expressed through its humanitarian aid to victims of violence and disasters. One example of America's support for disaster relief is a Facebook post from December 18, in which Secretary Kerry announced 25 million dollars in aid to typhoon victims in the Philippines. With regard to aid to civilians affected by violence and civil war, the unfolding humanitarian crisis in the Central African Republic (CAR) was most visible during the sampling period on America's social media channels. On December 5, the State Department tweeted that the "US is appalled by reports of the murder of innocent women & children outside of Bangui" in CAR.[9] On December 10, a video address by President Obama to the people of CAR appeared on both the State Department's Twitter and Facebook accounts. The tweet promoting the video read "President Obama: You-the proud citizens of #CAR-have the power to choose a different path. You can choose peace".[10] Rather than looking at this video through cynical eyes and calling for actions rather than tweets, we view it as a fascinating attempt by the US to reinvent itself as a superpower that respects other nations, and believes that they have the right to determine their own fate without having one imposed on them by the US. It is our opinion that America's attempt to regain its standing as the world's moral compass is a cornerstone of America's new selfie, given the fact that "moral leadership lends legitimacy to hard power" (Quelch and Jocz 2009, 167).

America's military might

What was most surprising about this theme was the overall lack of references to America's military might. During the sampling period, the US armed forces were mentioned in only 14% of all posts and 12% of all tweets analyzed. None of these tweets and posts demonstrated America's military strength, America's presence in Afghanistan or America's military superiority. US forces in Iraq were mentioned only once in a post from December 3, 2013, detailing the manner in which dogs are assisting soldiers in removing mines from southern Iraq. This post was accompanied by an image of a US soldier embracing an army-trained dog. [11]

Other mentions of the US army included a video message reordered by Secretary Kerry, which was to air during the traditional Army-Navy football game, and a post showing wrapped Christmas presents to be distributed by the US Marine Corps Toys for Tots program to underprivileged children in the US. Finally, in a post from December 25, President Obama and the First Lady wished US troops a merry Christmas, stating, "We want all of our troops to know that you're in our thought and prayers this holiday season".[12]

While the North American Treaty Organization (NATO) was mentioned during the sampling period on the State Department's Twitter and Facebook accounts, it was not portrayed as a military organization but rather as an international peacekeeping organization. Facebook posts published during a NATO summit on December 3 included a statement by Secretary Kerry saying that "#NATO will continue to protect freedom, continue to try to push for and bring about peace and it will do so for decades to come".[13] America's commitment to peacekeeping was further exemplified by a tweet and Facebook post from December 16, which dealt with the training of UN peacekeepers.

The final component of this theme includes posts and tweets in which the US expressed solidarity with victims of terrorism following terror attacks in Egypt, Israel and Russia. In our view, such tweets may represent a shift from a military-led war on terror to American-led solidarity in the face terror. As opposed to George W. Bush's famous "either you are with us, or you are with the terrorists", these tweets echo a different sentiment, one of a united world battling the horrific consequences of terrorism together.

We view the overall lack of references to the US armed forces, as well as the portrayal of NATO as a peacekeeping organization, as part of an effort by the US to alter its image as an imperialistic nation, which achieves its foreign policy goals through military confrontations. Pictures of soldiers embracing animals and gifts to be donated by the US Marine Corps may also demonstrate an attempt by the US to "soften" its global image following a decade of wars.

America's economic leadership

The fourth and final theme identified in our analysis of the State Department's social media channels deals with America's economic leadership. Surprisingly, only 11% of all tweets analyzed, and 13% of all Facebook posts analyzed dealt with America's economic leadership. Given the fact that "America's business is business", we expected that America's economic leadership would be more visible and would serve as a major component of the image it presents to the world. This finding could be attributed to the fact that the US is seen by many as responsible for the 2008 financial crisis. Moreover, while America is seen as the leader of the globalized economy, it is also seen as responsible for the environmental damages this economy has brought with it (Quelch and Jocz 2009).

Quelch and Jocz (2009) maintain that during the previous decade America was perceived as a greedy polluting superpower. The elements comprising this theme demonstrate an attempt to alter that image. Throughout the month of December, the US highlighted its investments in infrastructure in the developing world, be it in South East Asia or Africa. One such Facebook post, published on December 16, stated that "only 16% of #Africa is connected to high-speed Internet. What could be the impact of connecting Africa?" A tweet published during Secretary Kerry's visit to Vietnam on December 16 announced "$32.5 million in assistance toward maritime capacity building in Southeast Asia".[14]

On the December 12, the State Department tweeted that the US would financially support CASA-1000, a program that aims to create a shared hydropower electricity grid for the Kyrgyz Republic, Tajikistan, Afghanistan and Pakistan. The US support of the CASA-1000 program exemplifies important elements of the image the US is currently promoting on its social media accounts and that is America's newfound commitment to meeting the challenges of climate change. During a visit by Secretary Kerry to Vietnam, the State Department tweeted that the "US & #Vietnam are working together to tackle the most difficult environmental challenges of our day", and invited followers to "Read #SecKerry's remarks to students in #Vietnam about #climatechange and the environment".[15] The following day, a Facebook post stated that "70 million people rely on the #Mekong Delta for their livelihood. What will happen if the world's oceans rise 1 meter? #SecKerry spoke to students working on #climatechange in #Vietnam".[16] The US support of the developing world, along with its determination to tackle the challenges of climate change, may represent an effort by the US to rebrand itself as a conscience economic superpower which aims to integrate the developing world into the globalized economy while recognizing the effect this economy has on the environment.

The final component comprising this theme are tweets and posts which dealt with a trade agreement negotiated between the US and the European Union, known as the Transatlantic Trade and Investment Partnership (TTIP). In promoting the TTIP, the US State Department stressed that the agreement would benefit both Europe and the US. A tweet from December 19 read "#TTIP aims to lower tariffs, reducing costs for consumers on both sides of the Atlantic".[17] A Facebook post from the same day asked, "Can we increase trade and investment while creating jobs in both the U.S. and EU all at the same time?[18] That's the goal" of the TTIP. By promoting the TTIP agreement as one that will benefit both American and European economies, the US may be attempting to rehabilitate its image amongst European audiences who view it as responsible for the devastating 2008 financial crisis. We believe that this facet of America's image is meant to portray it as a responsible economic superpower.

Conclusion

For more than two decades, nation branding has attracted scholarly work from diverse fields, such as marketing, communications, public relations and international studies. Although researchers still dispute whether nations can be branded like products (Gudjonsson 2005), many have adopted the notion that nations have images (Papadopoulos and Heslop 2002; Kotler and Gertner 2002; Anholt and Hilderth 2005; Fan 2010). At times, nations may even have competing images – as for some, America may represent both a beacon of democracy and a self-serving superpower. However, once a certain image of a nation prevails, it becomes more difficult to alter (Kotler and Gertner 2002; Gudjonsson 2005). Using branding techniques to alter a nation's image and reputation is the very essence of nation branding.

Although the body of work on nation branding is both extensive and diverse, we find that few have attempted to illustrate how digital diplomacy, practiced through SNS (e.g. Facebook, Twitter) can serve as a tool for nation branding. In this chapter we attempted to fill this gap and extend the scope of nation branding to SNS. Our claim is that because nations' images are cognitive devices, nations' images are strongly rooted in peoples' consciousness. Moreover, we believe that nation branding achieved through digital diplomacy can assist nations in altering their images, thereby serving as a tool for change management amongst foreign policymakers.

Recently, nations of the world have flocked to SNS, such as Twitter and Facebook. By using such sites to promote their foreign policies, global actions, values, culture and economy, nations are already managing their image through digital diplomacy. Given that nation branding is an attempt by a nation to draw its portrait, and since self-portraits shared on SNS are known as "selfies", we refer to the practice of nation branding on SNS as selfie diplomacy. In this chapter, we attempted to analyze America's selfie.

We chose to focus on the US, given the continuing crisis in brand "America" and its negative image around the world. While the US once symbolized democracy, freedom and human rights, the 9/11 attacks and wars in Afghanistan and Iraq led many around the world to view the US as a greedy, polluting, self-serving, imperialistic and militaristic superpower (Silver and Hill 2002; Rawson 2007; Quelch and Jocz 2009). Given its negative image, we assumed the US State Department would be engrossed in an attempt to alter America's image around the world. Moreover, given the fact that the US State Department is one of the most active foreign ministries on SNS, we assumed that tweets and posts published during one month would provide sufficient data for selfie analysis. Our analysis was a qualitative one, and we employed thematic analysis in order to identify recurring themes within all Facebook posts and tweets published during four weeks on the US State Department's English Twitter and Facebook accounts.

Our analysis revealed four main themes. The first was America's attempt to mend its relationship with Arab and Muslim countries. During the sampling period, the Middle East was the most frequently mentioned region in the State Department's Twitter and Facebook accounts. The high visibility of this region and the frequent mentioning of Arab and Muslim countries (e.g. Syria, Iran, Palestine) serves to demonstrate that mending its relations with the Arab and Muslim world has remained an important US foreign policy goal. The second theme included instances in which America attempted to regain its reputation as the world's moral leader. An important component of this theme was the attempt by the US to rebrand itself as a beacon of democracy by calling for democratic reforms and safeguarding democratic processes in times of upheaval. Additional elements comprising this theme were US humanitarian aid for disaster relief and support for the protection of human rights. Some have maintained that the US's war on terror underscored America's position as the world's moral compass (Quelch and Jocz 2009). This theme indicates that America is now attempting to regain its moral standing.

The third theme identified was that of America's military might. During the month evaluated, there was little mention of the US armed forces. When the US military was mentioned, it was never in relation to American military conflicts around the world. We view the lack of references to American military might, and an emphasis on peacekeeping missions, as part of an attempt by the US to alter its image as an imperialistic state that relies mainly on its military to achieve foreign policy goals. The fourth and final theme identified in our analysis included posts and tweets portraying America's economic leadership. This theme included references to US investments meant to integrate the developing world into the global economy while taking measures to address the environmental impact of the globalized industrial economy. Herein lies an American attempt to present itself as a conscientious economic superpower. An additional element of this theme was a trade agreement negotiated between the US and the EU. We believe that by underlining the agreement's positive impact on Europe's ailing economies, the US is attempting to regain its standing with European allies who were negatively impacted by the 2008 financial crisis.

In summary, we found that America brands itself as an economically responsible superpower, guided by moral values and committed to diplomacy and building meaningful relationship with the Arab and Muslim world. As such, America no longer portrays itself as the world's policeman, but rather as the world's social worker. Interestingly, we found that America's selfie corresponds with Quelch and Jocz's article from 2009, in which they outline a roadmap for President Obama with regard to salvaging America's global image. The researchers called on Obama to fix three "major blemishes on the US's image": the military engagements in Iraq and Afghanistan, the violation of international law symbolized by the Guantanamo detention camp, and the US-originated recession that has impacted the world's economy (Quelch and Jocz 2009). In other words, they call on Obama to reshape America's image by regaining its position as a moral leader, by acting as a responsible economic superpower that is part of the solution to the global economic recession and by decreasing its reliance on military strength.

Interestingly, there was one element that resonated across all themes, and that is America as part of the global community. We found that in contrast to the Bush era, America is currently attempting to take its place in the international community. This was made evident by America's involvement in global initiatives such as the UN Human Rights Day, its support of international efforts to solve the Iranian nuclear crisis and its resolution to address climate change.

The elements comprising America's selfie are not necessarily new ones. America has been an avid promoter of democracy and human rights for nearly a century. However, by using digital diplomacy to promote democracy and human rights, the US may be able to directly reach a large audience, without the mediation of local institutions. Thus, it is able to strengthen the association between brand America and desired values, thereby mending its global image. By engaging with its global audiences and listening to their comments and criticism, the US can further evaluate whether its nation-branding campaigns are effective and, if not, identify which elements have been rejected by followers. Thus, the US can continuously "fine tune" its nation-branding strategies and increase their possible impact and acceptance. Moreover, by employing digital diplomacy at the embassy level, the US can tailor nation-branding campaigns to the characteristics of local audiences and the manner in which the US is perceived by such audiences. If engagement and listening can facilitate the acceptances of one's foreign policy amongst foreign publics (Hayden 2012; Metzgar 2012), they may also facilitate the acceptance of one's selfie amongst foreign publics. Herein lies the potential of nation branding delivered through digital diplomacy channels.

Like nation branding, selfie diplomacy also has its limitations, specifically when world events come to dominate news cycles and international diplomacy. However, our case study revealed that at times such events may be incorporated into the country's selfie. In December 2013, former South African President Nelson Mandela passed away. In tweets and posts published by the State Department dealing with Mandela's passing, Mandela was depicted as a man who fought for freedom, peace and human rights. In other words, Mandela epitomized the values promoted by the US on its digital diplomacy channels, and was therefore incorporated into America's selfie.

The emergence of selfie diplomacy necessitates that scholars begin to evaluate the impact of SNS on the art of nation branding. While selfie diplomacy may represent a conceptual shift in the practice of nation branding, its effectiveness remains unknown. Future studies should examine the extent to which local and international audiences accept nations' selfies. Barriers to such acceptance may be the belief that social media content published by foreign ministries is nothing more than propaganda. Likewise, studies should evaluate the effectiveness of nation-branding campaigns delivered through SNS as opposed to those delivered through traditional media (e.g. print, television). It is also of paramount importance to examine whether engagement and listening do indeed challenge people's stereotypes regarding certain countries, and whether engagement on SNS with a foreign diplomat is tantamount to a personal encounter with someone from a foreign country. Finally, nation-branding research should evaluate whether countries have been able to associate their brand with certain values by using selfie diplomacy (e.g. US and democracy).

While it is beyond the scope of this chapter to assess whether the US has been successful in altering its global image, such an assessment can be made by social media directors at both the embassy and ministry level. Doing so necessitates that operators of digital diplomacy accounts continuously monitor the manner in which nation-branding messages are received and further disseminated by their online followers. An example of such an analysis can be illustrated based on a tweet published by US First Lady Michele Obama at the time of the writing of this chapter. On May 8, 2014, the First Lady uploaded a selfie holding a sign with the hashtag #Bringbackourgirls, referring to more than 200 girls abducted by an Islamist group in Nigeria. The response to this tweet, which was published on the US State Department's social media accounts, was immediate, as countless individuals took selfies of themselves holding a sign with the hashtag #Bringbackyourdrones, referring to the frequent use of drones by the US military in killing suspected terrorists. Such online responses to social media content should be continuously monitored by ministries of foreign affairs as they may assist in analyzing the degree to which a nation's promoted image has taken root.

As Szondi (2008) writes, the ultimate goal of nation branding and public diplomacy is to reach foreign audiences, open channels of dialogue and build meaningful relationships with them. We believe this can be achieved primarily through engagement and two-way communication between foreign ministries, embassies and their online followers. Therefore, future studies should focus on examining the extent to which engagement takes place between ministries and their followers as well as the interactivity of messages, and how they are tailored and understood by local audiences. This calls for focusing on digital diplomacy at both the ministry and embassy level. Moreover, studies should examine the organizational processes of designing nation-branding messages, and whether the image portrayed on social media by a foreign ministry is indeed the result of a proactive attempt to manage one's image. This could be achieved by interviewing digital diplomacy practitioners around the world. Finally, researchers should evaluate whether nation-branding activities have actually led to the desired effect amongst the target population of digital diplomacy – followers of social media accounts operated by foreign ministries and embassies.

Notes

1   https://twitter.com/StateDept/status/415268124007481344
2   www.facebook.com/15877306073/posts/10151806559841074
3   US State Department English Facebook Account (www.facebook.com/15877306073/posts/10151794982071074) and (www.facebook.com/15877306073/posts/10151795038876074). Accessed May, 12, 2013.
4   https://twitter.com/StateDept/status/408324671394676736
5   https://twitter.com/StateDept/status/410635496528695296

6 www.facebook.com/15877306073/posts/10151805659566074
7 https://twitter.com/StateDept/status/410135298882822144
8 Statement published on Facebook: www.facebook.com/15877306073/posts/10151805158261074
9 https://twitter.com/StateDept/status/408626815675031553
10 https://twitter.com/StateDept/status/410269949538476032
11 US State Department English Facebook Account (www.facebook.com/15877306073/posts/10151790912936074). Accessed March 12, 2013.
12 www.facebook.com/15877306073/posts/10151832618426074
13 www.facebook.com/15877306073/posts/10151792544256074
14 https://twitter.com/StateDept/status/412616216583213056
15 https://twitter.com/StateDept/status/412646845878251520
16 www.facebook.com/15877306073/posts/10151817621901074
17 https://twitter.com/StateDept/status/413687670796070912
18 www.facebook.com/15877306073/posts/10151821476431074

PART II
Digital diplomacy
The institutional dimension

6

BUSINESS AS USUAL?

An evaluation of British and Canadian digital diplomacy as policy change

Amanda Clarke

Introduction

Typically under the remit of **digital diplomacy** initiatives, foreign ministries have begun integrating social media communications and monitoring, big data analytics, social network analysis and crowdsourcing into their larger toolkits. In these cases, foreign ministries are capitalizing on the social web, defined as the platforms of the 'read-write', interactive web (e.g. social networking sites, blogs, mobile applications) and the social phenomena associated with them (e.g. crowdsourcing, peer-production, citizen journalism, 'viral' information flows). On the one hand, the social web appears to find a natural home in foreign ministries. Networking, influencing and intelligence gathering and analysis comprise these organizations' key functions. The social web provides new and improved means of executing these tasks. According to this perspective, digital diplomacy extends naturally from traditional diplomacy, a logical and uninterrupted continuation of the 'business' of diplomats and foreign offices, but with a digital angle. On the other hand, digital diplomacy might be framed as a new and revolutionary development in which top-down, state-centric processes of international relations are increasingly replaced by a more networked, civil society-driven model of diplomacy. More specifically, according to this perspective, rather than being simply a case of 'business as usual', digital diplomacy signals a recognition amongst diplomats and foreign ministries that the social web has redistributed informational resources, ensuring that civil society – and not government – is best placed to perform the functions of networking, influencing and intelligence gathering and analysis that have long been the preserve of state actors as per the state-to-state, intergovernmental model of international relations (Huijgh 2013).

Does digital diplomacy represent the mere digitization of existing models of diplomatic conduct, or has adoption of the social web by foreign ministries been accompanied by substantive shifts in the ideas and practices shaping these organizations? Just how 'new' and 'different' is digital diplomacy from its analogue predecessor? In this chapter, I employ concepts from the **policy change** literature to evaluate the extent to which operations in the British and Canadian foreign ministries are becoming more open, networked and collaborative through their adoption of the social web. Canada's Department of Foreign Affairs, Trade and Development[1] (DFATD) and the UK's Foreign and Commonwealth Office (FCO) manage similarly sized budgets and staff,[2] operate under comparable organizational structures,[3] and represent countries with similarly high degrees of Internet penetration.[4] While the FCO is often cited as a leader in the area of digital diplomacy, and DFATD less often cited for its uptake of the social web, both ministries should nonetheless be viewed as early adopters, having since the mid-2000s steadily integrated social media into their operations, and with each ministry having developed centralized initiatives focused on the social web and its applications to the work of foreign diplomacy (in Canada, the open policy development model, and in the UK, digital diplomacy). Similarities across the two cases, and the approximately seven years of experience each has had with the social web, ensures, first, that they can be reasonably assessed in the same study and second, that their uptake of the social web is sufficiently well-developed to inform an evaluative assessment of the magnitude of the policy change it represents.

The chapter develops in four parts. First, I introduce concepts from the policy-change literature to frame an evaluative analysis of digital diplomacy's departure from, or adherence to, status quo models of diplomatic conduct in these two foreign ministries. Parts two and three present data generated through key informant interviews with civil servants in DFATD and the FCO, along with analysis of departmental documents describing initiatives related to the social web in each case. Part two explores a series of critical junctures referenced by interviewees and departmental documents which suggest that digital diplomacy has indeed developed from the departments' recognition that they must become more networked and open to collaboration with civil society groups to reach their objectives. Part three complicates this narrative, presenting evidence from interviews and documentary analysis which suggests that, in the end, digital diplomacy actually represents little by way of substantive change; here, digital diplomacy is described as 'business as usual' by civil servants in DFATD and the FCO. In an effort to cut through the mixed messages at play in the departments' own subjective perceptions of digital diplomacy (as explored in parts two and three), part four presents an analysis of each department's official Twitter accounts. I find that at least in terms of DFATD's and the FCO's departmental use of Twitter, digital diplomacy does not, in practice, signify the departments' willingness to engage in a more networked, collaborative mode of operations. In closing, I discuss the implications of these findings for the study and practice of digital diplomacy, and suggest avenues for future research.

Digital diplomacy as a policy change

Before the mid-2000s, foreign offices did not employ tools like Twitter and Facebook, nor did they engage in online crowdsourcing, social media monitoring and analysis of large-scale datasets generated through activities on the social web (big data). These activities are undeniably 'new' and 'different', but just how 'new' and 'different' are they?

We can begin to answer this question by first framing digital diplomacy as a policy change. Here I adopt Thomas Dye's definition of policy as "whatever governments choose to do or not to do" (Dye 2008, 2). Under this definition, policy not only refers to a government's stance on a given policy issue (e.g. the legalization or prohibition of prostitution). Rather, under this definition, policy also includes decisions related to operational concerns, or issues related to the management of public agencies. In this sense, when the social web is integrated into the operations of a foreign ministry, this is a matter of policy. And given that the social web, as discussed above, represents a 'new' and 'different' facet of the foreign ministry's operations, it accordingly represents a policy change.

With digital diplomacy defined as a policy change we can now set about measuring the magnitude of this change, following on Hall's schema of first-, second- and third-order policy change (Hall 1993). In this schema, policy change is defined according to the extent to which it departs from the status quo. First-order changes represent the smallest degree of change and are defined as routine adjustments to the settings of existing policy instruments. In Hall's example, focused on British economic policy in the 1970s and 1980s, adjustments to interest rates represent a first-order change. Second-order changes arise when a government adjusts the policy instruments it employs – altering, for example, the system used for controlling public expenditures – without changing the policy goals to which the instruments are directed. Such changes represent a greater departure from the status quo than first-order changes. Third-order changes represent the greatest degree of change and are defined as changes to the normative and ontological worldview of policymakers. These normative and ontological worldviews consist of policy paradigms (entrenched beliefs, values and ideas) and policy styles (enduring patterns of problem solving, or 'ways of working') in a given policymaking setting (Howlett and Ramesh 2003). In other words, third-order changes involve shifts in the taken-for-granted orthodoxy that defines how actors identify problems and solutions and define their role and the role of their organizations in the broader social, economic and political context in which they operate. In Hall's (1993) analysis, the shift from Keynesianism to monetarism in British economic policy in the 1970s and 1980s represented a third-order change.

In this schema, first and second-order changes occur more often and are easier to achieve by virtue of the fact that they flow naturally from existing policy paradigms and policy styles at play in a government setting. These changes involve "relatively minor tinkering with policies and programs already in place" (Howlett and Ramesh 2003, 235). This 'minor tinkering' is captured in the concept of

policy-oriented learning, in which policymakers refine or adapt their practices in order that they can more efficiently and effectively perform their roles and reach their objectives (Sabatier 1988; Sabatier and Jenkins-Smith, 1993). While policy-oriented learning enables first- and second-order changes, in the case of a third-order change, the well-entrenched and unquestioned policy paradigms and styles at work in a government organization must themselves change.

What enables these more substantive third-order changes to take hold? Authors describing the causes of third-order changes agree that these types of policy changes can only come about as a result of conditions emanating outside the policymaking environment. More specifically, authors argue that dominant policy paradigms and styles can only be disrupted when new information or actors enter the policymaking environment and cause policymakers to question, and adjust, the ideas and practices that shape their work. For example, Hall (1993) explains that the shift from Keynesianism to monetarism in Britain was only possible because of external events that violated the tenets of the Keynesian model (e.g. simultaneous rises in inflation and unemployment), which subsequently cast doubt on its predictive and explanatory power (Hall 1993). Likewise, Sabatier's Advocacy Coalition Framework posits that changing socio-economic conditions set the stage for third-order changes by causing policymakers to recognize that the entrenched ideas and practices shaping their work are no longer appropriate or adequate for the environment in which they operate (Sabatier 1988; Sabatier and Jenkins-Smith 1993). Finally, historical institutionalism, a body of thought with a much broader purview but which nonetheless speaks to questions of third-order policy change, notes how path-dependent trajectories in institutions can be disrupted by 'critical junctures' – external events, such as significant social, economic or political developments – which set the stage for new policy paradigms and styles to take hold in a given government setting (Capoccia and Kelemen 2011; Hall and Taylor 1996; Thelen 1999).

Turning back to the specific case of digital diplomacy as a policy change, we might anticipate that the emergence of the social web would qualify as one such critical juncture, or, more colloquially, as a 'game changer', capable of inducing third-order changes in foreign ministries. Social media, crowdsourcing and other forms of peer-to-peer collaboration amidst political unrest and in consular emergencies have demonstrated the instrumental role that non-state actors can play in contexts where foreign service officers have traditionally taken the lead. Most obviously, waves of protest in the Arab World – the so-called Arab Spring, initiated in 2010 in Tunisia – illustrated how groups of citizens can affect change in national governments by capitalizing on the social web as a platform for coordinating and executing mass protest (Howard et al. 2011). In addition to the impressive integration of the social web into social movements promoting democratic reform and regime change, citizens' engagement with the social web has also supported relief in the wake of natural disasters, uptake that again supports the work of the foreign ministry, in this case, its provision of consular services. During the 2011 Queensland floods, community-led Facebook groups served as venues for crowdsourcing updates from the ground (Bird, Ling and Haynes 2012). Victims tweeted within minutes of the 2010 Haitian earthquake striking, and in the first two days of the emergency, 36% of all posts on Twitter related to the situation in Haiti (Kodrich and Laituri 2011). Similarly, social web-enabled citizen reporting was evidenced in the 2010 California wildfires and during the Japanese earthquake of 2011 (Savelyev *et al.* 2011). And organizations like the Humanitarian OpenStreetMap Team[5] and Ushahidi[6] have demonstrated how social web technologies can produce accurate, timely maps and reports from the ground in the context of natural disasters and political unrest. Finally, as domestic populations take up the social web to connect with family and friends abroad, they have demonstrated how they can bridge the gap between foreign ministries and foreign populations, in some cases reducing the linguistic as well as spatial barriers that complicate **public diplomacy** initiatives (Eleta and Golbeck 2012; Karim 1998; Lazakidou 2012).

In these examples, a core assumption at play in the foreign ministry – an assumption which ultimately rationalizes its existence and value – is challenged; these examples illustrate that non-state actors enabled by the social web are capable of collecting, distributing and acting on information towards ends that traditionally were achieved by the foreign ministry, such as the promotion of democracy and human rights, and consular relief. Put differently, while the foreign ministry has traditionally been cast as a "knowledge-based" organization, a framing that induces actors both within and outside the foreign ministry to value diplomats for their unique ability to collect, interpret and distribute information in support of national priorities (Otte 2013), the social web indicates that this may no longer always be the case. Accordingly, the social web – more specifically, citizens' uptake of the social web – may qualify as a critical juncture that has the potential to induce third-order changes in this policy environment.

Digital diplomacy initiatives by which diplomats engage in open, networked collaboration with digitally enabled non-state actors represent one response to this critical juncture. Betraying the state-centric model of diplomatic operations, this shift would constitute a third-order change. However, an alternative response to non-state actors' impressive engagement with the social web might see diplomats either ignoring the social web altogether or integrating it into their operations to bolster their existing information gathering, interpreting and distributing functions, an outcome that would not constitute a third-order change, since core policy paradigms and policy styles would remain intact. Put differently, uptake of the social web by actors in the foreign ministry may simply represent a marginal departure from the status quo achieved through policy-oriented learning, in this case, as the social web is employed as a more effective means of performing well-established roles and achieving long-standing objectives in the foreign policy sector.

In the next two sections, the chapter brings forth empirical evidence to suggest which of these two possible outcomes has arisen in practice in the cases of Canada and the UK. This evaluative assessment relies on analysis of departmental documents and nineteen key informant interviews with current and former officials in DFATD and the FCO. The interviews were conducted in 2012 and 2013, in person in Ottawa and London and via Skype with officials posted overseas. An initial group of interviewees was identified through analysis of departmental documents, and snowball sampling was employed for successive interviews. Interviewees were drawn from a range of rankings (from ambassador-level officials to relatively new recruits, operating at lower levels of responsibility and authority) and from a range of functional areas (press office, communications, information management, foreign service officers and those explicitly engaged in the open policy development initiative [DFATD] and digital diplomacy [FCO]). As the ensuing two sections illustrate, we receive mixed messages when these interviewees are themselves are asked to define the magnitude of policy change accompanying their digital diplomacy initiatives.

Critical junctures: Digital diplomacy as a third-order policy change

Interviewees and departmental documents suggest that digital diplomacy does, in fact, represent a more substantive third-order change instigated by citizens' uptake of the social web. For example, officials in both departments emphasized that as more and more citizens integrate the social web into their own lives, citizens increasingly expect their foreign ministries to do the same. One DFATD official argued, "I want to be able to – I look at how I've changed, how I interact with companies or businesses and how I expect them to respond on social media. Why wouldn't I expect the same of my government?" (Personal communication, April 2012). A DFATD report on open policy development, a central component of Canada's digital diplomacy strategy, noted that "a digital public does not want to interact with an analog government" (Anonymized DFAIT official, 2012, p. 2).

But more than simply being the result of changing expectations, adoption of the social web has been driven by awareness that alternative, non-governmental sources of information are capitalizing on the social web to influence foreign policy processes to a degree not possible before, threatening the influence of these foreign ministries. An internal FCO document discussing "digital working" in the department notes the following:

> A key series of studies by the world's largest PR and lobbying company Edelman's shows the extent to which some of the people we seek to influence, in the Edelman's study specifically Political Advisors in the US and Europe, increasingly use the web and social media as their primary source of information in advising decision makers. UK and overseas Politicians and ministers are themselves increasingly ahead of officials in their own use of these technologies. It follows that by the time the people we seek to influence (and report to) hear what we have to say they will already have formed an opinion based on what they learnt via digital or 24/7 media. We

may flatter ourselves that the sagacity of our comment will overcome the comparative lateness of our intervention on their thinking, but there are more effective ways of operating that turn these new technologies to our advantage.

(Foreign and Commonwealth Office 2011, 7)

This passage illustrates not only that the department recognizes that its competitors are using these technologies to exert a more powerful influence over foreign affairs but also that this influence now competes with that of their own to a degree not seen before – a recognition that, in turn, calls into question traditional ways of thinking and operating in the department. In practice, this means that the department feels it must now be more open to collaborate with non-government actors who, as a result of the ubiquity of Internet access and the rise of social technologies, often have access to information and influence that state actors do not. As one FCO diplomat noted:

> The environment in which we operate today is very different. You weren't going to contact the Russians via Twitter. . . . We actually had better information than anyone else. That's not true anymore. That's what you saw with Somalia. We can't be in Somalia for more than one night – it's just too dangerous – but there's a huge Somalian diaspora in the UK. Thanks to the wonders of Skype they're in touch every night with those on the ground, with their families and friends . . . you have to be able to engage with a wider range of sources than ever.
>
> (Personal communication, October 2012)

Likewise, the FCO's review of "digital working" notes that the social web "has profound implications for journalists, diplomats and lobbyists who in the past drew their power and influence from the fact that information was a privileged resource where 'to be in the know' and to 'know who to talk to' was a fundamental part of how they carried out their professional tasks and their added value" (Foreign and Commonwealth Office 2011, 1).

Similarly, while commenting on the work of groups like The Standby Taskforce, who coordinate crisis mapping by collecting and visualizing the tweets, status updates and text messages of individuals in crisis situations, one DFATD official remarked, "I know how our own operation works. We can't do that. We can't be that. So they are better, faster, cheaper than us. And so we ought to learn from them, right, and we ought to leverage them. If there are people out there who want to do this, why not?" (Personal communication, April 2012). A Canadian document describing DFATD's Open Policy Development initiative also states that international ministries have to adapt "because there are individuals and organizations that have a greater capacity to influence the conduct of international policy than ever before" (Department of Foreign Affairs and International Trade Canada 2012, p. 3). One DFATD official echoed a sentiment expressed by many interviewees in both departments when he remarked "we've lost our . . . we kind of lost a privileged position" (Personal communication, April 2012). In sum, as citizens and non-governmental organizations have gained greater access to information through the growth of the social web, both DFATD and the FCO have indeed recognized that they no longer have a monopoly on information and the influence it enables, a recognition that they claim sets the stage for a new approach to their work to emerge, that is, for a more fundamental third-order policy change to arise. Non-governmental use of the social web – both the expectations it creates, the competition it introduces and the opportunities it offers for more effectively advancing national interests – has, according to officials in these departments, served as a critical juncture, highlighting to DFATD and the FCO that they must become more open, networked and collaborative if they are to survive as relevant, effective organizations in the digital age. In this sense, it appears that digital diplomacy has marked a more substantive, third-order policy change, resulting from changing external conditions which call into question entrenched ideas and ways of working in each department.

Yet, alongside these explanations, officials in both DFATD and the FCO have also been quick to assert that digital diplomacy is, ultimately, a natural extension of their existing work. In the next section, I explore this competing narrative, highlighting the 'mixed messages' at play in these departments' own perceptions of digital diplomacy as a policy change.

Digital diplomacy: The product of policy-oriented learning

As much as officials in DFATD and the FCO underscore the critical junctures challenging entrenched ideas and operations at play in the foreign policy sector and that accordingly rationalize the need for digital diplomacy, they also frequently explain that the social web is, in the end, simply a new and improved means of performing the traditional functions of diplomacy. According to this narrative, digital diplomacy results from processes of policy-oriented learning, and represents only a marginal departure from the status quo.

In some cases, policy-oriented learning takes place as well-established practices are transferred from the offline or static web context in which they used to take place to social media platforms. This is, to quote a former FCO official, "about achieving diplomatic objectives, just through a different means"; this is "an alternative way of doing the same thing" (Personal communication, May 2012). Similarly, an official from DFATD explained, "It's just a 2012 approach to a 1992 engagement method really" (Personal communication, April 2012).

For example, where the press offices of each department used to scan mainstream media, they now also scan social media, using a mix of manual and automated, computer-assisted approaches. Again, this is seen as a natural development of an existing practice. As explained by an FCO official, "We have traditional media monitoring in place. Well, that now has to be complemented by social media monitoring" (Personal communication, April 2012). In both cases, social media monitoring began in the press office but is now encouraged more broadly across the departments. Notably, DFATD granted department-wide access to social media sites at an early stage, while many other Canadian federal government departments and agencies restricted access due to security concerns, and a fear of employees wasting time. In the UK, access was originally restricted to a number of standalone computers in the press office, but in April of 2013, access was granted across the department, along with the suggestion that employees make use of Hootsuite, a social media monitoring tool. This level of access, and the encouragement of employee use of these platforms outside of the press and communications office, is not typical of other departments in the UK central government, but this has been framed by the department as a natural development, given that their employees' primary function is information collection and distribution (Foreign and Commonwealth Office, n.d.). This is reiterated in the FCO's social media guidelines for employees, which states: "All staff should use social media for listening, monitoring conversations, keeping track of news and building networks as part of their day to day work" (Foreign and Commonwealth Office, 2013c).

The same can be said for the use of social media by individual diplomats and trade commissioners as a networking tool. Social media sites become just another means of identifying and connecting with influencers, or promoting the national 'brand'. Trade Commissioners in Canada have formed an active community on LinkedIn to support their existing efforts to connect Canadian businesses with opportunities abroad.[7] As one official noted, "A lot of . . . you know, we've met important opinion-makers through our [social media] that maybe in an earlier era we would have met at a cocktail party or something like that" (Personal communication, April 2012).

While in this case core foreign ministry activities – communications and networking – remain relatively unchanged, in others, the 'value-added' from the social web is more striking. This has particularly been the case for public diplomacy initiatives in each department. In one case, an update on the Canadian Embassy to Beijing's Sina Weibo account advertising the ambassador's new car (a modest hybrid sedan) was originally intended as a light-hearted message, but it sparked a much larger conversation about accountability amongst high-ranking officials in the Chinese government, and scrutiny of the luxury European cars and private drivers they are awarded from the state. As described by an official in DFATD:

> So a dialogue that would normally be very difficult to initiate in China turned into just a fluke. That said that wasn't our intent at all. . . . We just simply were showing the ambassador with his new hybrid car . . . but then it became a pretty healthy dialogue on government transparency. . . . But you know, there's a new rule now that says Chinese government officials have to purchase domestic-made cars and such and such. So I don't know if it's been implemented yet, but . . . . And again, I can't say that it's . . . it's just

a very interesting coincidence if we didn't contribute to that. We definitely contributed to the policy discussion, let's put it that way. We contributed in a very high profile way to a policy discussion that seemed to result in a change of domestic regulations.

(Personal communication, April 2012)

Again, in this case, the core activity of Public Diplomacy – its aims, audience and outcomes – remains the same. But, through a process of policy-oriented learning, officials find a better way of performing this activity that capitalizes on the affordances of the social web. As explained by an FCO official:

Most of it, I mean in kind of creating this digital diplomacy function, we are really piggybacking on the public diplomacy. . . . That is really what we are using digital for is to do that kind of the engaging and influencing that was already part of different jobs and it was directly the job of public affairs offices and people in the embassies to do this.

(Personal communication, May 2012)

Likewise, these processes of policy-oriented learning are captured succinctly in the FCO's digital strategy when it states, "Given foreign policy is often about persuasion, influence and soft power, it is no surprise that in today's networked world digital and policy implementation are intertwined" (Foreign and Commonwealth Office 2012, p. 7).

In other cases, a more cynical perspective is adopted, as officials explicitly state that digital diplomacy is not the product of self-reflection on their changing external environment, and the related need for substantive reform, but is rather taken up because of enthusiasm for digital diplomacy in other jurisdictions, and the need to keep up with current trends in diplomatic activity. A DFATD official noted that interest in the social web was in large part sparked by senior officials who would complain: "You know, why doesn't our website look better? Why aren't we doing more of this? Why aren't – look at what the [United] States are doing" (Personal communication, April 2012). An official at the FCO argued:

I think it was born out of the need to be seen to be doing something, and I think that's true of a lot of organizations, where there is a kind of typical digital evolution, where for any organization they ignore it for longer than they ought to, and then feel that they ought to do something. And they always overcompensate by creating a department.

(Personal communication, August 2013)

These descriptions of digital diplomacy are a far cry from those explored in part two, in which digital diplomacy was framed as a remarkably unprecedented period of foreign relations, where the agency and influence of non-state actors had grown relative to that of the state, setting the stage for a more networked, collaborative model of foreign relations to emerge. Differently, here officials describe digital diplomacy as a natural extension of existing ideas and practices at play in the foreign policy sector. By this view, digital diplomacy has emerged because officials recognize that the social web offers new and improved means of executing traditional functions and reaching traditional objectives of diplomacy. In this characterization, digital diplomacy is simply 'business as usual', or, in Hall's (1993) language, uptake of the social web represents at most a first- or second-order change, as the settings of existing policy instruments are adjusted, or traded for more optimal, digitized versions.

It appears then that these departments' own perceptions of digital diplomacy can only take us so far in identifying the magnitude of change accompanying uptake of the social web in DFATD and the FCO. In light of this, the next section takes a different approach, measuring the magnitude of this policy change by evaluating one particular facet of each department's digital diplomacy initiatives – departmental use of Twitter – in an effort to settle the debate between the two competing perspectives explored so far. In other words, if the analysis presented above evaluates digital diplomacy by exploring what officials say it represents, the next section evaluates digital diplomacy by exploring what it looks like in practice, in an effort to bring more precision to our understanding of this policy change and its magnitude.

Departmental use of Twitter: Evidence of a third-order policy change, or the product of policy-oriented learning?

As one component of their digital diplomacy strategies, DFATD and the FCO have developed accounts on the popular microblogging service Twitter, both at their missions abroad and through accounts managed at headquarters, representing the departmental 'voice' on this social network. DFATD lists fifty-five Twitter accounts on its website,[8] while the FCO lists 246 Twitter accounts.[9] Given that Twitter has thus far proven the most commonly employed social media platform employed by each ministry,[10] this medium serves as a reasonable starting point for empirical analysis of each ministry's engagement with the social web. That is, focusing on the case of Twitter, specifically, we can ask: does DFATD and the FCO's uptake of the social web evidence the emergence of a more networked and collaborative model of diplomacy in the digital age? Or, as reflected in their uptake of Twitter, do these departments engage with the social web in ways that replicate more traditional, top-down, and state-centric models of diplomacy?

To answer these questions, I archived all content shared on central departmental Twitter accounts managed by DFATD and the FCO between February and June 2012.[11] In the case of DFATD, this produced a population of 612 tweets; in the FCO, this produced a population of 1,221 tweets. I generated a random sample of tweets from each of these populations, producing a sample of 389 tweets in the case of DFATD and 570 tweets in the case of the FCO (95% confidence interval, +/- 3%). Each tweet was categorized according to its content into one of three categories. 'Informational' tweets are those that issue information, such as the announcement of a new policy initiative, that highlight the work of a minister or which provide a travel advisory. 'Participatory' tweets support collaboration with non-government actors by inviting these actors to participate in policy development or service delivery. Tweets that foster amicable relations between the ministry and members of the public or the ministry and other governments using friendly or informal language were categorized as 'Amicable ties' (e.g. "@user Thanks for following us!"). In this scheme, Informational tweets are those that align most closely with traditional 'ways of working' in these departments, inasmuch as they represent tweets that issue information selected by DFATD and the FCO for distribution to domestic and foreign publics, organizations and governments. Differently, Participatory tweets and those which support Amicable ties depart from this tradition, and might be understood to signal the move towards a more networked and collaborative model of diplomacy emerging in the departments.

In both DFATD and the FCO, the majority of tweets were Informational, suggesting that traditional top-down, state-centric models of communication have merely been digitized, as opposed to being challenged, by the social web. In the case of DFATD, 86% of all tweets were Informational (n = 336); 10% of all tweets were Participatory (n = 37). In each case, these Participatory tweets directed users to a government consultation on the DFATD website or invited users to retweet messages related to consular service issues, in order to help the department expand the reach of the information they wished to share, in a co-productive effort. Four per cent of all tweets published by DFATD promoted Amicable Ties (n = 16). The FCO's results mirror those of DFATD, with only minor variation. Ninety-one per cent of all FCO tweets were Informational (n = 520). Only 2% of the FCO's tweets (n = 10) solicited the participation of users in the department's work (Participatory), through, for example, invitations to co-produce policies/services or participate in a consultation, while 7% consisted of efforts to promote amicable ties with the public (n = 40; see Tables 6.1 and 6.2).

TABLE 6.1 Tweets published by DFATD, February–June 2012

Content category	N	Percentage of total tweets
Informational	336	86%
Participatory	37	10%
Amicable Ties	16	4%
TOTAL	**389**	**100%**
Type of tweet		
Original	203	52%
Retweet	32	8%
@message	154	40%
TOTAL	**389**	**100%**

TABLE 6.2 Tweets published by the FCO, February–June 2012

Content category	N	Percentage of total tweets
Informational	520	91%
Participatory	10	2%
Amicable Ties	40	7%
TOTAL	**570**	**100%**
Type of tweet		
Original	157	28%
Retweet	217	38%
@message	196	34%
TOTAL	**570**	**100%**

While this analysis suggests that information provision, as opposed to open, networked collaboration, remains a prominent component of these departments operations when they use Twitter, this does not necessarily mean that the information shared follows the same top-down, government-directed patterns of previous periods. Rather, if DFATD and the FCO primarily retweeted other users' content, this would signal the departments' willingness to engage in a more networked, less government-directed model of information sharing, inasmuch as the content shared by the departments would be crafted by another user, granting these non-government actors control over the framing and content of official communications. Similarly, the issuing of '@messages' in reply to specific queries from other users ('@replies') or in an effort to direct tweets to particular users might evidence a greater willingness to network with non-governmental actors. Finally, if DFATD and the FCO used Twitter to share weblinks that direct their followers to non-ministerial websites, this might also evidence a new model of networked, less government-directed information sharing, since in this case, DFATD and the FCO would rely on other actors to provide information as opposed to directing users to an online information source created and managed by the department.

In the case of DFATD, 48% of tweets included in the sample were retweets or @messages ($n = 186$). In the FCO, 72% of all tweets were retweets or @messages ($n = 413$). This may suggest that a more networked, and less government-directed form of official communications has emerged (in particular, in the FCO), but before drawing this conclusion it is important to note which users' content was retweeted, and which users were referenced in the departments' @messages.

When DFATD retweeted, 50% of the time the retweeted messages were originally published by another Canadian government department ($n = 17$). Forty-seven per cent of the time, DFATD retweeted messages originally published by the department's minister ($n = 16$).[12]

Similarly, in the case of the FCO, 49 per cent of all retweeted messages were first issued by UK government departments ($n = 136$), while the second most commonly referenced users in retweeted messages were departmental ministers (38 per cent of all retweets, $n = 105$).

When these departments issue @messages, they primarily do so in response to, or to direct information to, departmental ministers and other domestic government departments. In DFATD, 80 per cent of all @messages cite its ministers ($n = 118$)[13]. Similarly, FCO ministers were the most commonly cited user in its @messages (48%, $n = 108$), while other UK government departments were the second-most cited users in its @messages (21%, $n = 46$).

Finally, when these departments issue weblinks through their tweets, they primarily do so to link users back to official government sources of information. In DFATD, 288 tweets included weblinks, all of which linked users back to Government of Canada webpages. In the FCO, 291 tweets included weblinks, 96% of which linked users to websites managed by the UK government.

And so, where DFATD and the FCO use Twitter to retweet others' content, to engage with specific users and to direct users to websites, they do so primarily to highlight content produced by their own ministers or their own governments, or to engage directly with these actors. In this sense, DFATD and the FCO's official communications may have become more networked via the social web, but the network itself remains state-centric; non-government actors continue to exercise little influence over the types of information shared by these foreign ministries, and are rarely the target of DFATD's and the FCO's efforts to engage more directly with specific Twitter users.

In sum, while the adoption of Twitter does indeed represent a new development, or a policy change, the data and analysis presented here suggest that this change represents only a marginal departure from the status quo. Information provided continues to be issued in top-down, government-directed ways, and the departments show little willingness or ability to engage in a collaborative, networked mode of operations in which non-government actors play a more central role in the departments' work. In the language of the policy change literature, this exploration of Twitter usage suggests that digital diplomacy results from processes of policy-oriented learning, in which the social web offers a new means of reaching old goals and performing established functions. In turn, the data and analysis presented here does not evidence a substantive third-order change towards a more networked, collaborative model of diplomacy, despite what public officials in both DFATD and the FCO have suggested.

Conclusions

Perhaps the most pressing issue in contemporary research on digital diplomacy is simply a definitional one. That is, at present, it is not entirely clear at what point digital diplomacy picks up and traditional diplomacy lets off. Inasmuch as adoption of the social web represents a 'new' and 'different' facet of the work of foreign ministries, digital diplomacy certainly represents some sort of policy change. Yet, it is not evident what this change consists of, or its magnitude. Until researchers clarify how digital diplomacy aligns with or departs from traditional models of diplomatic relations, any effort to theorize and track the implications of the social web for this policy sector will be stunted.

The findings presented here suggest that officials operating in this policy sector are themselves ill-equipped to define the relationship between digital diplomacy and earlier models of diplomatic relations. On the one hand, civil servants in DFATD and the FCO describe digital diplomacy as the product of changing social and technological conditions that mean foreign ministries can no longer reach their objectives without collaborating with civil society through open, networked web technologies. On the other hand, officials were also quick to assert that digital diplomacy is, in practice, adopted because the tools and practices of the social web are a natural fit for the well-entrenched communications, intelligence gathering and networking functions of diplomacy. Analysis of each department's central Twitter accounts provided a second route for evaluating digital diplomacy as a policy change, and suggested that in practice, digital diplomacy represents a mere digitization of traditional ways of working in DFATD and the FCO. Twitter was not used as a platform for open, networked collaboration with non-government actors. In this case, these findings suggest that digital diplomacy is simply 'business as usual'.

These findings represent only a modest attempt to define and measure the extent to which digital diplomacy initiatives depart from status quo models of diplomatic affairs. For instance, Twitter is only one piece of the broad range of platforms and tools that comprise the social web, and future studies should explore how other aspects of the social web are integrated into the work of foreign ministries, such as Facebook, blogging, crowdsourcing and big data analytics. It may very well be the case that the affordances of Twitter are simply ill-suited to a more open, collaborative model of diplomacy. Likewise, while the Twitter study presented here only addressed central, departmental adoption of the social web, scholars must also evaluate how individual foreign service officers and overseas missions employ the social web. It is possible that in these cases, diplomacy does become more networked, open and collaborative when it is digitized on the social web. Finally, while the Twitter data presented in this chapter focuses on the communications, or 'output' component of digital diplomacy, researchers should also address the extent to which the monitoring, or 'input' component of digital diplomacy departs from traditional ways of working in foreign ministries. It is possible, for example, that much of the networked collaboration associated with digital diplomacy happens not 'on the screen' in open exchanges but rather as foreign service officers collect intelligence from online communities of non-government actors. In short, the uptake of digital diplomacy initiatives presents researchers with a broad range of phenomena that is ripe for empirical analyses. Through rigorous studies that present these empirical analyses, researchers will be better placed to develop descriptive and explanatory theories of digital diplomacy which can be pitted against the 'mixed messages' we receive from diplomats themselves, extending our understanding of this increasingly prominent component of

126 Amanda Clarke

contemporary international relations. This chapter represents an early and modest contribution to this broader research agenda.

Notes

1. Note that prior to 2013, and during the time at which data collection took place, DFATD operated under the name the Department of Foreign Affairs and International Trade (DFAIT).
2. In 2012–13, DFATD comprised 12,383 full-time employees and managed a budget of $3.1 billion (Department of Foreign Affairs and International Trade Canada 2013a). In 2013, the FCO employed 14,087 full-time employees (Foreign and Commonwealth Office 2013b) and managed a budget of £2.1 billion (Foreign and Commonwealth Office 2013a).
3. Staff in DFATD and the FCO can be situated in either headquarters (Ottawa and London, respectively), in regional offices across Canada (in the case of DFATD) or in diplomatic offices abroad (embassies, high commissions, consulates, and other offices, including, in the case of the FCO, administrators in British overseas territories). DFATD manages 260 offices in 150 countries (Department of Foreign Affairs and International Trade Canada 2013b). The FCO manages 270 offices in 160 countries (Foreign and Commonwealth Office 2014).
4. In 2009–13, 86.8% of Canadians were Internet users; in the same period, 87%t of UK residents were Internet users. Source: World Bank http://data.worldbank.org/indicator/IT.NET.USER.P2
5. http://hot.openstreetmap.org/about
6. www.ushahidi.com/
7. See www.linkedin.com/groups?gid=1808582&goback=%2Enpp_%2Fpeter*5mcgovern%2F15%2F835%2F1b9&trk=prof-groups-membership-logo
8. See www.international.gc.ca/department-ministere/social-media_medias-sociaux.aspx#twitter
9. See www.gov.uk/government/organisations/foreign-commonwealth-office/about/social-media-use#twitter
10. As of March 2014, DFATD operated twenty-five Facebook pages, twenty-eight Twitter accounts, two YouTube channels, a Foursquare account, a Flickr account, a Sina Weibo account (a Chinese language microblogging service) and also led a Trade Commissioner Service group on LinkedIn (which included eight subgroups). Uptake of the social web in the FCO has advanced somewhat more quickly and evenly than in DFATD. The department operates a significantly larger number of social media accounts than its Canadian counterpart: 148 Facebook accounts, 246 Twitter accounts, 103 Flickr accounts, four Google+ accounts, three Storify accounts, two Pinterest accounts, three Tumblrs, and ninety-five blogs. These are in addition to single accounts hosted on YouTube, Instagram, Foursquare, LinkedIn, MixCloud, AudioBoo, BuzzFeed, Sina Weibo and YouKu (a Chinese video hosting service).
11. In the case of DFATD, the following accounts were included in the analysis: @DFAIT_MAECI and @TCS_SDC (the account of the Trade Commissioner Service, managed centrally in Ottawa). In the case of the FCO, @foreignoffice was analyzed.
12. Note that for each department the total number of users mentioned in retweeted messages exceeds the total number of retweeted messages because, in some cases, multiple users were referenced in a single retweeted message.
13. As above, note that for each department, the total number of users mentioned in @messages exceeds the total number of @messages because in some cases, multiple users were referenced in a single @message.

7

EVOLUTION, NOT REVOLUTION

The digital divide in American and Australian contexts

Stuart Murray

Introduction

Revolutions in information and communication technology (ICT) can have a profound impact on the relations between people, nations and institutions. Gutenberg's invention of a printing press with movable type (circa 1439), for instance, meant that European literature could suddenly be mass produced.[1] The technology transformed the speed and volume at which information was gathered, collated and disseminated – information which permeated then changed society. Similarly, the telegraph, telephone, radio and television dramatically altered the way disparate and estranged humans and states interacted with one another. Such changes were far reaching, but none are quite on the scale of the digital revolution in ICT.

Its origins lie in the nineteenth century, in Morse's electrical telegraph system and Marconi's wireless telegraphy; however, it wasn't until the launching of the first communications satellites in the late 1960s that the digital era began to significantly affect international relations. Satellites, as Dizard (2001, 59) notes,

> broke the mold of incremental network expansion by offering a means of connecting any two points on earth in ways that supplied services directly or by linking into ground networks. Its satellites released the global system from its primary reliance on earthbound wire technology.

This shift from physical, wire-based and land-based technologies to wireless, intangible bits, 0s and 1s, has been profound. Silicon-based semiconductor chips in the early 1970s, affordable home computers in the 1980s, the Internet in the early 1990s and social media in the 2000s propelled society from the modern, industrial to the postmodern, information age. Basic extrapolation such Moore's Law[2] or The Singularity[3] all suggest the revolution is by no means over.

The impact on the traditional Westphalian system of states has been far reaching. In the twenty-first century, states no longer possess a monopoly on information. Instead they co-exist in a plural, complex and increasingly competitive digital environment. Giant multinational corporations (MNCs) such as Google, Siemens and Microsoft drive the revolution, shape the digital world and as such are growing in political clout and diplomatic influence. Annually, the digital economy is worth some 20.4 trillion dollars, making it the largest sector in global trade, and in 2012 the number of people "using the Internet reached the milestone of 2.7 billion people", a remarkable figure but still much fewer than mobile cellular users, which reached "an estimated 6.84 billion by [sic.] end of 2013" (International Telecommunications Union 2013, 2–3). Bradley/Chelsea Manning, Julian Assange and Edward Snowden have easily bypassed the traditional diplomatic gatekeepers, more than amply illustrating that individuals also matter in the digital age. They are but part of a vast, multilayered network of civil society organizations (CSOs) which continues to grow in size, efficacy and interconnectivity.

As the US Department of State (2013) recently noted,

> the infrastructure that conveys goods around the globe has shifted over the centuries from ships to rail to highways. Our communications networks have gone from post to telegraph to telephone. And our mass media have moved from print to radio to television. Today, all three of these systems operate largely on the Internet. It is a triple paradigm shift converging on a common infrastructure for the first time in history (para. 3).

For the state and its diplomats, the impact of digital revolution is broadly understood as either monumental or relatively insignificant. Monumental because changes in how we use, share and securitize information is fundamentally altering the relations between states. Ergo, tech-savvy states that embrace **digital diplomacy** are gaining a comparative advantage over Luddite rivals, larger **public diplomacy** audiences at home and abroad and more diplomatic bang for fewer bucks, often at the click of the proverbial button.

On the other hand, traditionalists view the revolution as relatively insignificant because ministries of foreign affairs (MFAs) have weathered many similar ICT revolutions before. Diplomacy, "the conduct of relations between sovereign states . . . by official agents and by peaceful means," is first and foremost a profession carried out by human representatives and not machines (Bull 1977, 156). Moreover, realism, geopolitics and hard power – tanks, borders and bombs, tangible 'things' – and security dilemmas endure as the keystones of the anarchical international relations system. A few ambassadors tweeting is unlikely to persuade the Islamic State to desist from its medieval adventures, or Kim Jong-un to swear off the nukes. As the current United States (US) Secretary of State John Kerry (2013) recently commented, "the term digital diplomacy is almost redundant – it's just diplomacy, period" (para. 6). If anything, the digital revolution has created but one new conduit for diplomacy: an increased ability for state diplomats to communicate with large swathes of domestic and foreign publics.

These two positions inform what has come to be known as the digital divide, a widening gap between, on the one hand, states with advanced digital diplomacy operations and, on the other, e-dinosaur states somewhat unfairly described as "**Luddite holdouts**" (Hanson 2012a, p. 9). The 'have' state's operations are well funded and resourced, often with esoteric offices bustling with growing numbers of young, Web 2.0 tech-heads. A fecund diplomatic culture where diplomacy is valued as a key strategic asset and not a marginalized, backwater antique is important, as is a history of innovation, reform and openness to technological change. A realistic, consistent budget also helps, as does a pro-digital leadership (or at least a leadership that recognize the here and now of the postmodern global information age). In turn, this culture generates new methods for diplomacy: social media platforms with ministers, ambassadors and diplomats communicating with thousands upon thousands synergized public diplomacy programs or innovative two-way communication processes that allow ordinary people to, at last, feel part of a state's once rarefied and elitist diplomatic machinery. Simply, a 'have' state is one that exploits the digital revolution as a means to old and new foreign policy ends.

A '**have not**' state is, obviously, quite the opposite. It is yet to awaken to the digital age. A culture of resistance to change, innovation and technology pervades its ministry of foreign affairs. This culture is usually personified in its minister and government, which, in turn, regards diplomacy as a deliquescent institution and, as such, starves it of funding above the bare operational necessity. Thus, marginalized, anything 'e' or digital is regarded with disdain, nervous curiosity and trepidation. In 'have not' ministries, ambassadors and diplomats are forbidden to tweet or chat with foreign publics for fear of saying the wrong thing, of impinging upon historic, careful and intricate traditional diplomatic strategies, ossified relationships and anachronistic playbooks.

This chapter explores both of these positions by describing and critiquing the respective journeys of a 'have' state – the 'dataholic' United States of America (USA) and its Department of State – and a 'have-not' – Australia and its Department of Foreign Affairs and Trade (DFAT). For the former, "information edge" and "digital strength matter" so much so that "the one country that can best lead the information revolution will be more powerful than any other" (Nye *et al.* 1996, p. 20). The Australian story is, however, more familiar, one of tradition meeting and resisting innovation and change for a number of practical, time-honoured reasons. Primarily, the chapter seeks to address two simple questions: do the 'have' states possess a comparative diplomatic advantage over the 'have-nots'? And, therefore, is digital diplomacy a matter of relevancy or irrelevancy for foreign ministries in the global information era?

The 'haves' – the US information hegemon and digital diplomacy

Diplomacy is the "engine room" of international relations (Cohen 1998, p. 1). According to Bull, it has five core functions: "negotiation, communication, symbolism, the minimization of friction and information gathering and dissemination" (representation might be added; Bull 1977, p. 177). Of these, none is more important than information gathering and dissemination. Information is the base currency of diplomacy, the equivalent of the Higgs-Boson, or God particle, to quantum physics. It informs all other diplomatic functions, none of which would be possible without it. Information is vital to diplomacy. It is the cud that diplomats chew.

Since the end of the Cold War, the way governments use information to realize foreign policy goals has changed. In the information age, public diplomacy (PD) offices, programs and policies are commonplace. The stampede towards PD has been well documented by others and has significantly altered the conduct of modern diplomacy.[4] These days, diplomacy is "no longer a stiff waltz among states alone but a jazzy dance of colourful coalitions" with "public diplomacy . . . at the heart of its current rebooting" (Melissen 2011, p. 2).

The growth in PD coupled with the digital ICT revolution has created ideal conditions for the emergence of digital diplomacy (which is synonymous with e-diplomacy). The term can refer to more traditional digital channels for diplomacy (radio or television) as well as newer means of communication such as the Internet, YouTube or social media platforms. More specifically,

> 'e-diplomacy' describes new methods and modes of conducting diplomacy and international relations with the help of the Internet and information and communication technologies (ICTs). The term also refers to the study of the impact of these tools on contemporary diplomatic practices. E-diplomacy may be considered a sub-set of e-governance. Related (and interchangeable) terms include cyber diplomacy, net diplomacy, and digital diplomacy.
>
> (DiPLO, 2013a)

Others restrict the term to the latest wave on the digital revolution, defining it as "the use of the web and new ICT to help carry out diplomatic objectives . . . [which] escapes the tendency to confuse ediplomacy with social media tools alone" (Hanson 2012b, p. 2). Like PD, digital diplomacy stands to transform diplomacy from a stuffy, elitist, hermetic, secretive dialogue between rarefied, officially accredited representatives of states to something more 'jazzy', inclusive, public, open and plural.

Theoretically, however, the subject is only just catching on. There are only a handful of esoteric books, most of which focus on certain ministries. Dizard's (2001) *Digital Diplomacy: U.S. Foreign Policy in the Information Age*, Potter's (2002) *Cyber-Diplomacy: Managing Foreign Policy in the Twenty-First Century* and Stein's (2011) *Diplomacy in the Digital Age: Essays in Honor of Ambassador Allan Gotlieb* are good examples. Not many journal articles on digital exist, outweighed more so by chapters on the general impact of the Internet on diplomacy, think-tank policy briefs and government white papers, such as the Foreign and Commonwealth Office (2012) *Digital Strategy*. And it would be remiss to ignore the blogging, e-learning platforms and good work done by the nonprofit DiPLO, which "emerged from a project to introduce information and communication technology (ICT) tools to the practice of diplomacy", way back in 1992 (DiPLO 2013b).

Practically speaking and compared to CSOs or MNCs, foreign ministries have been caught lagging in exploiting the digital ICT revolution. Their tardiness can be explained by any number of reasons – bureaucracy, the size of the organization, the cost of reforming/updating ICT, or securitizing sensitive information and so on – however, they are rapidly catching up. The push has been led by the US Department of State (hereafter referred to as State) and, belatedly, the United Kingdom (UK) Foreign and Commonwealth Office (FCO).

The US was a late entrant to the digital age. Before the Second World War altered the balance of information power, the major players in international ICT were the British and the French, who used cable and telegraph networks to maintain control over colonies in Asia, Africa and further afield. However, by 1945 the prewar networks controlled by European countries lay in tatters, much like their physical infrastructure, war machinery and spirit. The timing for a large-scale, US global communications network was both ideal and necessary. As Dizard (2001, p. 23) notes,

> the United States emerged from the war as the unchallenged telecommunications power. Its base was the worldwide network built by the Army Signal Corps and the navy, with extensive help from AT&T.

Since then, the US has maintained a preponderance of information power, regardless of the digital technology: radio (1940s onward), coaxial submarine cables (1950s) or COMSAT technology (early 1960s). In the zero-sum game of international relations, information equals power, thus the country that can best exploit the latest ICT revolution will be more powerful than the one that cannot, a sentiment encapsulated by Nye (cited in Dizard 2001, p. 20), who writes that

> knowledge, more than ever, is power . . . America has apparent strength in military power and economic production. Yet its more subtle comparative advantage is its ability to collect, process, act upon and disseminate information, an edge that will most certainly grow.

That edge allowed the US to shunt the Europeans to the periphery of the nascent digital age, to out-communicate (or out-propagandize) the Soviets during the Cold War, and, subsequently, to extend First Amendment principles to the global, free flow of information (the unfettered right to send and receive information in any form across borders). These events dovetailed with a desire to reduce communication and information barriers to US international trade, which, in turn, drove the initial growth in the digital economy (which started in California's Silicon Valley in the early 1970s). Information thus became a key strategic aspect of US foreign policy, vital to trade, national security, human rights, energy resources and the environment, among other subjects. A superior, information and communications network also complemented softer policy objectives – the spread of liberalism, democracy, free trade, American cultural values and so on. As a result the "principle of open global communication was established as the cornerstone of American policy in global negotiations on the subject ever since" (Dizard 2001, p. 20). And in the 1990s, when the internet boomed, the US lay at the heart of a vast, global network of American driven ICT, so much so that scholars now write of the American ICT hegemon, the dataholic and/or the **information hyperpower** (Nye, 2000, p. 27).

Naturally, and in time, a love of all things information found its way into US diplomacy. State's digital diplomacy journey truly began when Secretary Powell took office in 2001 and sought funding for modern ICT to support America's diplomats. A year later he established the taskforce on e-diplomacy, which was later renamed the Office of eDiplomacy. Originally, the Office was charged with improving State's knowledge management – how information was retained, shared and optimized in the pursuit of national interests within the Department and government – and it was a small operation, maintaining a staffing level of around six. Powell's successor, Condoleezza Rice, dabbled with ICT; however, it was Secretary Clinton who aggressively pushed for more investment in digital diplomacy. Working under the world's first "digital President" in Barack Obama, she argued that State must complement "traditional foreign policy tools with newly innovated and adapted instruments of statecraft that fully leverage the technologies of our interconnected world" (US Department of State 2013, para 4).

Much of the early groundwork and proselytizing was carried out by three young, entrepreneurial Clinton disciples: Jared Cohen (policy planning), Alec Ross (Clinton's senior adviser for innovation from 2009 to 2013) and Anne-Marie Slaughter (director of policy planning from 2009 to 2011). Of these individuals, Ross, in particular, "has been on an endless international road trip evangelizing ediplomacy" ever since, applying ICT to public diplomacy, Internet freedom and – again – knowledge management purposes (Hanson 2012c, p. 3).

So far, the results have been impressive. First, a clearer role, mission and purpose of the Office of eDiplomacy have been realized. Now it seeks to advance

> diplomacy by providing effective knowledge-sharing initiatives, guidance on the convergence of technology and diplomacy, and first-class IT consulting . . . to support the convergence of technology and diplomacy. It cultivates the innovative use of technology to facilitate collaboration and the interconnection of people and information, with the goal of enabling Department personnel to find and share knowledge anywhere, anytime.
> (US Department of State, 2011, para. 4)

Second, and reflecting the prominence of all things 'e', the Office has grown in size: sixty-five individuals now work in knowledge management, sixty-one in public diplomacy, ten in Internet freedom and twenty-three listed as 'other'.

Third, the Office has been responsible for some terrific innovations. In 2004, it "established Radio Sawa, an Arabic-language radio network and its TV equivalent, Al Hurra" (Hallams 2011, p. 13). In addition, the Office manages a digital outreach team (DOT) – eleven bloggers who write in Arabic, Farsi, Urdu and other languages with the aim of countering online ideological support for terrorism. And, over the years, the Office has amassed a number of dynamic programs that extend the scope of US Diplomacy – Diplopedia (an internal unclassified online wiki), Corridor (an internal professional networking site akin to Facebook) and the Communities@State (issue specific blogs; communities discussing China's economic strategy or the Iran Watchers Page, for example).

State's successful experiment has other nations queuing up to emulate them. There are at least five reasons why. First, engaging with digital platforms for diplomacy embodies a proactive government response to the ill-founded notion that diplomacy is reactive, boring, irrelevant, obsolete and "dead" (Ramsay 2006, p. 273). By going digital, the culture, value and outlook of a state's diplomacy can change from aloof, rarefied, slow and fossilized to one that is innovative, proactive, dynamic and public (and fun even).

Second, and related, digital diplomacy creates pathways for ordinary individuals to participate in diplomacy. State's Virtual Student Foreign Service (VSFS), for example, offers nine-month "eInternships" for young, tech-savvy US and overseas students in "creating new forms of diplomatic engagement" and building web and social networking platforms, thus allowing more "college students opportunities to conduct digital diplomacy, reflecting the realities of our networked world" (US Department of State 2011, para. 13). Changed are the days from the old, hermitically sealed diplomatic institutions and their one-way (MFA to public) communication processes.

Third, digital diplomacy augments knowledge management and interagency communication between the domestic ministry, overseas posts and other agencies in Washington. This change came after 9/11, which revealed that various agencies "had the pieces but lacked the ability to put them together, questioning the Cold War concept of 'need to know' and the stove-piping on information" (Hanson 2012b, p. 8). In other words, digital diplomacy facilitates better flows and exchanges of information between State and other government departments.

Fourth, digitizing diplomacy increases the speed of diplomacy while reducing its cost. In these austere times of shrinking budgets, digital diplomacy is relatively cost-efficient, particularly for countries like the US that have advanced technology sectors. The US's Virtual Presence Posts are a good example, mobilizing "diplomatic outreach tools including travel, programs, media and technology to focus and improve our engagement with specific communities where the U.S. has no physical diplomatic facilities" (US Department of State 2011, para. 12). At the time of writing, State is responsible for approximately forty Virtual Presence Post communities.

Fifth, digital diplomacy amplifies the diplomatic message. State now has a presence on Facebook, Flickr, Twitter, YouTube and Instagram, and "effectively operates its own global media empire reaching more than eight million people directly through its 600 plus social media platforms" (Hanson 2012b, p. 15). These new channels dramatically increase the number of message recipients, be they states, corporations, media outlets or individuals. A single US diplomat can now communicate directly with hundreds of thousands of people through one of State's social media platforms.

Typically, where the information hyperpower leads, others will follow. In December 2012, the UK's FCO published its *Digital Strategy* (p. 7), arguing that it was

> essential in this more networked world to have the fullest possible picture of developments, to choose the right policy approaches, to influence those important to our getting our way [sic.], to communicate our policy most effectively and to deliver the most effective services for British nationals.

The Canadians are also 'logging on', for they have "the makings of digital diplomacy leader: a rich society with an educated, multi-ethnic, polyglot population; a talented diplomatic service; and access to cutting edge communications technology" (Paris 2013, p. 7). Other nations, such as China, Russia and Australia, are keen to catch up.

As the ICT revolution continues, digital diplomacy is the talk of foreign ministries the world over. Much of hype has been driven by practitioners, think tanks, so-called ICT evangelists and the data itself. In 1995, for example, there were roughly 16 million Internet users; five years later, 361 million people used the Internet and at the end of 2012, 2.7 billion were online (Internet World States 2013). Extrapolating from these data, Marshall McLuhan's 'Global Village' will soon become a reality and, for the first time in history, every place, down to the remotest yurt in the Gobi, will be linked electronically. This global network is in fact the end goal of Internet.org, a consortium of ICT business leaders established by Facebook CEO and founder Mark Zuckerberg who claims that a "connected world could address economic disparity and outlined a vision of even the poorest people connecting to low-cost, low-data versions of basic internet services" (Levy 2013, para. 4). Accordingly, international relations and diplomacy are experiencing an ICT *revolution*, an overthrow, repudiation or replacement of an established system by the people governed. Assuming the evangelists are aware of the gravity of the term, the system to be renounced is the centuries old rationalist Westphalian 'dialogue between states'.

In this context, digital have states like the US and the UK are set to gain a comparative advantage over the have-nots. For the latter, the usual bleak, irrelevant, underfunded and underappreciated future awaits. Ministries and departments that do not embrace digital diplomacy will be left behind, cut off and eventually wither away. As Hanson (2012b, p. 6) comments,

> for other foreign ministries . . . the message is clear. Ediplomacy has arrived. The choice for them is to either embrace the opportunities and advantages

ediplomacy presents or to be passive and be shaped (and sidelined) by this latest technological revolution.

Becoming digitally isolated is a common theme in the blogosphere. Hughes (2013), for example, blogs on the BBC that "in an ever more networked world, anyone trying to operate outside the network risks being left out of conversations that are increasingly taking place in public spheres" (para. 6).

But is digital diplomacy really that important? Writing on the Canadian experience, Fung (2012, p. 19) comments that

> part of what's driven the recent boom in digital diplomacy is as much an atmosphere of anxiety as of opportunity. Beneath the rhetoric about making new connections with people is a constant uneasiness that if we don't get this right, we'll get left behind. Never mind by whom; the fear alone – of missing out on conversations, missing out on telling people what and how to think, missing out on the prospect of leveraging a nation's collective voice for strategic purposes – is powerful enough to get governments scrambling to figure social media out.

The Australian Department of Foreign Affairs and Trade (DFAT) seems to fit the anxious category, complete with a small, indigenous church of evangelists, mainly from the Lowy Institute, Australia's leading think tank, who warn that digital diplomacy

> is no longer a boutique extra. Without e-diplomacy DFAT will be cut off from important audiences and find it increasingly hard to communicate its message and coordinate Australian foreign policy across government.
>
> (Hanson 2010, p. 8)

Rory Medcalf (2013), a former diplomat and now Lowy staffer also agrees, noting that "a 21st Century foreign service that does not seriously use social media is a bit like a pre-1914 diplomatic network that kept its hands clean of newspapers and the telephone" (para. 10). Using DFAT's recent trials and tribulations as a case study, the remainder of this chapter tests such claims: is digital diplomacy a matter of life or irrelevancy for foreign ministries?

The 'have-nots' – DFAT's digital diplomacy journey

A case study of DFAT's digital diplomacy experience is valuable because many ministries are currently wrestling with the same questions: is an esoteric 'e' or digital office necessary to stave off (further) irrelevance? Can digitizing diplomacy improve knowledge management or PD operations? Or, is digital diplomacy just another fad, more old wine in new bottles? Other 'have not' ministries can learn from and empathize with DFAT's journey, of radical ICT change sweeping an institution steeped in a tradition of resisting change.

DFAT is a normal middle power diplomatic institution. With a budget of just under $1 billion (AUD), it manages ninety-six overseas posts in five continents and has a staff of roughly 4,200 spread across in Canberra, state, territory and international offices. Its core work is typical: "to protect and advance the national interest through effective advocacy and overseas diplomatic activities which promote Australia's international political, security, economic and multilateral aspects" (Department of Foreign Affairs and Trade 2010, para. 1). Over the years, it has experimented with reform, merging the Departments of Trade and Customs and the Department of External Affairs in 1987 and, more recently, flirting with Public Diplomacy and the ICT revolution.

A final noteworthy characteristic of DFAT is that it exists in limbo, a sort of permanent state of crisis. For "more than two decades, the Department of Foreign Affairs and Trade has been chronically underfunded" and notoriously underfunded (Woodroofe 2012, para. 3). In the past fifteen years, "while the public service has expanded by more than 61 per cent across the board, including a doubling of Australia's AusAID agency, the foreign service itself has not grown at all" (Woodroofe 2012, para. 15). For too long, Australia's diplomatic network has been

> hollowed out by years of underfunding . . . It had not kept pace with our interests or with a changing world . . . our overseas representation compared very poorly with almost all other developed nations' . . . shortage in posts and of diplomats with critical skills shortages – particularly in foreign languages . . . public diplomacy was lackluster and use of new digital platforms almost non-existent. In short, our diplomatic infrastructure was in a parlous state of disrepair.
>
> (Shearer et al. 2011, 4)

While Secretary Dennis Richardson has breathed some life back into DFAT – the creation of Australia's first embassy in Francophone Africa (Senegal), Ethiopia and fifty new positions, for instance – digital diplomacy is not at the top of his 'to do' list. As such, DFAT's attitude towards the ICT revolution is constantly under attack. Those leading the criticism are twofold: Fergus Hanson, formerly of the Lowy Institute, and a Joint Standing Committee on Foreign Affairs, Defence and Trade.

It should come as no surprise that Hanson is "spruiking" digital diplomacy.[5] For one, he has a point: DFAT must do more with digital diplomacy. For a country like Australia that is geographically remote, digital diplomacy is an extremely cost-effective way of conducting foreign affairs. Hanson also has an inside perspective. He worked at DFAT from 2004 to 2007 and, more importantly, was the 2011 DFAT Professional Fulbright scholar based at Georgetown University, where he came into contact with Alec Ross, Jared Cohen and various other digital diplomacy luminaries. The Fulbright resulted in two widely read reports: *Baked and Wired: eDiplomacy@State* (Hanson 2012c) and *Revolutions@State: The Spread of Ediplomacy* (2012b). Since returning from the US, Hanson has been Australia's poster boy for digital diplomacy.

For Hanson, "a new technological revolution is bearing down" on DFAT yet the department is "cut-off", resisting change and lagging behind other nations, particularly the US(Hanson 2012b, p. 3). This resistance is a sign of "how hard it can be to foresee the advantages of new technologies, but also the cultural resistance they face in traditional organisations" (Hanson 2012b, p. 9). The point has now been reached "where a foreign ministry will fail the national interest if it does not adapt to this new operating environment" (Hanson 2012d, para. 4). DFAT's hopelessness projects "a quaint image of a neo luddite holdout . . . the shift to e-diplomacy at other foreign ministries is something DFAT needs to embrace, so Australia's overseas interests can still be pursued in a 21st century world" (Hanson 2012a, para. 4). Medcalf (2013, para. 4) also agrees that the advance of social media is "unstoppable"; it is a "process of creative destruction" where "diplomats who deem tweeting beneath their dignity . . . risk becoming the blacksmiths of the information age – heavy-handed, quaint and unviable." This all or nothing attitude seems characteristic of digital diplomacy revolutionaries, as does a nuance, a subtext: many of DFAT's problems can be solved with the click buttons.

Further pressure on DFAT came from the Joint Standing Committee on Foreign Affairs, Defence and Trade (JSCFADT), which was asked in 2011 by the Minister of Foreign Affairs to report on Australia's overseas representation, with specific reference to digital diplomacy. In October 2012 and after much consultation, JSCFADT tabled the report *Australia's Overseas Representation – Punching Below Our Weight?* The report began by acknowledging that "DFAT has experienced cuts and financial constraints through successive governments and this has resulted in a diplomatic network which is seriously deficient" and at least noted that "DFAT has made significant steps towards a greater online presence" however "the internet and social media remain underutilised, particularly as tools for public diplomacy" (Parliament of the Commonwealth of Australia 2012, pp. 7–9). The report cites DFAT's single, lonely departmental Twitter account and a mere four YouTube channels as evidence of such deficiency, noting that as of May, 2012, the account had a paltry 7,859 followers (somewhat small when one compared to one US embassy in Pakistan, which has just passed 1 million Facebook fans; Parliament of the Commonwealth of Australia 2012, p. 95). Ultimately, the Committee made three general recommendations for DFAT:

- "Recommendation 15: . . . immediately refurbish Australian embassy websites to make them more informative, attractive and user-friendly.
- Recommendation 16: . . . establish an Office of e-Diplomacy, subject to the external review, the Government White Paper and any increase in resources.
- Recommendation 17: . . . make better use of social media platforms to promote Australia's foreign policy, trade opportunities, and the Department's role to the wider Australian public and key audiences in Asia and the Pacific" (Parliament of the Commonwealth of Australia 2012, pp. 122–123).

In general, the Committee criticized the slow pace of ICT adaption at DFAT, risk aversion to social media, lack of engagement with the Australian Community (at home and abroad), and a failure to keep up with the leaders in digital diplomacy, namely the US JSCFADT strongly encouraged more staff (beyond the six or seven people currently working on digital), a "mix of policy and technical experts . . . people with specialist journalistic, social media and programming expertise" (Parliament of the Commonwealth of Australia 2012, p. 60). In the end, the report damned an already struggling DFAT, noting that their attitude to the ICT revolution, which is "quite old and tired . . . very basic and has no imagination" (Parliament of the Commonwealth of Australia 2012, p. 98).

In terms of official responses, DFAT had two, which speak volumes in relation to the have or have not conundrum. In January 2012, Secretary Richardson put his name to an extensive review of *Australia's Overseas Representation, Submission No. 28*, which illustrated the good ICT work DFAT was doing on a shoestring budget. Richardson highlighted that in early 2012 "two overseas missions were using social media tools . . . toward the end of the year twelve missions were pursuing active social media programs and a further six are expected to come online in the near future" (Richardson 2012, p. 12). In other words, DFAT was trying its best. Back off.

Second, in May 2013, DFAT and Government produced a specific response to the JSCFADT report and the three recommendations. Recommendation 15 (refurbish Australian embassy websites) was "partially supported", recommendation 16 (to establish an Office of e-Diplomacy) was gingerly "noted" (Richardson claimed the bases were covered) and recommendation 17 (make better use of social media platforms) – was "supported" (Richardson 2012, p. 18).

Speaking on the prospect of a US-style Office of eDiplomacy, Richardson stated that

> we are not at the forefront of it [e-diplomacy]. We do not have the resources to do it. If I had additional resources now that is not where I would allocate those additional resources. I would put people into Western China before I established an office of e-diplomacy. It is not to say an office of e-diplomacy is not important, but you have to make choices when you are running an organization . . . I would love the resources to open an office of e-diplomacy, but if I got 10 additional people tomorrow I would be allocating them elsewhere before opening such an office.
> (Parliament of the Commonwealth of Australia 2012, p. 118)

If ever there was a statement of new meeting old in an overworked and underappreciated department of foreign affairs, then this was it; the Secretary can almost be imagined throwing his hands in the air. Traditional concerns override innovation: more funding, more diplomatic leather-soled shoes 'on the ground' and more embassies in emerging/developing markets, notably Africa and China.

However, and perhaps to appease JSCFADT, DFAT has gone a little bit digital. The Secretary (Richardson 2012, pp. 21–29) reminded the Committee that DFAT is in the midst of a three-year reform of ICT strategy, continues to deliver "innovative and strategic public diplomacy as a core component of its daily work" and is well versed in digital and social media. DFAT also has a strong web presence consisting of over 100 separate sites that encompass the main DFAT website (with over 5 million visitors per year), the *Smartraveller* website (over 30 million hits each year) and overseas posts' websites. For the foreseeable future, DFAT is to "maintain a measured approach to adopting social media platforms" (Richardson 2012, p. 21). While encouraging, such data is unlikely to satisfy the digital diplomacy evangelists. Furthermore, DFAT's digital diplomacy experience alludes to a key question posed at the outset of this chapter: is digital diplomacy set to revolutionise the dialogue between estranged states, nations and people or is it simply a gimmick, a fad?

The digital diplomacy evolution

The evangelists are partly correct. States able to divert resources to digital diplomacy will enjoy certain immediate benefits ranging from enhanced internal and external knowledge management structures to 'jazzier', more innovative platforms for public diplomacy. As such, digital diplomacy 'haves' do have an edge over 'have-nots'; however, this edge is temporary and, in time, states such as Australia should modernize ICT capabilities and catch up. At the same time, traditionalists, Luddites and doubters also have a point: digital diplomacy will not *revolutionize* diplomacy, nor will it alter its key foundations (communication, negotiation, representation and so on) – what diplomacy *does*, in other words. As ever, it is important to inject a dose of reality to the hysteria that usually accompanies revolutions in ICT and their impact on diplomacy. Relativism, a sense of history and an awareness of the importance of tradition in diplomacy suggest that digital diplomacy is but the latest wave of a larger digital *evolution* whose origins lie way back in the nineteenth century.

It is easy to understand why the evangelists use the word revolution when thinking about the digital era. Quite simply, the data is staggering. Since the mid-1990s the volume of information has increased exponentially. Consider Nye (cited in Hanson 2012b, p. 21), for instance, who claims that,

> by one estimate, 161 billion gigabytes of digital information were created and captured in the year 2006 alone (that is about 3 million times the information in all the books ever written). In 2010, the annual growth in digital information is expected to increase more than six-fold to 988 billion gigabytes. This dramatic change in the linked technologies of computing and communications is changing the nature of government and accelerating a diffusion of power.

As previously noted, almost everyone on the planet is connected to a cellular phone network, and if Zuckerberg and Co. get their wishes, sometime in the near future we will all be connected to the Internet. This notion of *totality* is both mindboggling and unprecedented. However, just because everyone is connected doesn't mean they will all be glued to embassy webpages or tweets from random ambassadors lusting after relevancy. Also, and to paraphrase Asimov, who says that knowledge equals power and wisdom? And, hasn't diplomacy been through similar ICT revolutions before?

In fact, there are five general issues with the digital diplomacy evangelist's position, which perhaps account for the reluctance of institutions like DFAT to succumb to the revolutionary fervour. The first is semantic. What, actually, is digital diplomacy? It has been referred to as telediplomacy, e-diplomacy, 21st-century statecraft, cyber, open, net diplomacy and so on. In the book *Digital Diplomacy*, the first substantial work on the topic, Dizard (2001, pp. 1–2) writes that "electronic communications and information resources . . . access to computers, satellites, and other information technologies" result in a "distinctly different type of relations between nations – one that calls for a responsive *digital diplomacy*." He lumps changes in radio, television, telephone and facsimile under the heading digital diplomacy, arguing the revolution began in the 1960s with satellite, gathering speed in the 1970s with the emergence of the Internet. Others prefer the term *e-diplomacy*, defining it simply as "the use of web and new ICT to help carry out diplomatic objectives" (Hanson 2012b, p. 2). As the debate (to have or have not) intensifies, the definition keeps getting shorter, with Medcalf (2013, para. 1) defining digital diplomacy as nothing more than "the use of social media." MFAs such as DFAT can thus be somewhat forgiven for not jumping on the bandwagon. It is difficult to get excited about a revolution if those advocating change are unsure of what the theory and practice entails, or the key term actually means.

Second, and arguably, this lack of a succinct understanding stems from a lack of peer-to-peer scholarship on digital diplomacy. Without sounding the elitist call from the ivory tower, there can be no substitute for rigorous and methodologically sound inquiry. Epistemologically, the bulk of the rhetoric comes from nonrefereed blurbs, blogs and opinion pieces. In Australia's case, much of the evangelizing comes from the Lowy Institute, a privately funded think tank. Writing on the appearance of "young, amateur foreign policy commentators" thanks to digital diplomacy, Medcalf (2013, para. 7), a Lowy staffer and former DFAT employee, considered this "a commendable, natural development . . . when so many academics and experienced former officials fail to repay their training by helping society understand real-world policy problems." This is a good example of bad scholarship. Many former officials write books or enter into academia; and all academics educate thousands of students across society on real world problems (it's their job). Such rhetoric, combined with a limited amount of academically rigorous, peer-to-peer scholarship on digital diplomacy casts doubt on a revolution or fundamental paradigm shift in diplomacy.

As does, third, the empirical data supporters of digital diplomacy regularly trumpet. The US embassy's 'hugely popular' social media feeds provide one such example. Relatively speaking, the US Embassy Facebook fan page has 485,000 fans. To put this into quantitative terms, Indonesian motivational speaker Mario Teguh gets this many new Facebook fans every three months (he has 5.84 million fans). The latest Spiderman film had 2.5 million fans in Indonesia. So, Spiderman is five times more popular than Uncle Sam. US e-diplomacy needs to be put into perspective. There are 55 million internet users in Indonesia, which means that less than 1% of those are currently reached by the US Embassy. With a total population of 245 million, the US Embassy reaches only 0.21% of all Indonesians via social media.

(Smith 2012, para. 7)

The numbers, in other words, aren't that impressive.

Changes in how individuals and nations gather and share information are quite remarkable, but they must be considered in perspective. In 1971, for example, AT&T handled just twenty calls from the United States to China *annually*. Twenty. As alluded, the actual digital revolution (from slow, land-based wired technologies to faster, space-based wireless communications) began with Morse and Marconi in the mid to late nineteenth century. Since then, diplomacy has ridden out and benefited from several waves of ICT revolutions. The radio, for example, was one such dramatic change in how states and foreign publics interacted, as was the cable or the telegraph or the telephone or the jet plane. Take your pick! Evolution, therefore, is a far more appropriate, accurate and less dramatic term to describe the impact of digital changes on diplomacy.

Fourth and related, the digital revolution has not replaced, negated or swept aside more traditional elements of international relations. In a political sense, a revolution is an overthrow, repudiation and thorough replacement of an established government or political system by the people governed, a radical and pervasive change in society and social structure. A revolution suggests that the new brushes aside, replaces and/or repudiates the old. In the context of the digital diplomacy, this is incorrect. State-qua-state wars, hard power, guns, bombs, terrorists, tangible borders, geopolitics, economic, food and nuclear security, for example, will not cease to exist because of a revolution in social media, the Internet or how states gather and disseminate information. ICT, in this respect, is but a facilitator of change, not a causational factor of systemic or foundational change; it is a means, a tool or a method that affects the way information is shared, the way states and people communicate. Consider a nation's armed forces, an institution that has a history of proactively driving changes in ICT. The information revolution in military affairs has led to changes in *how* states fight wars (network centric warfare, effects based operations, fighting at greater distance with enhance precision and lethality, and so on) but not *why* states fight wars: to survive, to protect and promote national interest and to kill the "baddies" (Griffiths 2013). The same logic can be applied to diplomacy: evolutions in ICT change *how* states do diplomacy, but not *what* it is or *why* they do it.

One of those traditions in diplomacy is the gathering and dissemination of information. Because information comes from the press, internet and other forms mass media, scholars, writers and exchanges of private visitors and, these days, from the domestic and foreign public, there is a rather silly tendency to assume that the diplomat is endangered species. In the information age, however, a diplomat's ability to process large bodies of information matters more than ever. As Stein (2011, p. 3) comments,

> diplomats, in short, are not valuable because of the information they provide, but because of their authoritative knowledge and the quality of their analysis. Especially in the digital age awash in information, indeed drowning in information, knowledge and elegant analysis matter. They may matter even more that they did in the age of print, where editors traditionally assured the quality of what people read.

The diplomat is skilled in gathering a particular type of information and knowledge that their government masters demand. Besides elegant analysis, such knowledge can be one of personalities rather than of forces and conditions which influence a country's political direction over a given period. Moreover, the sheer volume of information does not matter. In diplomacy, quantity does not equal quality: knowledge, does not necessarily equal wisdom.

A sense of history, fifthly, would add much needed sobriety to the have/have not debate. From Palmerston to Queen Victoria to Zbigniew Brzezinski, a sense of hysteria usually accompanies changes in ICT for diplomacy. The practitioner's responses are almost clichéd in the canon of diplomatic studies. "My God," cried Palmerston, the British prime minister, on receiving the first telegraph message in the 1860s, "this is the end of diplomacy" (cited in Kurbalija 2013, p. 141). Regardless of the epoch, the narrative remains the same: a dramatic change in ICT occurs but diplomacy and diplomats are too archaic, elitist, traditional, change-resistant, fossilized, dead, etcetera, to realise the embrace that change. Irrelevancy becomes the institution and, in turn, diplomacy as an area of theory and practice becomes redundant and, eventually, deliquesces.

What utter nonsense. In a historical sense, diplomacy has survived similar revolutions before and no institution was cut off or left behind – nothing died. DFAT, for one, endured a similar period of histrionics when the fax machines came along in the 1980s. So-called revolutions are a common theme in the theory and practice of diplomacy. Scholars and practitioners are forever writing of the 'new' diplomacy yet the 'old' survives each time, waltzing to change in accordance with the unique organizational culture of diplomacy. A resistance to change is often misconstrued by outsiders as an inability to change. Ministries are unfairly portrayed as Luddite holdouts when an awareness of history reveals they do change, albeit slower than outsiders often desire. Such careful, considerate and measured responses to broader changes in society should be lauded, not lambasted. History informs that diplomacy has never been an institution that entertains kneejerk reactions, and fortunately so. The means of diplomacy may change, but its foundations (to represent and communicate a state's national interest, for example) do not and should not change. Besides, MFAs cannot change quickly; the size and scale of the operation, the cost of upgrading hardware and software across such a network, the nature of the information Ministries deal with, which often concerns sensitive materials conducive to national security, prevents dramatic change. Moreover, as in the case of DFAT, they often don't have the personnel, nor do they have the budget. A closer, balanced reading of history reveals that diplomacy always changes, but slowly.

Conclusion

For the evangelists, the latest wave of ICT could suggest that the machine may come to negate the physical diplomat. In what can only be described as moments of wild fantasy, artificial intelligence may usurp human intelligence, diplomacy could become computerized with **virtual embassies** ran on a form of telediplomacy controlled from the capital, "diplomacy conducted increasingly by remote control" in other words (Dizard 2001, p. 2).

There will be no such future. For diplomacy, tradition is every bit as important as innovation. Humans will always be required for good diplomacy, particularly in patching up the damage new technologies can cause. A study on the future of diplomacy by Georgetown University (cited in Dizard 2001, p. 2) agrees, noting that:

> the "global village" is a deceptively attractive term which obscures the real differences in peoples and governments. Foreigners will continue to live, think, and view events in ways that are foreign to us. We will continue to need diplomats pounding the pavements, talking to all sorts of people in foreign countries and analysing the significance of what why have learned.

DFAT's Luddite nature can thus be forgiven somewhat. Moreover, asking DFAT to do what the US has done is comparing apples to oranges. The US is a giant, wealthy nation of 310 million plus, a nation obsessed with upholding a preponderance of information hegemony, conducive to ensuring its position as a dataholic hyperpower. It has been a leader in all matters digital since the 1960s, can devote millions of dollars and hundreds of staff spread across twenty-five different nodes of government to its office of e-diplomacy, and has a culture and history of technological innovation. By comparison, DFAT is tiny. Pardon the pun, but it is not possible to 'cut and paste' State's digital diplomacy program.

To understand the impact of the ICT revolution on diplomacy is to think relatively, historically and less dramatically. Digital diplomacy is not the be all and end all for ministries. There is no digital divide, no world of haves and have-nots; no MFA will be cut off, left out to 'die'. When conceptualizing digital diplomacy it is more useful to think in terms of both continuity and change, trend and transformation, and tradition and innovation. While the latest wave in ICT will revolutionize the way people, CSOs and MNCs, for example, interact it will not fundamentally alter the key meaning of diplomacy, which has been the same since the days of the troglodytes as "the way in which relations between groups that regard themselves as separate ought to be conducted if the principle of living in groups is to be retained as good, and if unnecessary and unwanted conflict is to have a chance of being avoided" (Sharp 2003, p. 858).

Notes

1 The Chinese and Koreans had been using movable print since the thirteenth century.
2 Moore's law is the premise that in the history of computing hardware, the number of transistors on integrated circuits exponentially doubles every two years. It was named after Intel co-founder Gordon E. Moore.
3 The Singularity is a moment when artificial intelligence will progress and eventually surpass human intelligence, radically changing civilization and, arguably, the future of humanity.
4 Jan Melissen of Clingendael and Bruce Gregory of George Washington University, for example.
5 *Spruiking* is an Aussie slang term, meaning 'to speak in public.'

8

THE INTERNATIONAL CRIMINAL COURT

Using technology in network diplomacy

Karen L. Corrie

Introduction

The **International Criminal Court** (ICC, or "the Court") has become a significant institution in international diplomacy. Its work alters leaders' and states' reputations, and affects diplomatic relations. Yet the ICC is not simply an institution created by and for states, nor is it a passive factor in the international community. The ICC seeks to be a legitimate criminal court, and to accomplish this it engages in **network diplomacy**: diplomacy conducted through building sustained connections between governments, corporations, non-governmental organizations (NGOs) and individuals, which can be used to achieve common goals.

Network diplomacy theory highlights that actors must nurture their internal networks and find ways to facilitate information exchange internally, while also building and maintaining broader external networks with other actors. The ICC engages at both levels. On the one hand, it fosters internal communication and knowledge-sharing among its three organs, the participants in its court proceedings, and other internal actors, to facilitate efficient and effective investigations and prosecutions. On the other hand, the ICC builds and maintains a diverse external network of supportive states, NGOs, intergovernmental organizations and the public, who are necessary for the Court to successfully perform its work. Ultimately, these networks provide the ICC with both legitimacy and power.

Of particular relevance for this book, **digital diplomacy** is one of the ways that the ICC engages in network diplomacy to manage change. For the purposes of this chapter, "change" is looked at from two perspectives: how the ICC internally handles its endogenous ever-evolving casework; and how the ICC manages exogenous perceptions of its legitimacy and garners the external support crucial for its success. The latter is particularly important, given that the ICC is currently facing criticisms that undermine its position as a legitimate international institution.

To manage both kinds of change, the ICC uses sophisticated technologies to maintain, share and synthesize evidence and judicial documents, and to facilitate efficient hearings and trials. At the same time, the ICC uses a variety of Internet-based technologies to disseminate accurate and up-to-date information about its work, to enhance how it is received and understood as a legitimate actor by external actors.

This chapter outlines how the ICC uses digital diplomacy to manage internal and external change. Section II introduces the key features of the Court, as a foundation for what follows. Section III demonstrates that the ICC is indeed an international actor engaged in network diplomacy, reliant on both internal and external networks to manage change, i.e. to cultivate both its work and its legitimacy. Section IV describes the technologies that the ICC uses to handle both internal and external change.

Key background information about the ICC

The ICC is the first permanent and independent international criminal court. It was created by a treaty called the Rome Statute of the International Criminal Court, which went into effect on July 1 2002. The ICC is charged with prosecuting "the most serious crimes of concern to the international community as a whole" (Rome Statute 1998, preamble) namely genocide, crimes against humanity and war crimes, and may at some future point have jurisdiction to prosecute the crime of aggression (Rome Statute 1998, preamble, arts. 5–8bis, 15bis–15ter). The Court is based in The Hague, the Netherlands.

The ICC is built on the legacy of the prosecution of Nazi and Japanese war criminals after World War II, as well as the work of the Security Council's *ad hoc* tribunals, the International Criminal Tribunals for the former Yugoslavia and for Rwanda. However, the ICC differs from these institutions because it is permanent, and because it was not created to address only one conflict – it is intended to be a global impunity watchdog, ensuring that those who commit mass atrocities will not go unpunished.

Main organs

The ICC has three main organs: the Office of the Prosecutor (OTP), the Chambers, and the Registry. The OTP is responsible for receiving information about crimes within the ICC's jurisdiction, investigating them, and, where appropriate, prosecuting them (Rome Statute 1998, art. 42). It is headed by a prosecutor and a deputy prosecutor (Rome Statute 1998, art. 42(2)). The Chambers comprises the Court's judges, who make all decisions and judgments in legal proceedings before the Court, including on the innocence or guilt of the accused (Rome Statute 1998, art. 39).

The Registry is the Court's support organ; it is responsible for all nonjudicial aspects of the administration and servicing of the Court (Rome Statute 1998, art. 43), such as providing simultaneous translation during hearings and trials, providing security measures for witnesses, and facilitating access to counsel for accused persons. It also houses an Office of Public Counsel for the Defence (Regulations of the Court 2004, reg. 77), as well as an Office of Public Counsel for Victims (Regulations of the Court 2004, reg. 81), the latter of which is necessary because victims can participate limitedly as independent third parties in ICC proceedings (Rules of Procedure and Evidence 2002, rules 89–93; Corrie 2013).

Jurisdiction

The ICC does not have unfettered jurisdiction to prosecute crimes committed anywhere in the world. Rather, the ICC only has jurisdiction over crimes that occur on the territory of states parties, or that are committed by the nationals of states parties (Rome Statute 1998, arts. 12–13). Under these circumstances, investigations can be initiated in one of two ways: either (1) a state party refers the matter to the OTP for investigation and possible prosecution, or (2) the Prosecutor initiates the investigation with the permission of a Pre-Trial Chamber (PTC) (Rome Statute 1998, arts. 13–15).

There is a third option, by which the ICC can obtain jurisdiction over crimes committed outside of the territory of states parties and by non-states parties' nationals: the United Nations (UN) Security Council can refer any situation to the Court for investigation and prosecution, acting under its powers pursuant to Chapter VII of the UN Charter (Rome Statute 1998, arts. 12–13).

Because of the scope and nature of the crimes within the Court's jurisdiction, there may be hundreds, if not thousands, of perpetrators, from those who plan the crimes to those who physically commit them. Given the number of possible suspects, the OTP focuses its prosecutions on those who bear the greatest responsibility (ICC, 2014c): those senior planners and instigators who mastermind the crimes. It is hoped that states can prosecute the rest domestically. The ICC has indicted and is prosecuting, or has prosecuted, a number of important political figures and leaders of strong anti-government militias. For example:

- Germain Katanga, Thomas Lubanga, and Bosco Ntaganda, who were or are being prosecuted for crimes against humanity and/or war crimes, were senior Congolese militia leaders before their arrest and detention at the ICC.[1]
- Jean-Pierre Bemba Gombo, on trial for crimes against humanity and war crimes allegedly committed by his troops in the Central African Republic, was a wealthy politician, businessman, and former militia leader in the Democratic Republic of Congo (DRC) who came in second in the 2006 DRC presidential election.
- Three persons accused of responsibility for the genocide in Darfur include Sudanese President Omar Al Bashir, former Sudanese Minister of State for the Interior and for Humanitarian Affairs Ahmad Harun, and key Janjaweed militia leader Ali Kushayb.

- Accused persons Uhuru Kenyatta and William Ruto, who are currently appearing voluntarily at the Court to answer charges of crimes against humanity, are the current President and Deputy President of Kenya, respectively.
- Two persons accused of committing crimes in Libya were also senior leaders of the Gaddafi government, namely Saif Al-Islam Gaddafi, who was *de facto* prime minister of Libya, and Abdullah Al-Senussi, who was a colonel in the Libyan Armed Forces and the head of the military intelligence.
- Laurent Gbagbo, who faces charges of crimes against humanity, is the former president of Côte d'Ivoire.

Proceedings

Proceedings before the Court follow three phases: the pretrial phase, the trial phase, and the appeals phase. The pretrial phase includes the OTP's investigation of the matter. When the OTP is investigating a matter but has not developed any specific cases, the matter as a whole is referred to as a "situation." Charges brought against specific persons are referred to as "cases" that have "arisen" out of a particular situation. For example, in 2004, the government of the DRC referred the "situation" concerning crimes committed in its own territory to the OTP for investigation and prosecution ICC 2004). The "case" against Congolese warlord Thomas Lubanga "arose" from the investigation of that larger "situation."

The pretrial phase includes issuing arrest warrants and summonses to appear, as well as a milestone hearing similar to the American indictment process called the confirmation of charges hearing. If the PTC finds that the OTP has presented "sufficient evidence to establish substantial grounds to believe that the person committed the crime charged" based on documentary or summary evidence, including witness statements (Rome Statute 1998, art. 61), the case is set for trial. The trials, which procedurally combine a hybrid of common law and civil law legal systems, can last several years. The Prosecution and the Defence have the right to appeal the verdict.

The UN Security Council has the power to halt active investigations and prosecutions by issuing a one-year deferral, acting again under Chapter VII of the UN Charter. The Council can renew its deferral indefinitely (Rome Statute 1998, art. 16) – meaning that the Council has the power to essentially terminate ICC cases. The Council has not yet exercised this power.

Assembly of states parties

States parties to the Rome Statute convene as the Assembly of States Parties. (How votes are cast, however, can be highly political, influenced by state power and position.) The Assembly, *inter alia*, elects the Court's judges, prosecutor and deputy prosecutor, sets the Court's budget, and has the authority to amend the Rome Statute and the Court's Rules of Procedure and Evidence. ICC states parties also have an obligation under the Rome Statute to obey the ICC's orders, including a duty to execute ICC arrest warrants (Rome Statute 1998, arts. 59(1), 86, 89). The Assembly has a Bureau consisting of a President, two vice presidents and eighteen geographically representative members elected by the Assembly for three-year terms (Rome Statute 1998, ar. 121).

The ICC as a diplomatic actor managing change

The ICC and network diplomacy

ICC internal and external relations are best articulated through the paradigm of **network diplomacy.** Network diplomacy is used here as described by Anne-Marie Slaughter to refer to diplomacy conducted through building sustained connections between governments, corporations, NGOs, and individuals and from having the "knowledge and skills to harness that power to achieve a common purpose," where the actor "with the most connections will be regarded as the central player, able to set the global agenda and unlock innovation and sustainable growth" (Slaughter 2009, 94–113).

In one of the primary works on network diplomacy, Jamie Metzl (2001, 81) describes that network diplomacy involves both internal and external networks. Actors must "nurture their own internal networks," and, where they "amass a great deal of useful information in a multitude of areas," must find ways to "facilitate the exchange of information across agencies and hierarchies." At the same time, Metzl stresses the importance of states building and maintaining "broader networks outside of" themselves, including with foreign governments, civil society, and the public at large (Metzl 2001, 80–81, 85).

Benjamin Schiff argues that the ICC demonstrates a rise in network diplomacy.[2] He examines the Court's creation, noting that it prominently featured the collective efforts of like-minded states and NGOs to create a court opposed by traditionally dominant states, including China, Russia and the United States. He also writes that, since its creation, the ICC's record "demonstrates tensions between traditional state power . . . and the rise of global norms, multilateralism, and network diplomacy" (Schiff 2013, 745–748).

This chapter agrees with Schiff that the ICC demonstrates a rise in network diplomacy but examines this thesis from a different perspective, showing that the ICC uses digital diplomacy to foster its internal and external networks, particularly to manage the changes in both. In this chapter the term "change" is examined from two perspectives. First, the ICC must manage a kind of internal change: the progress of investigations and prosecutions. Second, at the same time, the ICC must manage a kind of external change: shifting perceptions about and support for the Court, or in other words – whether the Court is perceived as a legitimate actor by outside actors.

Internal

The ICC is a large, sometimes bureaucratic organization. Within its three organs are many divisions, subdivisions and hundreds of employees. All work towards one central goal: the thorough, effective and efficient investigation and prosecution of atrocity crimes. To do this, the ICC must internally share a great deal of information – particularly the evidence used in the ICC's cases, but also Court decisions, judgments and other documents.

At the same time, the knowledge that is shared is in constant flux. For example, the evidence collected for a situation or case constantly evolves. During investigation stages, evidence grows and must be regularly assessed and reassessed to develop case theories and identify those most responsible. When cases reach pretrial hearings and trials, the participants and judges must share and evaluate evidence from witnesses, documents, etc., which grows steadily. In addition to evidence, the participants and judges must respond to one another's motions and decisions, often within short deadlines, and react to new legal developments at the Court, such as decisions from the Appeals Chamber that can affect ongoing proceedings.

With twenty-one cases arising in eight situations before the Court and more sure to follow (as of August 2014), evidence to share from hundreds of witnesses and thousands of documents, a constant flurry of contentious motions practice, and regular important decisions from Chambers of the Court, efficient and effective knowledge management is key for the Court. As pointed out in Chapter 1 of this book, digital diplomacy can be used in knowledge creation, management and dissemination – the cultivation of knowledge as an institutional resource. This chapter supports that assertion: as is described in Section IV.A, the ICC uses digital diplomacy to manage and efficiently share the ever-changing situation-related and case-related information.

External

The ICC relies on external networks to succeed as a criminal court, because the Rome Statute does not give it the power to do what most national courts can do on their own. For example, the ICC has no standing police force, no guaranteed access to countries to conduct investigations, and limited resources to conduct investigations and prosecutions. As a result, the ICC can only be effective with help from others – and it relies on a network of states, international organizations, NGOs, and even public support for this reason. Put in other terms, the ICC relies on what Slaughter has called "collaborative power": the "networked, horizontal surge and sustained application of collective will and resources" (Slaughter 2011, para. 6).

States are arguably the most important group in the ICC's network. States parties, *inter alia*, fund the Court, make arrests, provide access to government records including criminal records and birth certificates, grant OTP staff entry to the country to perform investigations, and protect witnesses and their families. Without cooperation from states, the ICC cannot function. But other groups also have an important role to play. For example, the ICC relies on NGOs to lobby government support for its work, to increase public awareness about its activities and to facilitate investigations.[3] It also relies on international organizations and intergovernmental organizations to provide information, access to experts, etc.[4] And without public confidence in the ICC's ability to protect witnesses, secure convictions, and provide reparations, witnesses may be reluctant to give evidence before the Court.

The ICC must pay particular attention to fostering confidence from its external networks because, after roughly twelve years of operation, the Court faces criticisms that undermine its legitimacy. Chief among these are: that the ICC unfairly targets Africans; that it imposes Western notions of "justice" on non-Western societies; that it is inefficient and ineffective, having produced only three verdicts in twelve years; and that it conducts one-sided investigations and prosecutions, in some cases turning a blind eye to government atrocities in order to secure enough state support to investigate crimes committed by government opposition forces. The merits of these arguments have been debated vigorously in many fora, and so are not addressed in depth here (e.g. Robertson 2012, 554–9). Suffice it to say that many of these arguments are based on misunderstandings about the Court, while others have been perpetuated by those the ICC seeks to prosecute.

This **legitimacy crisis** becomes most apparent when states decline to cooperate with the Court, weakening it further and contributing to criticisms that the Court is ineffective. Although legally the Rome Statute requires states parties to cooperate with the Court (Rome Statute 1998, art. 86), and permits ICC cooperation with non-states parties (Rome Statute 1998, art. 87(5)), in practice cooperation is not always forthcoming. For example, although the ICC issued arrest warrants for Sudanese President Bashir in 2009 and 2010 concerning the Darfuri genocide – a situation that the ICC took up following referral by the UN Security Council in 2005 – Bashir remains at large. This is not because he has holed up in the Sudan; rather, he has enough support from the international community to continue to act as a legitimate head of state without being arrested, which has sufficiently trumped belief in the ICC's legitimacy to allow him to remain free.

For example, the African Union (AU) rallied behind Bashir, asking the UN Security Council to defer the ICC's proceedings in the situation in Darfur and calling on AU member states not to enforce the warrant for Bashir's arrest. Some ICC states parties have welcomed Bashir in their borders and have not arrested him, including Chad, Kenya and Malawi. States outside of Africa have also ignored the arrest warrants; for example, China, which is not a party to the Rome Statute and which buys significant amounts of the oil produced in Sudan, has offered support to Sudan, urged the Court to drop the warrant, and even hosted Bashir in China without arresting him. This is despite the fact that China, a permanent member of the Security Council, bears some responsibility for the UN Security Council referral of the Darfur situation,[5] and might be expected to want to see Council decisions enforced.

The legitimacy of the Court was further called into question by African states in 2013, following a push by the Kenyan government to combat the cases against its president, Uhuru Kenyatta, and deputy president, William Ruto. These efforts culminated in the AU holding an extraordinary summit in October 2013, before which it was rumoured that the Kenyan government would encourage African states to withdraw en mass from the Rome Statute. The outcome, though certainly less dramatic, was nevertheless problematic: the AU issued a decision that heads of state and other senior state officials enjoy immunity from prosecution before international courts (in direct opposition to Article 27 of the Rome Statute), that the trials against Kenyatta and Ruto should be suspended, and that Kenyatta would not appear before the ICC until the Security Council had ruled on a request from the Kenyan government to defer prosecution of the cases.

The ICC did not initially face these issues. When it was first created, the ICC rode a wave of support derived from the Security Council's creation of *ad hoc* tribunals for Yugoslavia and Rwanda and an apparent international commitment to the pursuit of justice. Twelve years later, practical and political realities have shifted the nexus of state support, and there is a need for greater cooperation and mutual understanding between states and the ICC (e.g. Bjola and Kornprobst 2013, 194). As discussed in Chapter 1 of this book, digital diplomacy can be used as a form of public diplomacy. This is certainly supported by the practices of the ICC. As is discussed in Section IV.B, the ICC uses a variety of primarily Internet-based resources as one way to try to manage exogenous change, with an emphasis on sharing accurate and up-to-date information about the Court's work.

Technologies the ICC uses in digital diplomacy

Given the pace at which ICC cases develop and external partners' relationships with the Court evolve, the ICC has developed many methods for managing these constant changes. This chapter focuses on how the ICC uses digital diplomacy for these purposes – facilitating faster, more accurate and more secure investigations and prosecutions, while at the same time managing perceptions of its work to consolidate external support and cooperation.

Fostering internal networks

Metzl highlights that governments should cultivate their internal networks in part through using enhanced computer systems, coupled with training for all staff on how to use them (Metzl 2001, 81). Though he discusses this in the context of sharing comprehensive information about government agencies' skills and capabilities, it is equally applicable in the ICC context – to sharing evolving information about ongoing investigations and prosecutions as well as the development of jurisprudence, and to facilitate court proceedings.

E-Court system

The ICC uses electronic management systems to collect, store, and provide access to all orders, decisions and judgments of the Court, the filings of the participants, and evidence submitted by the participants, as well as transcripts of the proceedings (Regulations of the Court 2004, reg. 26(1); Regulations of the Registry 2006, reg. 10). This system is called the **e-court system**; it is really a collection of systems, including:

- TRIM (Total Record Information Management), a software produced by Hewlett Packard,[6] to store all filings, decisions, etc.;
- Ringtail, an evidence storage and management tool produced by FTI Consulting (see Section IV.B.2); and
- Transcend,[7] an application produced by Legal Craft, to manage and store transcripts from hearings and trials (see Section IV.B.4).

The Registry is responsible for this system (Regulations of the Court 2004, reg. 26(2)). Access is limited to participants in the proceedings, including judges, OTP staff, defence staff, and victims' representatives (Regulations of the Registry 2006, reg. 10(2)).[8] Once a situation or case has been initiated, parties and participants file materials in the record of the case by submitting them to the Registry. Electronic filing is preferred.[9] When documents are filed with the Registry, it notifies relevant participants that the document has been filed by email (Regulations of the Court 2004, reg. 34(1)).

Evidence management: Ringtail

The ICC stores and manages electronic copies of evidence – including searchable-text files, photographs, pictures, maps, audio recordings and videos – using an evidence management database called Ringtail. Once material is uploaded to Ringtail, metadata can be attached to provide important historic information about it, such as the date of collection, the name of the person who collected it and the name of the witness or other entity that provided it. The text of uploaded materials and the metadata can be searched,[10] and the results saved. Additionally, the Ringtail system can isolate sets of documents into electronic "binders" as necessary.[11]

Effective use of Ringtail requires training and practice. Some ICC staff find it difficult to use and as a result do not rely on it or rely on other staff members to review the database for them. This may have greater effects on the defence than the OTP: while some OTP staff regularly use the Ringtail system, defence teams that are new to the ICC may not know how to use it and will need to take time and resources away from other work to learn it.

Ringtail also facilitates redaction and disclosure of documents – in other words, knowledge sharing between the participants and judges for court proceedings. The ICC follows a complex and burdensome regime of redaction approval, where participants must obtain permission from the Chambers for every redaction of materials being disclosed.[12] The Ringtail system has been used to accommodate redaction and disclosure: it includes a function to highlight portions of the electronic version of evidence to propose redactions to them. Once the relevant

Chamber approves the redactions, the participants can convert the highlighted portions into blacked-out redactions that others cannot lift.[13]

The process of reviewing documents and redacting them can be time-consuming and often requires the attention of a significant number of staff members, especially under short Court-ordered deadlines. Without an electronic system, this would be virtually impossible, and thus Ringtail is essential for the ICC to bring accused persons to trial "without undue delay" (Rome Statute 1998, art. 67(1)(c)).

OTP evidence assessment: CaseMap[14]

Because it investigates large-scale crimes, the OTP collects and must synthesize high volumes of evidence for each case. One way the OTP tackles this is with case assessment software called CaseMap, produced by the company LexisNexis.[15] OTP litigation teams working on specific cases input all key facts from the evidence into one CaseMap database for each case. Each "fact" is entered separately and linked to the piece of evidence it comes from, until the team amasses a database of thousands of facts. Multiple team members can enter evidence into and edit entries in CaseMap at the same time.

In addition to facilitating input of facts, CaseMap contains interlinked spreadsheets that provide the framework for organizing and evaluating critical case knowledge.[16] The OTP primarily uses two spreadsheets: the "object" spreadsheet, which lists relevant persons, locations and items in the case; and the "issues" spreadsheet, which lists the crimes that the OTP has charged in a particular case, with a hierarchy of sub-issues for the elements of each crime. The list of crimes and their elements in the issues spreadsheet is referred to as the "issue tree."

CaseMap allows "tagging" of evidence based on criteria that are important for the case, including "objects" and "issues." Facts can also be searched, filtered to show only those that contain one or more issues or objects, or sorted by criteria such as the date of the fact (e.g. only facts for a particular date, all facts sorted chronologically) or the witness providing the evidence.

CaseMap facilitates different stages of OTP knowledge management. OTP teams use CaseMap during the pretrial phase to, *inter alia*, assess the strength and quality of the evidence, structure a theory of the case, etc. The OTP also uses it during trial, inputting testimony from witnesses and other sources to determine what elements of what crimes have been proved. The OTP can do the same if the accused presents evidence, to determine how it has impacted the OTP's case.

The OTP has also used CaseMap to produce "in-depth analysis charts" ("IDACs"):

> comprehensive in-depth analysis chart[s] of the evidence included in the list of the evidence upon which [the Prosecution] intends to rely . . . , wherein each piece of evidence is linked to each constituent element of the crimes charged, and, wherein each piece of evidence concerning the alleged criminal responsibility is presented with respect to each suspect separately.
> (*Situation in the Republic of Kenya*, "Corrigendum to Decision" 2001, 9)

Chambers have asked the OTP to provide IDACS prior to confirmation hearings and trials (e.g. *Prosecutor v. Bemba*, "Decision on In-depth Analysis Chart" 2008; *Prosecutor v. Ruto et al.*, "Prosecution's submission" 2011). CaseMap significantly facilitates IDAC production because CaseMap allows teams to export reports of facts organized by the issues in the issues tree. This gives the judges and participants lists of all facts that allegedly prove all elements of the crimes charged. Without CaseMap's export function, IDAC production would be unmanageable.[17]

Evidence management at trial

The participants submit evidence in electronic format[18] and it is used electronically during hearings and trials (Regulations of the Registry 2006, reg. 52(1)). Participants give the materials and relevant metadata to the Registry,[19] which will upload the material to Ringtail (ICC, 2014e, paras. 5–6). When evidence is used at trial,[20] the Registry registers it with additional metadata, including: the name of the participant tendering the evidence or an indication that the evidence was produced upon order of the Chamber; the date when the evidence was tendered; whether the Court admitted or excluded the evidence; a brief description of the evidence; the name or pseudonym of the witness through whom the evidence was tendered in Court; whether an objection was raised against the relevance and/or admissibility of the evidence, and if so, by whom; and the level of confidentiality, if any (Regulations of the Registry 2006, reg. 28(3)).

Having all of this information attached to each piece of evidence facilitates evidence review. It helps the participants know what they can rely on to argue their case, and helps the Chambers determine what evidence can be relied on to render verdicts. At the same time, ensuring that the metadata is accurately filled out is a time-consuming job for Registry staff, and the participants may feel compelled to check that the correct metadata has been inputted with evidence they tendered, which can be a burdensome task.

To share evidence quickly among the judges, participants and witnesses during hearing and trials, the ICC has established the most technically advanced court rooms in the world. For example, there are computers at all participants' and judges' tables, as well as the witness stand. Evidence displayed electronically on these computers (Regulations of the Registry 2006, reg. 52(1)). Witnesses can use smart boards to mark the evidence, which is electronically captured and stored. Other technical advancements in the courtroom include: simultaneous interpretation in English, French and any language chosen by a witness and the accused; live digital audio and video archiving and playback; delayed and distorted video and audio broadcast; and multipoint video conferencing for judges, counsel submissions and witness testimony.

Additionally, participants can follow real-time transcriptions in both English and French via Transcend. Transcripts are an important tool for trial knowledge management because they are a primary record of the evidence presented at trial, especially from witness testimony. Transcend allows participants to annotate transcripts electronically while in court, without other participants seeing those annotations. Teams can flag evidence for, for example, items to review or follow up on, inconsistencies between witnesses' statements and their testimony in court or key pieces of evidence that will be relied on in closing briefs.[21] Transcend also saves historic transcripts, allowing participants to review them immediately after hearings are over. This can, for example, help a lawyer determine what further evidence to elicit from a witness in the course of the witness' testimony.

Additionally, technology is used to provide security for witnesses who present evidence in court.[22] ICC hearings and trials are, for the most part, open to the public and broadcast live on the Internet (see Section IV.B.1), but, due to the nature of the crimes within the Court's jurisdiction and the station of accused persons, some witnesses may be placed in danger by giving evidence publicly, or by having their identities revealed to the public. Technological measures that can be taken in court to protect victims and witnesses (Regulations of the Registry 2006, reg. 94) include:

- Videoconferences, where the person takes part in the proceeding via a direct video link;[23]
- Facial distortion, where the image of the person is rendered unrecognizable by an electronic mosaic in the audio-visual feed; and
- Voice distortion, where the voice of the person is rendered unrecognizable by electronic means in the audio-visual feed.

External network building: Technology for ICC public information sharing

Beyond cultivating its internal networks through efficient knowledge management and sharing, the establishment of "appropriate network links outside of" itself is "critical to [the] effectiveness and relevance" of the Court (Metzl 2001, 82). According to Metzl, liberal external information sharing is preferred (82). Absent the need to withhold information to protect the safety of witnesses and ongoing investigations, this is certainly true for the Court. The Court must share as much information as it can about its work, so that it can be seen to be fair, transparent, and without prejudice, and so that it can avoid misunderstandings about its work that could weaken public support. This **openness** ultimately enhances the ICC's legitimacy and encourages cooperation from the Court's external network.[24]

In 2005, the Court adopted an "Integrated Strategy for External Relations, Public Information and Outreach" (ICC 2005, 3). The Registry's Public Information and Documentation Section (PIDS) is response for implementing this Strategy, in close cooperation with the OTP's Public Information Unit (PIU), the OPCV and OPCD, and others (ICC 2010c, para. 13). The ICC's plan for sharing information with the public recognizes that the methods used depend on the target audience, who may be in areas far away from the seat of the Court in The Hague, and which are unstable, unsafe, lack access to electricity or the Internet, and/or have large illiterate populations (ICC 2005, 4).

Given these issues, the ICC uses a number of different methods for sharing information about its activities with the public. In communities affected by the crimes being prosecuted at the Court, the Court tends to rely on outreach tools such as town hall discussions, seminars and workshops in affected communities, radio broadcasts, pamphlet and poster campaigns, etc. (ICC 2005, 7) to try to provide information about its work to the widest possible audience.

At the same time, the ICC also relies on Internet-based technologies for sharing public information (ICC 2010c, para. 8(b)). In this respect, the ICC engages in digital diplomacy as **public diplomacy,** as is discussed in the first chapter of this book. Chinese scholar Xiaoying Jiang has recognized that those engaging in digital diplomacy "include not only state governments but also international organizations, transnational corporations, nongovernmental organizations and individuals" (2013, 9). The most prominent Internet and social media tools on which the Court relies are discussed below.

ICC website

The ICC maintains a website that is accessible in English and French (www.icc-cpi.int). It provides comprehensive information about the Court, including: the structure of the Court and its three organs; the situations and cases before the Court; access to public documents in the record of each situation and case, including orders, decisions and judgments of the Court, the filings of the participants, etc. (but not evidence); information about visiting the Court; job openings at the Court, for all organs; and a visual tour of all areas of the Court that are open to the public.

Unfortunately, the author has heard many criticisms of the ICC's website, most commonly that documents related to situations and cases are difficult to find and that key information about cases is not uploaded to the website contemporaneously. In one recent example, in the case against Kenyan Deputy President William Ruto, the case resumed from its 2013/2014 winter recess on January 17, 2014. New rules concerning the accused's appearance at trial on a summons to appear are being tested in Ruto's case, and so many in the diplomatic community have been interested in the status of his voluntary appearance at trial. This information is difficult to find on the ICC's website. There was a page titled "Trial in the Ruto and Sang [Ruto's co-defendant] case: Relevant information and materials" (ICC 2014d) but as of February 2, 2014 it stated that "hearings in the case *will resume* on 16 January 2014" (emphasis added), giving no indication that the trial had in fact resumed on January 17. The page also informed that, pursuant to an oral ruling, Ruto was excused from continuous presence at trial except during a set list of hearings, but did not set out the full parameters of the order and did not provide a link to the transcript of the oral ruling, which could have clarified the issue.[25]

Moreover, though trial had proceeded since January 17, by February 2 the most recent trial transcript was from January 15 – in other words, two full weeks' worth of transcripts were not yet available on the ICC's website. Although PIDS produces an "ICC Weekly Update" each week, it did not make clear that Ruto's trial had resumed: the report covering the week of January 13–17 did not mention Ruto's case (ICC 2014a); the report covering the week of January 20–24 did not mention whether Ruto's trial had resumed (ICC 2014b); and, as of February 2, no report was yet available for the week of January 27–31. As of February 2, 2014 it was easier to obtain up-to-date information about the proceedings in Ruto's case from blogs that follow the trials.

On the other hand, the author has also heard positive comments about the ICC's website from non-experts. For example, the author was told by a student who was new to international criminal law that the ICC's website is easy to understand for a non-lawyer, suggesting that it avoids complex legal jargon.

Besides providing public information on the Court's proceedings, the ICC uses its website to bring the public closer to the Court by streaming hearings and trials live on the ICC's website, also in both English and French. Live audio streams are used for all public court proceedings, including witness testimony, oral arguments and other statements by the parties, and the rendering of judgments and verdicts by the Chambers of the Court. The proceedings are typically streamed with a thirty-minute delay, which allows for redaction of the audio or visual display to ensure that confidential information, such as protected witnesses' identities, is not made public (Regulations of the Court 2004, regs. 21(1), 21(7)). Some ICC staff have questioned whether thirty minutes is enough time to identify an inadvertent disclosure during a hearing, inform Registry staff, and have the video redacted before the information is broadcast.

YouTube account

In addition to its website, the ICC maintains a YouTube account (www.youtube.com/user/IntlCriminalCourt). The ICC uses this to post a number of different kinds of videos. For example, the ICC posts clips of hearings and trials, often with explanatory summaries narrated by the Court's judges. It also includes videos where staff members of the Court explain complex decisions so that laypersons can better understand the proceedings (e.g. ICC 2013a). In particular, the ICC produces an "Ask the Court" radio and television program that is available on YouTube, where the ICC's spokesperson answers questions related to recent events at the Court, and address issues of concern to the public such as whether the ICC's Prosecutor has taken certain actions "because of political pressure" (e.g. ICC 2013b). It also contains a video that generally explains the ICC, including its origins, the crimes it can prosecute, the scope of its jurisdiction, and the structure of the Court (ICC 2011). There are also videos that explain the work of the different participants. For example, the ICC has posted statements recorded by the Prosecutor (e.g. ICC 2013c), as well as a video titled "A Day with Defence Counsels," which shadows defence counsel representing accused persons before the Court (ICC 2014a). English and French versions are provided for many of the videos.

The YouTube account can be a good source for up-to-date information about the Court's proceedings when the website is not current. Taking the example of Ruto's case from above, though it was difficult to find information on the website indicating that Ruto's trial had resumed in 2014, the ICC posted a video to its YouTube account (set to rather melodramatic music) on January 31, 2014, recapping the trial proceedings from January 17–28, 2014 ICC 2014b). However, videos are not as efficient for finding information as documents, because, while documents can be searched and skimmed for relevant information, videos must be carefully watched to see if they contain the information one seeks – especially where the ICC does not provide a written synopsis of the information in videos.

Twitter accounts

The ICC and some of its staff maintain Twitter accounts. The ICC's Twitter account tweets in both English and French (https://twitter.com/IntlCrimCourt). The ICC uses Twitter to, *inter alia*: provide updates on proceedings in the Court's situations and cases, with links to relevant documents or videos of public proceedings; disseminate links for e.g. new significant reports from the Court, new informational videos on its YouTube account, and public statements by senior Court officials; and to inform of key upcoming hearing and trial dates. As of April 2014, the account has over 91,500 followers, which include various countries' foreign affairs ministries and diplomatic missions, UN officials and agencies, civil society, academics, journalists and interests members of the public. The ICC's recruitment section also maintains a Twitter account (https://twitter.com/icc_jobs).

Additionally, some top ICC officials maintain Twitter accounts, such as the president of the Assembly of States Parties from 2011–2014, Ambassador Tiina Intelmann (https://twitter.com/TIntelmann). Intelmann's account, for example, provided a live Twitter feed of the public sessions and some side events at the 2013 session of the Assembly of States Parties; this especially helped some smaller government and NGO delegations to keep abreast of public sessions when they could not be present due to negotiations and other commitments. The account has produced similar live tweets from UN events relevant to the work of the Court and international criminal law more broadly.

Blogs

In partnership with the UCLA School of Law's Sanela Diana Jenkins Human Rights Project, the OTP also organizes regular online blogging sessions through the ICC Forum (http://iccforum.com). The Forum is intended to allow members of the legal community, governments, academics, and others to debate complex issues of international criminal law faced by the Office of the Prosecutor in the course of its work at the ICC. The Forum addresses one substantive legal issue at a time, in the form of a question, together with relevant documents such as ICC filings and decisions. Legal experts are invited to give their opinions, after which the issue is open for public discussion.

Legal tools

The ICC also seeks to help country-level practitioners develop domestic capacity to prosecute the crimes within the ICC's statute. In this vein, the ICC provides a service called the Legal Tools. The Legal Tools strives to be the leading information services on international criminal law, providing legal information, digests and an application to work more effectively with core international crimes cases. The information is freely available to anyone with Internet access. The goal of the Legal Tools is to "democratize access to international criminal law information" and thereby "empower practitioners and level preconditions for criminal justice in both richer and materially less resourceful countries" (ICC 2014f).

The Legal Tools consists of three legal research platforms (ICC 2010b, 2014f). First, there is a Legal Tools Database, a searchable database that claims to be the most comprehensive and complete database within the field of international criminal law. It contains more than 70,000 documents, including ICC documents, such as foundational texts and situation-related and case-related documents; preparatory works from the creation of the ICC; selected documents from other international courts; selected documents from national criminal jurisdictions, including national instruments implementing the Rome Statute and relevant decisions from domestic courts concerning atrocity crimes; and selected international treaties, decisions of regional and international human rights bodies, websites and academic works relevant to public international law, international human rights law, international humanitarian law and international criminal law (ICC 2010b).

The Legal Tools also contains two digests: the "Elements Digest," a "commentary on each element of the crimes and legal requirement of the modes of liability in the ICC Statute;" and a "Means of Proof Digest," a "detailed digest of international criminal jurisprudence showing the type or category of facts which could potentially constitute evidence for the existence of specific legal requirements of an international crime or mode of liability."[26]

Finally, the Legal Tools provides a "Case Matrix":

> A law-driven case management application that provides an explanation of the elements of crimes and legal requirements of modes of liability for all crimes in the ICC Statute, serves as a user's guide to how one could prove international crimes and modes of liability, and provides a database service to organise and present the potential evidence in a case.
>
> (ICC 2010a)

While the rest of the Legal Tools are publicly available, the Case Matrix is only made available to those who specifically request it and make an agreement on its use with the ICC.

The Legal Tools were first developed by the OTP, but its maintenance and development is now coordinated by a Legal Tools Advisory Committee with representatives from all Court organs as well as participants in ICC proceedings. They are maintained by outside partners at no cost to the Court, supported by voluntary contributions from several ICC states parties (ICC 2010b).

Conclusion

It has been said that power today is "as much about promoting ideas and norms of behaviour as it is about projecting military might," and that, under these circumstances, "the real struggle consists of projecting values, promoting interests, and ultimately setting the global agenda" (Metzl 2001, 79). If this is true, the ICC may yet fulfil its mandate to ensure that the most serious crimes of concern to the international community do not go unpunished. The ICC represents ideals of international justice, and it can only succeed where states put humane values above protectionism and national self-interest. To increase its chances of success, the ICC must rely on its external networks to enhance its legitimacy and increase cooperation, and on internal networks to make sure it can handle the constant and rapid change inherent in the investigation and prosecution of mass atrocities.

To build and strengthen internal and external networks, the ICC has invested extensively in various technologies to facilitate its work and to share information about that work publicly. Internally, the ICC relies on a number of technologies to review, share, and use the ever-growing and evolving quantum of evidence and key jurisprudence governing proceedings among participants, judges, and relevant ICC staff. Externally, the ICC uses a variety of Internet-based social media to communicate externally about its work, under the belief that sharing timely and accurate information will enhance support and cooperation from states, international and inter-governmental organizations, NGOs, and the public, and will ultimately increase their perceptions about the ICC's legitimacy.

Despite their importance, complaints about these technologies persist, and their use (or misuse) is often part of the problem. The system needs more focused attention from senior management to ensure that the technology is used well and produces the desired results. As digital diplomacy becomes an increasingly dominant tool in international relations, the Court must continue to position itself to leverage it effectively in the international criminal law domain.

Notes

1 Lubanga was found guilty on March 14, 2012 of the war crime of enlisting and conscripting of children under the age of fifteen years and using them to participate actively in hostilities. Katanga was found guilty on March 7, 2014 of one count of crime against humanity (murder) and four counts of war crimes (murder, attacking a civilian population, destruction of property and pillaging). Ngudjolo was acquitted of all charges on 18 December 2012.

2 This is in contrast with "club" diplomacy, which has been defined as an exclusionary system based on a common membership sense shared within elites and professional diplomats, where diplomacy is the role of duly appointed foreign officers, and where external relations are conducted by ranking ambassadors with the support of a plethora of hierarchically organized attendants (Heine 2006, 4–5).
3 For example, the Coalition for the International Criminal Court and Parliamentarians for Global Action lobby and work with governments to help new states become parties to the Rome Statute, while the Open Society Justice Initiative monitors proceedings in some of the cases before the Court and provides easy to understand synopses of important events, testimony, judgments, etc.
4 For example, Justice Rapid Response, an intergovernmental facility that manages the rapid deployment of criminal justice professionals from a stand-by roster, has mobilized experts to assist the ICC.
5 China abstained during the vote on the resolution referring the situation, when it could have blocked the referral with a veto.
6 Hewlett Packard recently changed the name of this software to HP Records Manager, but the ICC adopted this software when it was called TRIM and this is the name ICC staff use for it, so that it how it is referred to here. More information about TRIM is available here: http://h18000.www1.hp.com/products/quickspecs/13507_div/13507_div.pdf.
7 More information on Transcend is available here: http://legalcraft.com/.
8 Each participant gives the Registry a list of persons who have or have had access to the most sensitive materials. All materials submitted to the e-court system must be clearly marked with the level of confidentiality required (Regulations of the Registry 2006, reg. 14).
9 Until recently, the standard procedure was for the Chambers and participants to send all filings, orders, decisions, and the like to one central email address in the Registry – judoc@icc-cpi.int (Regulations of the Registry 2006, reg. 24(5)). The Registry is replacing this with a system where the person filing the material can upload it on the ICC's intranet.
10 Ringtail supports Boolean, proximity, fuzzy, wildcard, synonym and phonic searches, and searches involving multiple criteria, helping to narrow down key pools of evidence.
11 The OTP is currently rolling out an updated version of Ringtail that includes an analytics function, providing linguistic analysis to find dominant concepts in documents, and clusters documents based on common concepts. This is a purely animated process, which will hopefully reinforce the accuracy and thoroughness of disclosures, and can be especially helpful to cull high volumes of documents.
12 Every redaction must be individually justified, based on whether its disclosure may "prejudice further or ongoing investigations" (Rules of Procedure and Evidence 2002, rule 81(2)) or whether the redactions are necessary to "protect the safety of witnesses and victims and members of their families" (rule 81(4)). This becomes increasingly cumbersome when a participant discloses video and audio recordings that need to be redacted. It can also be extremely difficult where an accused – who is legally entitled to have the evidence translated into a language which he understands – speaks a language that is oral only and not written (Rules of Procedure and Evidence 2002, rule 76(3); see e.g. *Prosecutor v. Banda and Jerbo*, "Prosecution's Proposals" 2011; *Prosecutor v. Banda and Jerbo*, "Order on translation" 2011 (where the accused speaks only Zaghawa, an oral language)).
13 The disclosing participants must be sure to redact both the face of the documents and the metadata associated with them, because both are disclosed and may include sensitive information.
14 This article focuses on OTP evidence assessment because of the author's experiences working in the OTP. Defence teams and victims' representatives may use the same or different methods to assess evidence.
15 More information is available here: www.lexisnexis.com/casemap/casemap.aspx.

16 More information is available here: www.lexisnexis.com/casemap/casemap.aspx?content=features.
17 Because of the volume, complexity, and limited utility of the IDACs, the OTP argues against their use, and has proposed producing a Document Containing the Charges (DCC) whose footnotes are hyperlinked to the evidence cited. This would allow the OTP to produce an elements-based chart containing hyperlinks to the cited evidence (*Prosecutor v. Jean-Pierre Bemba Gombo et al.*, "Prosecution Response" 2014, paras. 17, 20). At least one Chamber of the Court has approved the use of hyperlinked DCCs (*Prosecutor v. Jean-Pierre Bemba Gombo et al.*, "Decision on the 'Defence request'" 2014).
18 The Registry has created a "Unified Technical protocol for the provision of evidence, witness and victims information in electronic form" (ICC 2014e). This Protocol is used as a general guideline for the Court, but the Registry provides the judges and participants working on a specific situation or case with a unique e-court protocol that defines the standards for those particular proceedings (Regulations of the Registry 2006, reg. 10(4); e.g. *Prosecutor v. Muthaura and Kenyatta*, "Order on the E-Court Protocol" 2012; *Prosecutor v. Muthaura and Kenyatta*, "Registry submissions" 2012). Material collected in physical form (documents or tangible objects) must be converted into a "Standard Image Format" by scanning or other digitization. This includes providing an OCR text file for materials containing text including for any translation thereof, which is useful because it allows the participants to electronically search text documents uploaded to the Court's e-court system. Participants must submit the evidence with specific metadata attached to each item, and with a unique document identification number ("Doc ID") created by the participant that will be used before the item is entered into evidence in the case (ICC, 2014e, paras. 4, 15.1, 17–20, 21(1), 27–29).
19 Parties and participants can provide the Registry with evidence on one or more CD ROMS or DVDs, or by using the Court's internal electronic infrastructure (ICC, 2014e, para. 13).
20 The Registry assigns new ID numbers to evidence tendered at trial (Regulations of the Registry 2006, reg. 28(2).
21 In some cases, team members who are not present in the courtroom may also have access Transcend in their offices, and can participate in real-time review and annotation remotely.
22 Under the Rome Statute, the Court is obliged to "take appropriate measures to protect the safety, physical and psychological well-being, dignity and privacy of victims and witnesses" (Rome Statute 1998, art. 68(1)-(2); Rules of Procedure and Evidence 2002, rule 87(1)).
23 The Registry arranges for witness testimony via video link. The witness must be able to see and hear the judges, the accused and the person questioning him or her, as well as the relevant evidence as submitted in the courtroom. Likewise, the judges, the accused and the person questioning him or her shall be able to see and hear the witness as well as evidence submitted from the remote location (Rules of Procedure and Evidence 2002, rule 67(1); Regulations of the Registry 2006, regs. 45(1), 46(4); *Prosecutor v. Bemba*, Transcript 2013).
24 The ICC's ability to share information publicly is constrained by its responsibilities as a judicial institution, including "confidentiality, preserving integrity of investigations, protection of victim and witness security and well-being, [and] the rights of the accused." (ICC 2005, 3).
25 The transcript of the oral ruling is available on the ICC's website (*Prosecutor v. Ruto and Sang*, "Transcript" 2014).
26 There is also a "Proceedings Digest" that "provides an analysis of key legal issues that are relevant for proceedings before the ICC," but it is only available in the Office of the Prosecutor.

9

WHEN DOING BECOMES THE MESSAGE

The case of the Swedish digital diplomacy[1]

Jon Pelling

Introduction

Just like communication is driving change in organizations, and in their relation to the civil society, **public diplomacy,** which aims at increasing a nation's leverage and impact abroad, is experiencing transformation. A range of subcategories has emerged in the field of public diplomacy, creating new language and symbols to allow for adaptation and effective outreach. These include the concept of **digital diplomacy**. Apart from the technological approach to adaptation, which embeds the use of digital technology in the work of foreign policy, the concept also deals with the shift in power and influence from hierarchical structures to citizens and grassroots. This shift may at times provoke institutional tension and unease, but also awakens the curiosity and energy required to stay on top of change and to find new strategies for adaptation in a global context. This raises the important question of how diplomats can embrace change in a way that minimizes institutional resistance and helps foster new methods for communication and relationship building in a global context. The chapter suggests that the behaviour of diplomatic institutions and the way in which things are done, is increasingly becoming part of the message it wants to convey as this allows for new forms of engagement and communication, thus creating trust, influence and legitimacy.

Digital diplomacy as a concept plays a crucial role in sending internal signals about the importance of embracing change with genuine interest. I am here borrowing from Dale Carnegie's classic set of principles for influence. His recommendations include showing genuine interest in other people, sincerely making people feel important and being a good listener (Carnegie 1936). These recommendations are still relevant, as the way in which an organization acts is increasingly linked to the message it wants to convey and how it comes across. Its behaviour determines the effectiveness of its communication. As pointed out in the introductory chapter of this volume, in many ways "digital diplomacy" works as a bridge between old structures and new, making it possible for different stakeholders to connect in pragmatic ways around creating new solutions for change. As smaller actions of individuals in the organization become part of the content on which the communication is based, the communicator's role is increasingly that of an in-house consultant's, fostering new mind-sets to allow for co-creation and **openness**. To some extent this allows the organization to change structures from the inside through capacity building and empowerment, and thus contributing to further institutional change.

This chapter aims to reflect on the implications for institutional adaptation in the wake of digital transformation. It describes recent digital diplomacy initiatives at the Swedish Ministry of Foreign Affairs (MFA) that are indirectly designed to explore the shifts in hierarchies and global culture. By serving as platforms for meetings and ideas where content is created in collaboration, Diplohack and the Stockholm Initiative for Digital Diplomacy represent new instruments used by the Swedish Ministry to approach foreign audiences and stakeholders in novel ways. At the same time, these projects prepare the organization for new forms of engagement and communication, where learning and sharing are important tools for influence and relationship building.

The chapter is structured as follows. It starts with describing what drives the interest in digital diplomacy at the Swedish MFA. After a brief outline of the historical meanings of connectivity and openness in Sweden, it describes how Swedish public diplomacy plays out in a digital landscape. The chapter then discusses the challenges facing hierarchical structures when they attempt new forms for collaboration and engagement and explains why *doing* is increasingly becoming the message. Thereafter, the chapter focuses on the importance of new vocabulary and discourse to allow for institutional adaptation. The chapter ends with descriptions of the Stockholm Initiative for Digital Diplomacy (SIDD) and Diplohack, a collaboration between the Dutch and Swedish embassies in London, and concludes that clarity of values and ideas is key for anyone who wants to achieve goodwill and influence in collaboration with others.

The drivers behind Swedish MFA's interest in digital diplomacy

A wide range of new stakeholders has emerged in the field of foreign policy. Accordingly, in order to learn and to reach out, diplomacy needs to adapt, allowing for a more casual and activist approach in which nonhierarchical collaboration and innovation become more important (Copeland 2009). Those who fail to get to grips with the networked environment run the risk of falling behind, losing trust, and subsequently influence and legitimacy. This process of managed change overlaps with traditional diplomacy, but does not replace it. Tradition is still important, but new methods of influence and interaction are quickly overtaking. The risks of sticking with the status quo are likely to be greater than those of learning through trial and error. As Davidson notes, "the ability to construct networks through cultural relations will be a key component of the conduct and future development of public diplomacy" (Davidson 2008, 77).

Sweden may be a sparsely populated country in the North, but it is historically well connected internationally through technology, trade, migration and aid. An important feature of its government is a deeply rooted tradition of transparency.[2] The first Swedish Freedom of Press act was enacted in 1766. Public access to governmental documents has since been a key feature of the Swedish democratic model, making politicians and civil servants accountable for their actions. At the same time, public investments in connectivity, such as subsidies for personal computers and fibre broadband, have created a nation of early adopters with a high demand for online services. Sweden has twice topped the global Web Index ranking (Web Index 2012) launched in 2012 to measure the World Wide Web's contribution to development and human rights globally.[3] Similarly, Sweden is often noted for its innovative and creative business climate. This context has led to high domestic expectations that the diplomatic services should keep up to speed with the rest of society. The Swedish effort to break new ground in the field of digital diplomacy should be seen in this light.

In recent years, Sweden's MFA has increased its efforts in the field of digital diplomacy, as part of a wider push for public diplomacy. Civil servants have been encouraged to make use of social media and to find new ways of interacting with the public through co-creation and collaboration. Apart from improving the organization's speed in gathering, analyzing and sharing information, this initiative has allowed the ministry to engage with nontraditional stakeholders, and to better reach out with Swedish positions and perspectives. Sweden can now amplify conversation in the social media space in ways which were impossible only a couple of years ago. Through learning, the Swedish MFA has become more responsive and more adaptive to change, making it better prepared for diplomatic engagement and relationship building in the twenty-first century.

The Stockholm Initiative for Digital Diplomacy (Regeringskansliet 2014) was launched, for instance, as a co-creative forum for knowledge exchange in January 2014. In the autumn of 2013, a joint project between the Dutch and the Swedish embassies in London led to the development of Diplohack (Diplohack 2014) a toolkit for change and outreach based on collaboration, innovation and co-creation, which produced valuable insights in the field of method development, innovation and engagement. Other recent Swedish initiatives for public diplomacy with a digital angle include Curators of Sweden (Swedish Institute 2011), where the official Swedish Twitter handle @Sweden is run by the citizens on behalf of the Swedish Institute. Also, in 2014, the Swedish Embassy in Lusaka hosted Sweden@ Zambia (Swedish Institute 2014), a solution-orientated co-creative event that drew together experts and entrepreneurs from different fields to encourage new forms of collaboration between the two countries, and at the same time inspiring gender equality and emancipation. These projects can all be described as tools for institutional adaptation as well as for communication in the field of public and digital diplomacy, where values and identity such as openness and equality are of increasing importance.

The process of modernization at the MFA accelerated considerably after the devastating Asian tsunami of 2004, which killed over 230,000 people, approximately 550 Swedish citizens among them. The perceived insensitivity and lack of active response from the Swedish MFA angered the public and undermined trust at a national level. The catastrophe and subsequent negative media coverage caught the civil service unprepared and kick-started a transformative process focussing on crisis management and communication, as well as better explaining the work of the Foreign Ministry to the public. Among the main lessons drawn from the catastrophe were that the government cannot afford not to adapt to ongoing changes, and that internal priorities need to reflect public expectations. Thus, attitudes changed. Consular work, which to some extent had been internally overlooked, now in many ways became the priority. The realization hit home that trust and legitimacy are linked to capacity of communication and action; that is, *doing*.

These processes of institutional adaptation and increased availability in turn affect the way in which Sweden projects itself, not least through its work with digital diplomacy. Sweden wants to be perceived as a country open for collaboration around future challenges. In their work on media as a mechanism of institutional change and reinforcement, Coyne and Leeson (2009) outline interesting perspectives on how the mass media can hinder, catalyze or reinforce institutional change by introducing individuals to new ideas, meanings and alternatives. Their analysis identifies a paradoxical relationship whereby the media simultaneously reinforces and induces change in existing institutions. To some extent, the same perspective can be applied to any organization adapting to social media. The learning process drives change, and thereafter reinforces the new normal. As an illustration of this point, the Swedish embassy in London's readiness to respond to the public via new platforms has resulted in more interaction and invitations to take part in events outside of the embassy. This change in organizational behaviour represents the values of openness and accessibility that the embassy wishes to represent, putting pressure on individual members to become even better public communicators, and on the organization to give up some control over information flows in order to increase its agility. This is likely to have improved the embassy's capacity to cut through the noise and make its message heard.

In this cultural shift, curiosity, tonality and perceptiveness are crucial assets to maintaining influence through engaging with a new set of stakeholders. Just as successful media corporations and other organizations have relinquished their privileges as agenda setting one-way broadcasters, the Swedish Foreign Ministry is looking for new ways of liaising with the public. To quote the blog of the Swedish ambassador to the United Kingdom: "Foreign ministries have to be fast learners to stay relevant in this busy and competitive marketplace. We can only understand the culture of two-way Internet if we are part of it" (Clase 2012, n.p.).

Swedish public diplomacy goes digital

The Department of Communication at the Swedish Ministry of Foreign Affairs is in charge of developing the tools needed for its staff to become successful digital and public diplomats. The diplomatic objectives are to enable the Swedish MFA to effectively project Swedish values and political interests abroad, as well as maintaining relationships with the public and other governments. A recent governmental inquiry (Egart 2011), tasked with answering the question of what type of foreign service Sweden needs for the future, concluded that the Swedish MFA needs to seek cooperative solutions with like-minded countries. "This can concern just about everything from building alliances to jointly pursue an issue, to creating effective local solutions and operational synergies with other missions" (Egardt 2011, 53). In short, Sweden needs to be an attractive partner, engaging in the right conversations.

This objective is pursued via a multitrack strategy of institutional adaptation focused on transforming the organizational culture, fostering better institutional coordination and integrating digital tools in the day-to-day diplomatic activity.

The guidelines for communication furthermore acknowledge, for instance, the importance of well-functioning internal communications, as well as the need to adapt to a world where the internet has rendered one-way communication from traditionally closed institutions obsolete (Swedish Institute, 2011). Individual responsibility for communication is increasing as the civil service is expected to engage and exchange feedback with the public. Learning requires practice, and co-workers are encouraged to actively use new tools for communication. In January 2013, foreign minister Carl Bildt used the Statement of Foreign Policy to instruct all Swedish embassies to open Facebook and Twitter accounts before the end of the month. "We must be at the absolute cutting edge in digital diplomacy efforts," he declared (Bildt 2013, 12).

The symbolic value of these instructions cannot be underestimated. They obliged the whole organization, over a very short period of time, to become an active learner and to create a new ecosystem for digital communication, thus changing the behaviour of the ministry. A part from clarifying any doubts over the need to take the new media culture seriously and pushing staff out of their comfort zone, the whole shift energized the organization. Discussions on content creation and the use of different tools became commonplace at many embassies and got priority in the day-to-day activities at the ministry. Thanks to the initiative, a sense of urgency to learn and understand social media and the surrounding culture emerged, and with it important discussions on tonality and on how to use the new tools. The change in culture also seem to have given more leeway for further innovation and experimentation, a crucial asset for an organization which aims at being at the forefront in an culture which is still quickly developing.

From an institutional perspective, it should be noted that the National Board for the Promotion of Sweden was created by the government in 1995, to strategically coordinate the promotion of Sweden abroad. Apart from the Swedish MFA, the Swedish Institute and the tourist agency Visit Sweden, members of the Board include Business Sweden as well as the Ministries of Enterprise, Energy and Communications, and Culture. A central tool for coordination is the joint platform for communication and a strategy to promote Sweden abroad. The vision for this work is to build on Sweden's history as a free and open society and to act as a workshop, or greenhouse, for innovation and co-creation. Four profile areas have been agreed: innovation, society, creativity and sustainability (Presenting Sweden 2014). There is a generally high interest in Sweden's welfare solutions, including its salient policies on gender equality, parental leave and child-care systems, as well as for its handling of the global economic crisis. Similarly Sweden is often referred to for its active involvement in climate and environment issues.

The booming creative, tech and fashion sectors, with companies like Spotify and artists like Avicci and Max Martin, are also part of the narrative around Sweden, as is innovation from a broader point of view in fields ranging from telecommunications to life science. The aim of the joint platform is therefore to encourage new thinking and collaboration in key areas where Sweden's particular strengths are internationally recognized and can contribute to an accurate representation of a modern and progressive society. With the ongoing change in global culture, where social media transforms collaboration and representation and let messages take on new meanings while they make their way to a fragmented set of audiences, this work will in itself need to continuously evolve in order to be efficient.

Earlier example of prosperous campaigns with a digital angle include the launch of the "Second House of Sweden" in the virtual world of Second Life, based on the House of Sweden in Washington DC. The **virtual embassy** in Second Life, created by the Swedish Institute and inaugurated by the Foreign Minister in the form of an avatar, received much attention but also pushed the creative boundaries for **nation branding** in a digital space. Bengtsson (2011) have evaluated this campaign from a virtual branding perspective and found that apart from receiving substantial international coverage, the project clearly connects Sweden's brand to the future, rather than emphasising a glorious past. This is all in line with an overall ambition to be part of a wider change, rather than resisting it.

Another bold campaign, Curators of Sweden, was launched in 2011 as a collaboration between the Swedish Institute and Visit Sweden. Here, the official Swedish Twitter account @Sweden was handed over to the citizens in order to establish an image of Sweden, different to the stereotypes usually seen in traditional media:

> Sweden's development and future prosperity depend on strong relations with the outside world and a more active exchange with other countries in many areas. This is only possible, if more people are familiar with Sweden and become interested in the country and what it has to offer.
> (Swedish Institute 2011)

The success of the project can be linked to the ability to give up control over the message and let the public regulate the image and learning process through conversation and debate.

However, in terms of communicating political values, distinct from the broader themes for which the Swedish Institute has responsibility, the Swedish MFA, in collaboration with relevant parties, has begun to take a more active approach. The topic was prioritized under foreign minister Carl Bildt, himself an early adopter who took part in the first email exchange between heads of government when he, in his then role of prime minister, in 1994, emailed President Bill Clinton. Apart from the Swedish MFA's focus on trade and international development cooperation, this work generally conforms to the government's political priorities, including, for instance, a strong interest in policy related to freedom and security on the Internet. An integral part of the public diplomacy strategy designed to enhance this work was the launch of the Stockholm Internet Forum (Stockholm Internet Forum 2013), bringing together policymakers, civil society representatives, activists, business representatives and the technical community.

The work on several diplomatic levels at the same time is likely to have contributed to the resolution on freedom of expression online adopted by the UN Human Rights Council on June 29, 2012, when the Council unanimously affirmed that "the same rights that people have offline must also be protected online, in particular freedom of expression" and recognized the global and open nature of the Internet as a driving force in accelerating progress towards development in its various form (United Nations General Assembly, Human Rights Council 2012). Other examples of political priorities promoted by the foreign ministry in the digital environment include support for the implementation of the Millennium Development Goals, not least in the field of maternal health and rights to sexual rights and reproductive health. Here, communication has for example been driven around the Conference on the implementation of the ICPD Programme of Action (IPCI 2014).

In regards to digital diplomacy, Carl Bildt has argued that talkers and thinkers need to co-ordinate in order to have an impact, especially in the field of public diplomacy. "When we talk about digital issues and diplomacy . . . it is essentially about communications, about human minds getting together sharing information and then, as we all do when we get better informed, changes the way in which we think, in which we act and the things that we do" (Bildt 2014, n.p.).

Digital hierarchy, collaboration and innovation

In a series of articles on various aspects of engagement and public diplomacy, commissioned by the British Foreign and Commonwealth Office, Brian Hocking examines challenges relating to the increased preoccupation with public diplomacy after the terrorist attacks in September 2011, as they drew attention to the centrality of values and identity (Hocking 2008). The text indicates the crucial differences in appropriate methods, depending on whether the aim is to persuade or to convince. This may seem to be a subtle difference, but in winning the hearts and minds of opponents, the method of action is likely to affect the result. Whereas persuasion requires tenacity and force, convincing requires arguments and intellectual honesty. A point can be conveyed successfully by actually making a difference, in collaboration with others. Doing something in new ways can in itself become the message, initiating change and enabling further relationship-building.

The practitioners of traditional state-to-state diplomacy are experts in the field of power liaison, accustomed to a competitive process of "negotiation between political entities which acknowledge each other's independence" (Watson 1984, 33). These skills are key to any state's capacity to conduct official relations with "intelligence and tact" (Satow and Bland 1957). However, relating to the public in a networked space with a strong culture of sharing, open source and collaboration, these methods may be counterproductive. Indeed, the systematic formalities of official administration can easily quell progressive and innovative impulses. Although the complexities of the diplomatic process prepare civil servants to analyse information and act in abstract systems, unorthodox approaches to problem solving outside the formal environment are sometimes met with hesitation: "As a diplomat you might make mistakes, but you cannot afford to make the wrong mistakes" (Clase 2014, n.p.).

Hocking identifies two interlinked but distinct, perspectives on engagement within the discourse of public diplomacy. The first reflects a traditional concept of diplomacy as a fundamentally "hierarchical and intergovernmental process . . . predominantly in terms of top-down information flows, using techniques founded on theories of strategic political communication" (Hocking 2008, 64). The second perspective sees public diplomacy in a context where international policy is increasingly conducted through complex policy networks. In the latter, the public are partners in and producers of diplomatic processes. The first perspective is based on "state centred models in which people are seen as targets and instruments for foreign policy" (Hocking 2008, 65). The second network model, on the other hand, focuses on "managing increasingly complex policy environments through the promotion of communication, dialogue and trust" (Hocking 2008, 64). While either approach may be appropriate for a given purpose, it is in the latter where Sweden through its work with new platforms is trying to adapt.

According to Hocking, the difference between the two perspectives highlights the fact that globalization has not, as predicted by some, rendered national governments irrelevant. Instead, it has "highlighted their deficiencies in terms of knowledge, flexibility and speed in responding to global problems, and often the limits of their legitimacy in the eyes for whom they claim to act. The more diverse membership and non-hierarchical quality of public policy promote collaboration and learning, and speed up the acquisition and processing of knowledge" (Hocking 2008, 64).

At the same time, in a hyperconnected and increasingly multipolar world, the need to find new ways of joint problem solving is increasing. As most challenges facing us are transnational, Davidson argues that, in cultural and other long-term contexts, mutually beneficial relationships . . . can contribute to the development of solutions by building the networks through which diverse communities can develop new approaches. . . . It achieves this by connecting people, emphasising a willingness to listen, and focusing on mutual benefit.

(Davidson 2008, 77)

Finding new ways to flexibly engage with stakeholders is rapidly becoming a key skill for building trust, driving change and impacting the political agenda. Organizations that truly target this kind of capacity building will have to think carefully about the nature of training and recruitment.

Joseph S Nye's concept of soft power (Nye 2004), defined as the ability to get what you want through attraction rather than through coercion or payment, indicates another key challenge for diplomacy in a digitally networked society. Influence, Nye argues, is built through the attractiveness of culture, political ideals and policies. If a nation's leverage depends on the perception of its policies as legitimate in the eyes of others, a country's relative soft power will depend on how its national ideas and values are represented in practice by its officials. The successful projection of these values will increasingly depend on the ability to communicate ideas in a more inclusive way, online as well as offline. A static, top-down approach is likely to alienate audiences, and official communication from ministries can often reinforce a top down perspective rather than opening up for engagement in more subtle ways. A negotiated balance between coordination and autonomy is the best way to achieve an impact in a genuine way as it empower the sender. At the same time it is important to realize that the borders between digital and analogue are merging. Content needs to be formulated in an attractive and engaging way from the start, no matter which is the outlet. A basic rule of thumb should be to focus on narrative, to be aware of why a particular story would be worth spreading.

This, in turn, introduces another interesting debate, related to the focus on metrics. In some cases, overemphasis on measurable results and the value of reach per se has tended to cool the expression of different ideas before discussions around genuine content creation can be initiated. Projects are sometimes designed in order to satisfy the need for quantifiable results, rather than to attract the right audiences. A more "oblique" approach might be more effective in achieving foreign policy goals in a fragmented and unpredictable environment. In his book *Obliquity*, John Kay (2010) argues that our goals are best achieved when we approach them indirectly. This requires other forms of evaluation, since the success of traditional diplomacy is judged on different grounds. The tone of the content and the ability to engage convincingly in broader discussions will ultimately count as much as reach.

Just like other large institutions and businesses, foreign ministries still have some way to go in order to encourage "intrapreneurship". **Intrapreneurship** is short for *intra*-corporate entre*preneurship,* and is considered key for organizations aiming to turn new ideas into profitable new realities. This also goes for the public sector. Without empowered entrepreneurs, organizations don't innovate (Pinchot and Pellman 1999). Intrapreneurship is defined as behaving like an entrepreneur while working within a large organization and allowing for different thinking within the existing structures. This concept has many similarities with the field of social entrepreneurship, where individuals use their entrepreneurial energy to create innovative and scalable solutions to pressing social problems.

Working with communication and institutional adaptation in the public sector requires many of the same tools, not least the tenacity and empowerment required for anyone pushing ideas for change in larger systems. Communication departments ought to focus their efforts on enhancing new forms of collaboration and problem solving, setting positive examples for new methods of interaction, and push for change and adaptation together with other actors.

When doing becomes the message

As capacity building proceeds at the Swedish MFA, a number of interesting questions arise on how to manage and create content for engagement in this new ecosystem, and how to draw on these newly won skills to build new networks and relations for diplomatic purposes. As Marshall McLuhan pointed out five decades ago, the medium itself becomes part of the message as it "shapes and controls the scale and form of human association and action" (McLuhan 1994, 2). In a fragmented information landscape where conversations and relationships take place in real time, the form in which we participate matters. Mobile technology and the Internet have extended our senses. In some ways, social media projects virtual representations of individuals and organizations, extending the meaning of avatars. People and nations are increasingly becoming "present" in the lives of others through dual representation online. This reality is very different from the world of engagement and influence pre-social media.

Although the message in itself needs to be correct, particularly in a diplomatic setting, it may struggle to cut through the noise unless it is formulated in a way that takes into account the meaning the message takes on through the medium and become attractive.[4] Similarly, it is not necessarily the government which is the best sender of a message. As seen in the project Curators of Sweden, citizens and networks can often work together with institutions if the content is relevant and attractive enough for them to take part in. For diplomatic services, where public servants are traditionally trained in exchanging and adapting information for governmental use, this aspect of communication can be hard to embrace, as it requires a fairly spontaneous approach to interaction with a heterogeneous set of stakeholders. As noted by the Swedish diplomat Jon Åström Gröndahl, diplomats, who often come from competitive environments, are high achievers, on one hand used to teamwork, on the other to negotiating and officially representing their governments. (Åström Gröndahl 2014). But in order to actually connect with networks, a far more informal and collaborative approach may be needed.

Digital diplomacy to some extent accommodate this challenge as the active use of social media results in changes to both the organization and its image, and make new ways of interaction more common. Behavioural change can at times be achieved through the creation of new platforms allowing actors to co-create and engage with each other around shared values and challenges. If designed well, these events can by themselves become relevant content for communication and relationship building in networks. From a communications perspective, the perceived magic and mystery surrounding diplomacy is also, if used in contrast to expectations, an important element when it comes to amplifying a discussion on relevant policy issues, as it often attracts interest and awakens curiosity. What is clear is that it is becoming harder for organizations that want to influence and be part of events to control and broadcast information in a traditional manner.

In order to maximize outreach and impact, the diplomatic craft needs to foster internal cultures of intrapreneurship and collaboration to be able to connect with and understand its surroundings. This challenges status quo, but is to some extent already happening. An initiative's actual impact depends on other stakeholders willingness to interact around the cause as a way to jointly achieving change. This also requires an organization with confidence and readiness to expose itself to new environments. The ability to argue and interact around values and democratic ideas will determine success and legitimacy. Importantly, this change in behaviour is not going to happen by default, or by responding to events alone. Instead, it will require coaching and approval from the top, as well as practice on the ground through doing things in new ways. Internal signals encouraging the embrace of innovation are therefore an important asset for organizations who want to increase their impact.

Discourse and vocabulary for digital diplomacy

There are already many interesting schools of thought formulating discourse for a more activist approach to diplomacy, adapted to the digital age. Many of them aim to create a parallel language which allows for an expansion of the diplomatic self-concept, a symbolic upgrade of the skill sets required by diplomats in the field. British Ambassador Tom Fletcher has launched, for instance, the concept of Naked Diplomacy. Fletcher presents an activist approach to diplomacy that merges communication, networking and nation branding:

> In the past we could meet people, do traditional media, map influence, engage civil society. But social media changes the context completely – we no longer have to focus solely on the elites to make our case, or to influence policy. This is exciting, challenging and subversive. Getting it wrong could start a war: imagine if a diplomat misguidedly tweeted a link to that offensive anti-Islam film. Getting it right has the potential to rewrite the diplomatic rulebook.
>
> (Fletcher 2012, n.p.)

Keeping up with technology and new forms of engagement is key if diplomacy aims to remain relevant as a profession. Fletcher favours interaction over transmission, and points out that diplomats needs to be confident about what they stand for when they communicate with a wider range of interlocutors. Philip Seib, of the University of Southern California's Center on Public Diplomacy, talks about "Real-Time Diplomacy" in the context of the Arab Spring and warns policy makers to avoid being mere spectators (Seib 2012). Meanwhile, Alec Ross's definition of 21st Century Statecraft' accounts for the technologies, the networks and the demographics of the twenty-first century. He asserts that a big shift is taking place in geopolitical power, not from the west to east, but in power from hierarchies to citizens and networks (Ross 2013, 2014).

Another interesting contributor to the field of new discourse is the analyst and former Canadian diplomat Daryl Copeland. Without glamorising globalization, he outlines a method for "Guerrilla Diplomacy" to keep up with change in a world where a different "set of challenges and threats have emerged, in tandem with multiplying media and unexplored possibilities" (Copeland 2009, 5). Here, the connectedness that globalization offers as geographic distances decrease offers new possibilities for cooperation. Diplomats, Copeland writes, need to learn how to operate in amorphous horizontal spaces, but are currently "more attuned to and adept at working in the familiar vertical mosaic of the apparatus of the state, where official designations and hierarchic social relations are the norm" (5). Although Copeland, who places his concept at one end of a scale with traditional diplomacy at the opposite and public diplomacy somewhere in the middle, doesn't explicitly target preparing foreign ministries for digital diplomacy, he highlights skill sets suitable to the new breed of diplomats he wishes to see. Some of these are also relevant for communicators in uncertain and moving contexts, such as autonomy, personal and situational sensitivity, cultural awareness, energy and an affinity for collaboration, teamwork and improvisation (Copeland 2009, 206–7).

From a Swedish perspective, there is a clear understanding of the importance of taking initiatives to kick-start processes, as this generally lead to further engagement and interaction. By inviting new networks and connectors to the table and driving discussions on topics of future concern, content is created which can feed in to both offline and online contexts and establish new relationships. Rather the being a top down sender, the ministry can act as a node or an overlapping network, taking part in a process together with others.

Sweden's platforms for ideas and collaboration – innovation for change

For the communications team in Stockholm, a key approach to enabling the organization to develop in the field of digital diplomacy is to take new initiatives for networking, collaboration and learning, and to create new symbols and associations around the potential of communication in a digital and networked society. Apart from coaching the organization in how to handle new tools and find its way in a digital landscape, the department engages with the public through its official platforms like blogs and social media campaigns. Furthermore, a lot of thought is being put into how to connect with different actors in the field of digital diplomacy, and how to become a platform for non-hierarchical engagement with other actors. The Swedish MFA is well aware that smaller stakeholders and governments will struggle to make a real footprint on their own.

In January 2014, a year after the instructions in the Foreign Policy Declaration to increase efforts in digital diplomacy, the Swedish MFA organized the first Stockholm Initiative for Digital Diplomacy (SIDD) to investigate the implications for the future of diplomacy in a growing culture of digital participation. The event brought together key movers and shakers in the field of digital diplomacy for a period of twenty-four hours. The process was designed to be as disruptive as possible in order to allow for listening and mutuality, and turned into a conceptual debate around the future of a traditionally secretive world in the very public age of social media.[5] SIDD also resulted in new informal networks and had a somewhat empowering effect on the participants, many of whom were used to challenging organizations from within in order to make them more flexible and adaptable to change. The SIDD initiative was combined with a TEDx Salon broadcast from Stockholm. Speakers included Carl Bildt; Moira Whelan, Deputy Assistant Secretary of State for Digital Strategy at the US Department of State; and Andreas Sandre, from Italy's Embassy in Washington.

For the Swedish MFA, the project has worked as an experiment and a stepping-stone from which to continue building solutions around communication in collaboration with others. It showed that there is a demand for new forums where collaboration and the future of engagement in the social media age can be discussed and new methods encouraged. The initiative was designed as a pilot project, but resulted in a wave of interest to attend in diplomatic circles concerned with the future on digital diplomacy. It resulted in the creation of new relationships and subsequent collaboration in the field of communication. Attendees appreciated the fact that the forum was organized in a manner that rather reminded of an un-conference than a traditional roundtable or conference, as this allowed for a less static interaction and encouraged exchange of ideas and experiences. External process leaders led the event which focused on ideation. Here, as we will see with the case of the Diplohacks, it is important to make sure that challenges or problems are formulated as specifically as possible and not to underestimate the need for a developed design process, with a clear focus on results, although the form of collaboration by itself leads on to the creation of new forms of collaboration.

There sometime exist a somewhat equivocal belief that social media, engagement and method development comes free, as the user subscription services are free of charge and the concepts at times are abstract, just as they can be in diplomacy in general. In order to create solutions together, research questions or problems need to have set parameters and be well prepared beforehand in order to become executable. In the environment of foreign policy and institutional adaptation this may be easier said than done, but is still worth exploring and developing. The learning from the project has proved valuable for the organizers who continue to build on the platform and to develop working methods. Natural next steps would be to broaden the set of stakeholders outside the diplomatic community and to co-create around a political agenda for change, possibly linked to the UN's Post-2015 Development Agenda, where Sweden has a strong interest in making a difference.

The inclusive nature of SIDD, where different partners from different fields can come on board, means that the Swedish MFA has the chance mitigate between different stakeholders and to allow for collaboration in new ways. In collaboration, the impact of a policy agenda set out as above is more likely to make a footprint. SIDD, it must be remembered, is however just one initiative to allow for new ways of doing things, a complement to a wide range of other platforms for diplomatic interaction that already exists within the fields of traditional and public diplomacy. That said, the concept makes an important contribution to the toolkit of symbols, platforms and language required for the Swedish MFA to refine and develop it's capacity to engage and influence in novel ways.

Diplohack (http://diplohack.org) is another recent contribution to the field of digital as well as to the toolbox for institutional adaptation. The idea behind the event began as a discussion between the communications teams at the Dutch and Swedish Embassies in London. We wanted to connect our embassies to new networks and create replicable methods for collaboration with NGOs, social entrepreneurs and other stakeholders in horizontal ways. Similarly we saw the benefits of pooling recourses and ideas. The underlying aim was to create a discussion around public diplomacy agendas prioritized by our governments, including freedom of the internet and sustainability; but also to engage through learning and reversed mentoring in a digital setting.

From the start we had planned to organize a co-creative digital event coinciding with London's Social Media Week to create content for the online discussion surrounding it. We needed to do something autonomous and attractive enough to make sure that dynamic stakeholders wanted to engage with us on the same platform. The project required quite a bit of research, and the actual process of organising meant that we had to contact people and organizations that we didn't already know, making friends as we went along. We connected with Hub Westminster, part of a global network of collaborative working spaces, and MakeSense, an open-source global community of volunteers who use their skills to tackle problems facing social entrepreneurs. With their help we then designed the first Diplohack, with the ambition to *do* something rather than just talk, and to play on the perceived contrast between innovation and tradition.[6] The event was organized in collaboration using Google hangout and other shared platforms, and was heavily informed by the methods used by MakeSense to tackle challenges and find solutions facing social entrepreneurs. Two positive and inclusive challenges were agreed: "How can creative collaboration in the arts enhance freedom of speech and tolerance?" and "How can open data and technology improve sustainability in the food supply chain?" Thereafter, several NGOs and social enterprises were invited to take part in the ideation phase, which lasted a day and resulted in several ideas for apps related to the defined challenges. Among the participants were diplomats, NGOs like Article 19 and The Swedish Society of Songwriters, Composers and Authors, as well as companies like the mobile broadcaster Bambuser.

The feedback from the participants was generally positive, highlighting the need for innovation in policy and outreach. At the same time, the event showed that there are new ways to work for civil servants who want to reach out and engage in more agile ways. The hashtag #diplohack got 118,000 hits during the first week after the event. This confirmed our theory that new ways of doing things would also make an impact in terms of communication, and amplify the online discussion around policy in networks where embassies are normally absent. Since the first Diplohack in London, similar events have taken place in Tallinn, Tbilisi and, London, spreading learning and collaboration through the system and creating new solutions. A method toolkit has been developed for Dutch and Swedish embassies that want to go ahead and explore local opportunities for collaboration and content creation, based on the following principles:

- A Diplohack aims at solving problems of global concern for the benefit of citizens worldwide or locally.
- A Diplohack brings together the unique skill-sets of several fields (tech, NGOs, social entrepreneurs, enterprise) with those of diplomats.
- A Diplohack should involve a) either Dutch or Swedish diplomats (it's a *diplohack*, after all); b) at least as many outside participants as diplomats, preferably more; and c) social entrepreneurship.
- The challenge to be solved at a Diplohack needs to be a) clearly defined, b) solved in a limited time-frame, and c) solved through an ideation and design process/hackathon/ideathon.

The broader goals of the concept, it self a result of doing things in a new way, are to create collaborative and creative methods for diplomacy and to familiarize civil society and the tech industry with diplomats and diplomacy through co-creation. The aim is also to familiarize diplomats not just with social entrepreneurship, social media and open data, but with the tech industry and their start-up culture, and to actively look for added value in technology and social entrepreneurship for diplomacy.

When implemented well, the model has the potential to result in implementable solutions contributing to solving problems in new ways. This requires project leaders with a clear mandate to innovate and explore new terrain and stakeholders with resources and willingness to implement the result. An important aspect to take in to account when organizing, is to plan for the outcome: which stakeholders will be able to follow up and execute the results, how do you maintain an informal community, etc. A Diplohack can also work as a freestanding platform for collaboration between different stakeholders that need to be able to talk to each other. In the case of urgent global challenges, for example the Ebola outbreak of 2014, the method could be used to bring heterogeneous actors together, including local expertise; congregations, artists, diplomats, media leaders, universities, NGO's and multilateral organizations that urgently need to find new ways to reach out with a narrative or a message. It is however important to constantly evaluate and refine methods and concepts through exchange of experiences, and not to have allow the expectations from the surroundings to put to much pressure on the process.

A pedagogical challenge is to explain the concept for traditional actors and to encourage them to take full part of the process. It has therefore been encouraging to see that the Diplohack concept has inspired individual actors to bring the concept with them as a tool for engagement and creation. Similarly, a positive side effect is that the concept of Diplohack has been replicable enough for others to take after and initiating similar processes on their own. Rather than being part of a grand plan the concept has been spreading as an oblique idea between intrapreneurs in different locations who have identified topics and issues that they wish to tackle in new collaborative ways. The concept has in this sense worked well for learning and relationship building, as every new organizer needs to connect with new stakeholders and methods locally, and thus automatically project a new image which signals a will for engagement and collaboration. What was particularly interesting in London was the energy that the process leaders managed to create in the process and the effect it had on the participants. Part of this was due to another important component, the mixture of people representing different fields coming together in the same room.

The methods for ideation applied meant that all contributors had the chance to contribute with the respective expertise, allowing for a genuine exchange of ideas in a nonhierarchical way. In many ways the first Diplohack also served as an opportunity for reversed learning, where diplomats involved got acquainted with the opportunities offered by doers in other fields and vice versa. From an organizers perspective, the most important insight came in form of the understanding of importance of planned ideation process management. The process leaders from MakeSense helped planning every step of the ideation process in detail, allowed for contributions of ideas beforehand and had systematic ways of incorporating these throughout, as well as for refining and structuring the resulting ideas and concepts. If similar methodology were to be used more widely in the field of policy making, it would definitely be able to effect the outcome of policy process and at the same time create a basis for communication and advocacy. The way in which this work was done, would in itself become an important part of the message.

Values and collaboration – where do we go from here?

This chapter aims to put Swedish initiatives for digital and public diplomacy into context, and to explain why the above mentioned projects can be seen as the starting point of a journey of adaptation to allow for new forms of engagement. An important benefit has been to learn from the projects and to build on the experiences from the same. The world is already digital and is becoming connected in new ways by the minute, transforming patterns of human behaviour. Any discussion about diplomacy and digital diplomacy need to take this as a starting point. Coming from a communications perspective, I have focused on the organizational dimensions of the digital transformation rather than the practical application of digital services and technology. I have also argued that smaller nations who are already used to horizontal organization and openness may have a comparative advantage when it comes to adapting to change. The process of "doing "things differently can in itself become an important part of the narrative about a country, and in this way increase its influence.

All larger organizations are currently going through changes to adapt to the new environment. To be successful, this requires a flexible mindset. It is clear that diplomacy in itself is platform-neutral. Therefore, its practitioners are asked to embrace news ways of operating when required. As hierarchies and cultures change, this will require new ways for engagement and learning, based on genuine curiosity. The ability to influence is directly linked to the capacity for understanding and keeping up to speed with other actors. Sweden aims to be an active learner and node in this networked environment. Strong values inform this process. The latest initiatives for digital diplomacy have served the Swedish MFA well. Its agility and capability to respond to opportunities arising have increased. With a new set of platforms, the next step will be to use this capacity to push political agendas. With a clear vision for change making, based on strong values, the Swedish MFA can convert these new channels into strong tools for democratic engagement.

Notes

1 The views expressed in this chapter are those of the individual contributor and the Swedish MFA is not responsible for the content.
2 For more information, see Government of Sweden, Sweden's democratic system, April 16, 2004. Accessed January 12, 2015. http://www.government.se/sb/d/2853.
3 This index assesses eighty-one countries using four categories: universal access, freedom and openness, relevant content and empowerment.
4 For an interesting discussion on the challenge of making an impact, see "What's Next for Foreign Policy Think Tanks?" www.huffingtonpost.com/robert-muggah/what-next-for-foreign-pol_b_5762832.html.
5 Liat Clark's articles in *Wired UK* from January 2014 on this event offer an external observer's impressions (www.wired.co.uk/news/archive/2014-01/20/swedish-diplohack, www.wired.co.uk/news/archive/2014-01/17/carl-bildt-digital-diplomat).
6 A description on the *ideathon* can be find in *Wired UK* (www.wired.co.uk/news/archive/2013-09/27/diplohack).

10

THE POWER OF DIPLOMACY

New meanings, and the methods for understanding digital diplomacy

J. P. Singh

Introduction

Old-fashioned diplomacy worked within an important context: one where nation states understood their interests and identity, and furthered the former through strategic tactics. In highly interactive and information-rich environments, especially fostered through digital technologies, identities of actors and their interests change, and the task of diplomacy becomes difficult. For example, the United Nations Development Program (UNDP), relatively a new actor in global politics, has led the move to redefine security, traditionally understood as threats to nation states, towards a definition of human security, which speaks to the threats to the material comfort and dignity of human beings (UNDP 1994). Any understanding of human security would be incomplete without reference to the diplomatic corridors since the early 1990s, when UNDP coined this concept and advanced it through international meetings.

Diplomacy practiced through information-rich, highly interactive environments is termed **digital diplomacy** in this volume. The editors conceptualize digital diplomacy as strategies of change management through internal and external changes in the system. The external changes of important concern in this chapter are informational and communication technologies broadly understood through human history, and not just in the current social media era.

This chapter forwards a conceptualization called '**metapower**', suitable for understanding the interactive world of digital diplomacy. It also advocates a few methods for practitioners and scholars to understand the new meanings arising from digital diplomacy. The chapter takes a historical approach to demonstrate that the key to understanding digital diplomacy is communication and human interactions. Metapower, therefore, speaks to actors in communication who give rise to new meanings through their understandings of themselves, each other and the meanings of issues over which they interact.

The logic of metapower is simple: human conversations allow for interactions among actors and for new meanings to arise. Thus, *the more interactive an environment, the more we would expect new meanings.* Interactions are collective processes and lead to collective meanings or understandings. That successive interactions might affect identity and preferences will come as no surprise to a child psychologist. Human interactions can reproduce and rest upon existing cultural practices, but they can equally lead to new or hybrid ones. The concept of metapower helps us understand how human interactions create new meanings in our global politics.

The role of digital technologies in the context of global interactions is especially important in understanding global transformations: Buzan and Little (2000, 286–8) note that communication technologies greatly enhance the "interactional capacity" of the international system, and therefore the possibilities of transformation.[1] Thus, the conversations that take place among diplomatic participants are at the heart of understanding **metapower.**

Context for power

Diplomacy, commonly understood as the art of polite persuasion in international affairs, arose as a modern-era institution in Western Europe, although some form of diplomatic conduct can be found in the Greek city states and the tablets of ancient Sumeria. While popular accounts of diplomacy liken it to anything from Machiavellian manipulation to Byzantine intrigues, diplomacy has also generally been understood as a 'civilized' polite alternative to war for the realization of particular interests. Sir Harold Nicholson (1969), with this historical context in mind, wrote that the Italian state system that emerged in the early modern era relied on diplomacy as a source of power rather than using power to realize diplomatic interests. Nicholson, in fact, believed that the need for diplomacy came first from the commercial interactions that developed and that the security interests, with which diplomatic interests are commonly identified, arose later. One of the first professional diplomatic corps, the Venetian diplomatic service, was a commercial service.

Diplomacy and its counterpart negotiation, the tactical repertoire underlying diplomatic conduct, are often described in terms of power. Therefore, understandings of power form the core of this chapter. Related questions in the context of digital diplomacy include the following: what should we make of the changing identities of the various actors who practice diplomacy and that of the issues themselves? And, how should we recognize or analyze these new diplomatic interactions.

A sense of historical context is important in understanding the evolution of (national) interests in diplomacy. During the Hellenistic period, city states were known to send several ambassadors to another Polis to represent the various political factions from their home state (Leguey-Feilleux 2008). While this seems extraordinary, it was a solution to a problem that continues to exist. How does a diplomat speak to 'a national interest' when the factions at home warrant against a singular definition? Today's diplomats still struggle to contain the internal divisions of the polities they represent: thus, the so-called national or another interest represented at one time is always open to redefinition at another. The national interest can also change not just through domestic changes but also international interactions.

Diplomacy as strategy and persuasion, especially among nation states, can be understood within the traditional confines of an instrumental conception of power about resources, but such instrumentality breaks down in a changing and interactive environment. In a world of multiple actors and continually redefined issue areas, such as security or human rights, it is not always clear how we should understand the identity of the actors or the issues that they represent. International relations are no longer solely about nation states and issues are redefined continually: security is no longer just about territoriality or commerce just about goods. When the International Campaign to Ban Landmines (ICBL) or Amnesty International puts forth ideas about security in the international public sphere, they are redefining the boundaries of who represents these issues and how these issues are to be represented; in simpler terms, who tells the story and what story gets told. Thus, it is now common to find debates on state security, defined in territorial terms, being overlapped by an ICBL or Amnesty's preference to speak of this issue in human-security or human-rights terms. Similarly, commerce is as much about goods as it is about services and movement of peoples. Recent debates at the international level have sought to redefine poverty from a dominant focus in material terms to recasting it as a human-rights violation (Pogge 2007). At a broad level, the practices of diplomacy might provide a new meaning to what it means to be a nation state or, as in the current era, to various other types of diplomacy – such as citizen diplomacy, digital diplomacy and cultural diplomacy, to name a few.

In order to understand these changes in identity, I advance here an altogether different conception of power, one where power arises and is understood in the course of diplomatic interactions and conversations. Here power is a *process* rather than a *resource,* as in most traditional understandings of power. As a process, power shapes the meanings of the issues being discussed and the identity of the actors discussing them. This is different from traditional understandings, where power is generally taken to provide the input or resource for diplomacy or associated negotiation strategies and tactics: the output is governance in the form of negotiated international rules, treaties, charters, conventions or nonbinding recommendations, Memoranda of Understandings or declarations. This is power understood in an instrumental sense of X shaping or constraining Y's ability to do something. Bargaining power, a slippery concept that measures diplomatic outcomes in terms of the bargaining resources – in this case that of X or Y – is an example of instrumental power.

The concept of metapower understands the role of power in diplomacy in its deepest, most transformational sense. Power is often understood in the way that it instrumentally enhances, or structurally restricts, capabilities, but we need to also understand the way that it transforms the meanings of politics. The latter is conceptualized as a form of *metapower*. Briefly, metapower illustrates transformations in identities and interests as a result of international interactions.[2]

Metapower is antecedent, and the word *meta* is employed in this antecedent sense, to traditional understandings of power. Metapower *processes* shape the identity of issues and actors. Traditional or instrumental notions of power, which focus on *resources* – to persuade or constrain others, for example – take identities and interests as given. Dominant issues in diplomacy include security, property and rights. However, security will mean different things to different groups of actors. Its affixation in territorial security terms can be traced back to diplomatic interactions (or metapower processes) such as the 1648 Treaty of Westphalia, which made nation states the guardians of the dominant (territorial and national) forms of security. However, rival conceptions of security, such as human security, mentioned earlier, or networked security, often referenced in the information age, continue to come about through other metapower processes. If we solely focus on how nation states exercise traditional power to preserve territorial security, we miss the metapower processes antecedent to affixed meanings.[3] Similarly, in an era of complex globalization, we can continue to think of international trade and associated commercial diplomacies in 'national' terms, but what does national trade or comparative advantage mean to a multinational corporation, which now operates with complex value-chains in several 'national' markets. To take another example, the idea of universal rights, often protected through nation states, is now being contested in diplomatic negotiations around cultural rights or rights of particular groups, that may or may not obey 'national' logics.

Conceptualizations of power as social processes that constitute the identities and interests of actors provide a useful way of understanding digital diplomacy.[4] Barnett and Duvall's (2005) concept of productive power is a variant of power in a constitutive sense, in explaining social meanings. Productive power is imagined as a discourse, that is "the social processes and the systems of knowledge through which meaning is produced, fixed, lived, experienced, and transformed" (55). However, metapower as conceptualized here is different from productive power because it is antecedent to the exercise of other forms of power, follows from intensive and extensive communicative interactions and has a normatively positive and transformative dimension.[5]

In short, traditional power centres on nation states and national meanings of security, commerce and rights, and diplomacy is the instrument of persuasion to deliver on existing meanings. Metapower processes are antecedent to these understandings. They show us how these 'national' understandings arose in a prior era and how they are being overlapped with new processes (human security, transnational commerce and cultural rights) in our current era. Diplomacy and negotiations are, thus, not merely guides to understanding strategic interests or behaviour but, in the context of communication environments, interactive processes of debate, deliberation, problem solving and argumentation that transform the very interactions, identities, and interests underlying the negotiations.

Two different types of conversations

Let's start with two familiar diplomatic conversations, one old and one new, to understand the workings of diplomacy. The first, the Melian Dialogue, from Thucydides' *Peloponnesian War*, is a well-known example of power used as a resource for realizing previously specified interest. The second, a set of commercial diplomatic interactions that served to define what is now known as the global services economy, shows how metapower explains the meaning of the issues being discussed and, instead of prespecified interests, how interests arose during the diplomatic interactions.

The Melian Dialogue is an iconic account of strategic or instrumental conversations. Imagine yourself, at the beginning of fifth century BC, listening to the famous Melian Dialogue from Thucydides' *Peloponnesian War*. The war was fought between 431–404 BC in ancient Greece, in a world with a number of city states, or the polis, from which we get the term *politics*. It's an important precedent-setting conversation.

You are on the island of Melos in the Aegean Sea, barely sixty square miles in size, and inhabited by less than 3,000 people. The Melians are of Spartan descent, but they would like to stay neutral in the conflict between the Athenians and the Spartans during the Peloponnesian War. The Athenians not only do not understand the Melian perspective but they denigrate it. They ask the Melians to actively assist them in their cause against Sparta and its allies. You sit up to listen. The Melians all but admit to the Athenians being morally superior and the force of good in Greece. However, they do not want to be part of the conflict on mainland Greece far away from their tiny Cycladic island, many days journey by ship to Athens. We can be your friends, they tell the Athenian generals, but we cannot be your allies. The bare volcanic rocks and the steep beaches of Melos are hardly desirous, and the tiny population of Melos has little to offer. Yet, the Athenians will not hear of Melian independence – or of their friendship. You cannot even see the Greek mainland from where the Athenians arrived even if you stand on the highest peak in Melos, 2,400 feet high.

You hear the Melians being given a choice by the Athenians. You can join us and subject yourself to our authority, or you can friend the Spartans, and we will annihilate you. Joining us is a better choice, they counsel the Melians. "Because you would have the advantage of submitting before suffering the worst, and we should gain by not destroying you." The Athenian generals also tell the Melians that Athens' enemies will judge their independence as a sign of Athenian weakness rather than Melian neutrality. Your heart cringes at Melos' plight and you already know of Athens' military superiority.

You are, therefore, surprised, that the Melians do not submit to the Athenians. Is it because they are descendants of Sparta, Athens' mortal enemy, you ask yourself? Or because they really want to stay independent and think they can? The motives do not really matter in this story, especially in hindsight. During the war, the Athenians demand tributes from the Melians, establishing suzerainty after a brief military operation. Soon after the war with Sparta is over in 416 BC, they overcome Melos, killing its men, children and many others.

The Melian Dialogue in diplomatic histories is described in various ways. It is about might makes right. To the victor belong the spoils. The strong do what they can and the weak suffer what they must, writes Thucydides himself. We continue to praise ancient Athens for the moral superiority of its vision. With such a powerful vision, guided by Athenian democracy – in fact those ancient Athenians, we say, invented not just politics but also democracy – we are likely to forget the objections from tiny Melos. In the world of global politics – if you can think of Ancient and Hellenistic Greece being one such world – there is no place for neutrality. The prerogatives about power are lent towards knowing who you are and acting accordingly.

This is one of the interpretations of the Melian dialogue and it is commonly found in political texts. It repeats itself in Machiavelli giving advice to Prince Lorenzo de Medici in the mid-fifteenth century. It is better to be feared than to be loved, writes Machiavelli. Friendships based on attraction and love is useless in politics. In many ways, we continue to live in that unchanging world of power politics. An ex-Israeli diplomat had the following to say of PM Benjamin Netanyahu's reluctance to negotiate on Palestine after a fiery speech in the US Congress: "Everything is changing but he is determined that everything stays the same."

Before describing why this world *as we see it* has little to do with metapower, let me now turn to the kinds of conversations that we find at an everyday level in everyday lives or in our literary texts. Here we begin to understand ourselves through our conversations, we begin to imagine the world differently as we interact with each other, and we see our roles and identities change as a result of these interactions. The reason that everyday conversations are more apt for understanding metapower than the Melian Dialogue is because the latter does not make anyone question the world in which they find themselves. The Athenians, the Spartans, and the Melians know who they are, and they must act according to the historically prescribed interests and preferences ascribed to them. They know they are governments – city states or island states or, in Greek terms, *poleis*. They have clearly defined interests, increasing their security, which have to be met in a particular way. Metapower is about discovering the origins of these interests, the origins of the identities of the actors themselves, and the underlying coded meanings of the actions that follow.

I now turn to a more recent conversation in global diplomacy that comes close to the notion of metapower being advanced here, and one with enormous implications for understanding digital diplomacy. In the 1980s, diplomats in Geneva were meeting on a continual basis to give shape to global rules to regulate and shape what has come to be known as the global services economy. Services include just about anything we buy, sell or consume that is not quite tangible – our phone and media services, digital television and film programs, airline journeys, bank accounts, education and tourism activities are all part of the global services economy. Nearly three-fourths of the US economy is driven by services. Even among the poorest countries of the world, nearly half their economy may be made up of services. Did you know that tourism is the biggest industry in the world, employing nearly one in every ten people? I suspect that most people reading these words are employed in the global services economy or that they are its avid consumers. However, popular wisdom is that services are a high-tech economy and at the global level, the US was alone in pushing negotiations on this issue in the 1980s. Initially, the Europeans resisted these moves, and countries such as India and Brazil came out vociferously against the idea of even discussing services at the global level. Services were portrayed in the world of diplomacy as a high-tech issue, mostly of concern to the Americans. But by 1995, the world's trading countries signed a far-reaching agreement called the General Agreement on Trade in Services (GATS) that now shapes the global services economy. GATS liberalized over 500 subsectors listed on the so-called Services Sectoral Classification List governing the framework, signed by the 160 members of the World Trade Organisation, and its rules now govern everything from how many films China will import from abroad each year (twenty, at present) to how many foreign providers can provide landline services in the US (none were allowed). GATS is the governance framework for nearly two thirds of the global economy.

Between 1985 and 1987, a group of countries met to brainstorm and problem-solve rules that could govern the global services economy. There were disagreements and pressures applied, but, generally, the framework was about problem solving, in which there was no one particular prespecified outcome towards which any country would move. They did not even know what to call the global services trading framework initially until the term GATS began to be floated around. The surprise was that when the GATS framework was finally signed, the US, which had led the moves to have it adopted, was somewhat unhappy with the way things came about. Equally surprisingly, India was ecstatic: US was getting cold feet about participating in the global services economy with the emergent GATS framework; India would later emerge in our own century as a services powerhouse, partly due to its participation in the GATS talks. All those stories you hear about outsourcing and off shoring information technology, banking, health and other services were made possible for India and other countries through the GATS framework.

US, Europe, India and Brazil talked about a new issue in the mid-1980s, after an old one of manufacturing and agriculture was no longer the one that was making the world economy move. These were new conversations. India assumed a new identity after this conversation. It began to see its future in delivering services to the world. Many countries would no longer play the roles assigned to them. Metapower in this case helps us decode and decipher the meaning of the issue, trade in services, as it first came about on global stage, and also how the identity of the actors driven by services changed as a result. Metapower itself arises out of the conversations and interactions among the players.

Metapower has been around since the dawn of time, but we have, well, not talked about it – biased by Thucydides and his followers to only notice traditional instrumental power. The latter is always about resources and the ability to get others to do something they otherwise would not. Even soft power or persuasion, which is often the subject of many headlines or talk shows these days, is also an instrumental understanding. It is about persuading someone to do something you want them to do through talking and other "soft" means, such as the use of cultural products. Thus, for example, US could use Hollywood and its music industries to get people to like the country. Soft power is not about emergent issues that lack a meaning or a name.

Beyond traditional power

Metapower, as noted earlier, is antecedent to instrumental power: the identity of the actors and the issue they transact is set prior to the use of resources or instruments. But in highly interactive circumstances these old identities can come undone, and metapower becomes important again. It is no wonder that often the conversations of digital diplomacy preface **public diplomacy** – how people think and act about one another – and involve, literally, the hearts and minds of people.

We need to move beyond traditional instrumental understandings of diplomacy of the 'who does what to whom variety' to account for its transformative contexts. Diplomacy changes things. Seeing diplomacy as an instrument does not help us understand these changes. Instruments allow us to do things – to calibrate, measure or tune things – but not change their meaning altogether. Thus diplomacy understood in an instrumental fashion can allow us to understand the enhanced or diminished capabilities of actors and their desired or limited strategic courses of action. On the other hand, while capabilities also may be enhanced or diminished by interactive contexts, seen as sources of metapower, interactions may also change the very nature of the game being played.

The following analysis details the instrumental context of power and, subsequently, analyzes the collectively held 'intersubjective' contexts, described herein as a form of metapower. Details of instrumental power contexts highlight the way actors choose strategies given prespecified diplomatic environments, but, in a dynamic context, they may also show how these strategies and the underlying interests might change, at least in limited ways. Power configurations that embody instrumental and structural possibilities therefore provide a good point of entry. They show why the developing world dug in its heels during the feisty UN debates during the 1960s and 1970s, or why arms races and arms negotiations together governed East–West relations during the Cold War.

Most accounts of diplomatic interactions take the actors interests to be constant, and diplomacy is practiced in such a way that each move has a particular payoff. Thus, diplomacy is a strategic endeavour constrained by the environment in which it is practiced. Dynamic models of strategic intent are sophisticated in their attempt to call attention to the evolution of diplomatic interactions, but nevertheless limited in their understanding as a result of two assumptions: Change in the environment is almost always exogenous to the system, and actors always act strategically.

Literally in a *fast changing world* of digital diplomacy and communication networks, taking the underlying context to be unchanged is myopic, to say the least. With such lenses, we do not see that actors other than nation states might be practicing diplomacy or that the issue means something quite different to them than what it does to state actors. The notion of security mentioned above is one such example. In a broad sense, liberal theories lack a deep understanding of interactions if actors' interests and identities remain unchanged through these interactions (Singh 2010). I make this point almost in a common-sense way. Through conversations and interactions we formulate a notion of ourselves and our identities and our interests are shaped accordingly.

The conceptual suggestion that instrumental power specifies a point of entry for our analysis is predicated on two givens: the shared understanding of the issue in question and the interest of the actors as a result of a given issue need to be prespecified. To understand the origins and effects of these understandings, we need to detail metapower or the power of interactional contexts to change the self-understandings of the actors with respect to the issues and environment in question.

Diplomacy, and the set of strategies and tactics known as negotiation associated with it, can transform the collectively held understandings informing the identity of actors and issues. Thus, metapower works at both ends: it specifies actor understandings prior to diplomatic interactions and, second, more importantly, the understandings are amended as further interactions take place.

Metapower is a process that speaks to transformations in collective identities of actors and their interests in the context of international interactions. International interactions, especially as enhanced through communication technologies and diplomacy, socialize actors while also leading to transformations in terms of actor identities and their interests. However, the transformative possibilities of these interactions must be distinguished from both the limited and expansive uses of the term "transformation" in speaking of the collective dimension of power.

In an expansive sense, Buzan and Little (2000) note that the interactional capacity of the system that should account for transformations in the modern world has increased. However, even in their account, the transformational possibility might still be limited (Buzan and Little 2000, 351). For example, the intensity and velocity of global communications may have increased exponentially, but that does not mean that the international system is qualitatively different from what it used to be. If states still dominate the system of interactions, or they are primus inter pares, in international relations, then we cannot speak of fundamental transformations in the system. They, however, agree with Ruggie that the potential for international transformation with information technology enhancing interaction capacity might be in the "economic sectors" where "its most likely effect would take the form of a serious assault on the territorial organisation of politics and culture."[6] Nevertheless, the thick descriptions of these interactions, as presented in terms of diplomatic interactions, are missing. Buzan (2004) himself seems to have moved forward to delineate the possibility of a world society of multiple actors as a fundamental transformation from the international society of the interstate system.

Metapower locates the transformation in the micro contexts in which actors' identities and their interests are embedded. In Ruggie's (1993) analysis, for example, the fundamental transformation from the medieval city state system to the Westphalian sovereign state system could be noticed in the micro-level trade fairs outside city walls. These fairs were giving rise to a new commercial class that asked for new forms of organizing authority that would grant them necessary property rights or incentives for economic ownership and conduct.[7] The empires of the world at that time were constantly shifting in terms of territoriality, and granted property rights sparingly usually only to the landed aristocracies. Thus, through a new form of interaction, commercial classes and later manufacturers, obtained new forms of property right. Eventually, new forms of political organisation arose altogether, which would 'fix' political boundaries around nation states.

The metapower context is understood through interactive negotiations of actors that lead to new collective understandings. The technological roots of these understandings provide a related point. For example, information technologies are networked technologies. Networks enhance, deepen and extrapolate international interactions. The technological basis of metapower is undeniable. Nevertheless, technology is merely one of the bases of metapower. Information technologies enhance the interconnectedness of people as well as the meanings and representations that flow across them.[8] So does the mere act of human speech and it can be taken as another basis of metapower. Therefore, this chapter takes diplomatic interactions as an important arena in which we notice the workings of metapower.

Metapower in its boldest sense is about various forms of communication and the possibility of "discursive consciousness", as noted by Anthony Giddens (1984, 41–5) or "consciousness awakening" as noted by Paulo Freire (2000). Only through discursive consciousness can we describe the constitutive processes of social phenomena: "'Consciousness' in this sense presumes being able to give a coherent account of one's activities and the reasons for them." Paulo Freire goes a step further by situating "consciousness awakening" in dialogic practices through which subjects come to know one another and themselves: "In this theory of action one cannot speak of *an actor*, nor simply of *actors*, but rather of *actors in communication*" (Freire 2000, 129). Taken together, technology and diplomacy thereof facilitate the rise of metapower in human interactions, but especially in those informed by information networks, as *actors in communication*.

New methods

What methods are best suited to understanding and practicing digital diplomacy? Clearly, the method of strategic persuasion, the instrumental power variant, works well when the environment is stable and as in the modern era, nation states are the primary actors and practice diplomacy with each other. How should diplomats understand the transformations in diplomatic practices that pose a challenge to their old repertoires?

I start with the assumption that methods that help us with understanding the terrain of diplomacy will provide better answers to good practice as well. Former Secretary of State Hilary Clinton asked in the *2010 Quadrennial Diplomacy and Development Review*: "How can we do better?" The QDDR

> is a sweeping assessment of how the Department of State and the United States Agency for International Development (USAID) can become more efficient, accountable, and effective in a world in which rising powers, growing instability, and technological transformation create new threats, but also new opportunities.
>
> (US Department of State 2010, 1)

The QDDR sets forth "a series of reforms and recommendations" on how the US should deploy the civilian power of diplomacy.

The QDDR does not concern itself much with how to understand this world: its chief concern is what to do with it. A policy report that was uncertain about the means and ends it analyzes would be viewed as equivocal and ambiguous. Nevertheless, QDDR sets forth recommendations that speak to known interests and outcomes, along with a set of tools that can measure the efficiency of the future diplomatic practices outcomes, without first really taking note of the new world in which US diplomacy now operates where known interests and effective outcomes are no longer clear. In this sense, the QDDR continues, rather than departs from, traditional diplomatic practices. Taken to extremes, for example, in traditional diplomatic practices a terrorist *network* is conceived as a threat emanating from specific *nation states*, against whom a war must be waged. An alternative understanding might emphasize the conditions under which human beings join global terrorist networks and policy responses that seek to address those conditions.

Diplomacy is the art of persuasion, and this art must reflect the prerogatives of its age. As times change, so do the prerogatives. When François de Callières wrote *On the Manner of Negotiating with Princes* in 1716, he was writing about a set of practices that were fast becoming norms for understanding the relations among emerging European nation states. Therefore, de Callières' persuasion speaks to national interests and the diplomats' skilfulness in tempering out the conflicts; he advises diplomats to "win everyone's good graces." In our current era, this persuasion must address new issues, understandings, and actors in global affairs. It is no longer clear how to do the persuading and who is to be persuaded. The old diplomacy practiced among nation states has not faded, while new forms overlap and intersect the old forms.

François de Callières (1963, 121) suggests: "One of the most necessary qualities in a good negotiator is to be an apt listener." The diplomat should listen closely and fit practices to that of the learned culture in such a way that they seem to be effortless: "By this means your influence will spread gradually through their minds almost unawares." As compared to what de Callières recommends, the QDDR is less about listening and more about action: what the United should do and how it should be done. The QDDR is not situated in an anthropology of cultural listening. The following subsections chart a few methods for listening.

Field notes

In an age of emergent phenomena and transformational diplomacy, the task of gathering cultural intelligence is a salient concern. Intelligence is more about contacts and listening than about lecturing and making people listen.

The first methodological task for the new ediplomat – from a nation state, an international organization, or a civil society organization – must be immersion into the cultural practices of our times, not as a study of exotic others who must be made legible and translated through a known set of codes but as emergent phenomena whose codes are not yet known. An anthropologist decodes a culture with "participant observation" and "field notes." Surprisingly in an age that had not yet invented anthropology, de Callières (1963, 139) writes that "the diplomatist will find it useful to make a daily note of the principal points of which he must render an account. . . . This diary, which is a valuable part of diplomatic engagement, will greatly assist him in composing his dispatches, and will give him a means of correcting his own memory at any later date."

The point being made here about cultural listening is more encompassing than that of composing a diplomatic dispatch. The diplomatic dispatches from the 20,000 officials of the US State Department are greater than any news gathering abilities of any of the big international news organisations. The point about cultural listening is about getting deeper into the cultural practices of the world to understand change at its most abstract. The scholar James N. Rosenau (1997) once wrote that understanding change must come from the art of generating puzzles, or "puzzlement", as he called it. He distinguishes between anomalies and puzzles: "anomalies are exceptions to known pattern, whereas puzzles derive from known patterns in which the dynamics that sustain them are perplexing" (16).

In the context of this chapter, there are many known patterns, which include the practices of diplomacy, the world of multiple actors, and new threats and challenges. What is not known is how effective our diplomatic practices are in dealing with these known patterns. The corrective impulse in diplomacy is to look into the repertoire of possible choices to bring about "effective" outcomes. Puzzling is antecedent to a repertoire of choices: puzzles help us ascertain the usefulness of our repertoires in the first place, and to look for unknown patterns. We are not good at looking for unknown patterns: international relations scholars predicted neither the fall of the Soviet Union nor the Arab Spring.

Social media provide two choices for cultural listening to look for patterns. One is surreptitious listening, or mass surveillance, and it seems that the United States is adept at this, gathering big data from social media firms such as Google and Facebook. Clearly, the resources of listening have been thrown in this direction. The second direction is public diplomacy where the United States listens carefully to figure out how to understand and engage global publics. Judging from the meagre budgets thrown at the latter, this type of cultural listening is not yet popular. Cull (2013) has argued that the US public diplomacy initiatives were slow to utilize social media tools and, when they did, they emphasized the one-way broadcasting rather than the two-way 'relational aspects' of social media.

Ethnography

There are other methodological practices, apart from cultural listening as field notes, that would generate puzzles from known patterns, and one of them is participant observation.

Participant observation comes from cultural immersion and listening. Rather than proceeding with known hypotheses and known phenomena, an ethnography finds patterns through "thick description" that come from the analyst's skills.

Digital diplomacy operates in a networked environment. The ethnographer's task thus becomes complicated as meanings must be understood through interconnected field sites. The new meanings of security, commerce and human rights, as mentioned earlier, now arise out of networked environments. For example, in order to understand the meanings of cultural rights and identity for the Sami people in Nordic countries and Russia, we must now understand similar meanings arising out of indigenous peoples movements worldwide. Old fashioned diplomacy often relied on knowledge of discrete units – a nation state, an institution or a set of people. However, now more than ever this knowledge arises from networked practices, making the task of the ethnographer both challenging and difficult. Again, François de Callières' (1963, 11) words are prescient:

> We must think of states of which Europe is composed as being joined together by all kinds of necessary commerce, in such a way that they may be regarded as members of one Republic, and that no considerable change can take place in any one of them without affecting the condition, or disturbing the peace, of all others.

Fortunately, anthropologists are already working to develop the techniques of a multisited ethnography that "moves out from the single sites and local situations of conventional ethnographic research designs to examine the circulation of meanings, objects and identities in diffuse time-space" (Marcus 1995, 96). Multisited ethnographies can help us understand the new meanings and challenges that are arising for security, commerce and human rights. One way to do conduct multisited ethnography is through old-fashioned intelligence from networks. However, as the case of Edward Snowden from the US National Security Administration shows, such intelligence gathering is an inherently risky, if not an unethical activity. There are intelligent ways of gathering information. More recently, defence and intelligence agencies of the US government have turned to anthropologists to decipher cultural meanings. It is time for the state department to do likewise.[9]

There are two ways through which anthropologists can specify meanings for digital diplomacy. First, there is the ethnography for the analyst who tries to find meaning in cultures, and, second, ethnography can be the metaphor for guiding the practices of diplomats themselves, such as the kinds of diaries that de Callières advocated for diplomats.

An ethnographer, writes Clifford Geertz (1973), does not study a village but studies *in* a village. "Cultural analysis is (or should be) guessing at meanings, assessing the guesses, and drawing explanatory conclusion from the better guesses, not discovering the Continent of Meaning and mapping out its bodiless landscape" (20). This is fair warning to not try to impose pre-fabricated systems of meaning upon phenomena that are new. For most analysts, this is hard.

Most scholars and diplomats are trained to think of negotiations in game theoretic terms and proceeded with a prefabricated vocabulary to try to uncover moments of strategic diplomatic conduct. Instead, in the interstices of these diplomatic processes, one can discover the cultures of diplomacy: shared professional norms, professional courtesies and, most importantly, collective problem solving. Remember that in a prisoner's dilemma or Rousseau's stag hunt, the theorist's imagined world reaches inefficient outcomes because there is no collective problem solving. Each person's strategic interest is such that he or she defects. In a diplomatic culture of shared norms, there may be several opportunities for problem solving that an analyst would miss if our lenses are only attuned to noticing strategic conduct.

The art of puzzlement combined with the art of thick description might be apt ways of understanding new cultures through which diplomacy operates. As Rosenau notes, puzzling comes from recognising patterns. The UN Security Council is the epitome of strategic conduct and its formal decision-making procedures or votes are often the subject of analysis. Yet, new research shows that informal dialogue processes among the P5 countries have been important for resolving deadlocks or reaching consensus (Prantl 2005). The idea of the UN Peacekeeping Force, for example, after the Suez Crisis in 1956 arose from such informal consultations, especially between the Soviets and Americans, and can be understood as problem solving: it assured the Egyptians that Israelis, British or French forces were unlikely to march across the Sharm-el-Sheikh with UN peacekeeping forces in the way.

Elite interviews

Related to detailed ethnographies is the value of elite interviews or conversations with diplomats. Most diplomats operate in a messy and complex world of multiple issues and actors where their choices are not always clear. Lengthy conversations with the diplomats and negotiators throw light on the ways in which these diplomats reach decisions and the kinds of heuristic, mental short-cuts or narratives they might use in situations such as these.

A rule of thumb for these conversations is that they allow negotiators to tell their story. The analyst must provide cues to the story, if necessary, but the analyst is not a journalist: her task cannot be to pin the negotiator against the wall in the hopes of getting a hidden answer with a set of investigative techniques. In other words, the analyst's task is to listen and provide cues. "When you were in Montreal for the Uruguay Round meetings in April 1989, can you tell me how you proceeded with the intellectual property negotiations?" I asked this question of India's intellectual property negotiator for the Uruguay Round. Received wisdom on this issue is that India signed away its fortunes in IP to get concessions in textiles and agriculture, and that it got nothing in return. Instead, what I heard from the negotiator was something altogether different. There were no consultations among the textile and intellectual property negotiators. If there were any trade-offs, she conjectured, they might have been among heads of states, but not among the Montreal negotiators themselves. More importantly, she heard from her Canadian colleagues that US law allowed national security bodies such as NASA to break foreign patents to meet security requirements in the US. The Indian negotiator used this knowledge to frame article 31 of the Trade-Related Intellectual Property Services (TRIPS) agreement, which allows for abrogation from patents in practices known as compulsory licensing and parallel imports (Singh 2008, Chapter 3). Article 31, in fact, served as the basis of the well-known Para 6 of the Doha Health Declaration in November 2001, which asked the TRIPS Council to look into the questions of national health emergencies and the need for poor societies to get around expensive patents from developed country firms.

While elite interviews may be structured around particular negotiations, there is also need for histories from diplomats of their experiences in general. Fortunately, this need is beginning to be met through projects in various institutions on diplomatic oral histories.[10] The relevant toolsets here are historical and archival.

Case studies

Most centres studying diplomacy now maintain case histories.[11] Rich case histories of diplomatic or negotiation episodes outline the 'story' or 'narrative arc' of these episodes, usually chronologically, to pinpoint the actors, the issues, the challenges and tipping points or deadlocks. They provide a rich texture for understanding the cultural practices of diplomacy. There is every reason to do the same for digital diplomacy environments.

While the case study method is still in its infancy in most schools of international relations, this has changed in business schools where the case study method is regularly used for role play, problem solving and entrepreneurship. The case is presented as the cues for an unknown landscape where a variety of outcomes is possible. It might be that the field of international relations has still not come to grips with the role that diplomacy or negotiations play in shaping global outcomes. When we believe that habits of antagonistic conduct or that of habitual cooperation are the structural realities of the global order, as in realist or liberal analyses, respectively, the role of diplomacy in these endeavours is merely posited as smoothing out the crinkles rather than shaping substantive outcomes. Therefore, the deference given to case studies in business schools versus the relative indifference towards them in teaching diplomacy: business schools utilize the case to teach fundamental business skills. Interestingly, courses in diplomacy and negotiation play second fiddle to those outlining power and known interests in training diplomats, and thus rich case studies on diplomacy are seldom used.

Case studies in digital diplomacy can show both how new meanings arise in information-rich environments and how diplomatic actors can influence (or even create) new meanings. For example, case histories on public diplomacy can show the context in which it is successful and the types of social media that are most effective. Although not quite case studies, the many research themes explored at USC's Center for Public Diplomacy explore such possibilities. These include digital diplomacy, cultural diplomacy, and non-state public diplomacy.[12]

These case studies can in turn be used in the training of diplomats. The case study method approximates experiential learning. It draws upon "real world" cases to teach diplomats to think about the perceptions, motivations, interests, and actions of actors in information rich environments. Through simulations, the case study methods allows for role-play and problem solving. Therefore, the case study method is an effective way of becoming empathic and for learning to listen.

The case study method holds tremendous potential as a pedagogy for a transforming world. Holding diplomacy as secondary to power-based outcomes or always reflecting strategic conduct is not optimal for a world in which these practices are needed to respond to transformations and challenges. The methods used to analyze diplomacy need to catch up to the real world of diplomacy. Otherwise, the limits of diplomacy become like a self-fulfilling prophecy: if we teach diplomats that diplomacy is secondary to traditional power, then we are hardly asking them to be creative or being at the forefront of understanding or managing global transformations. We need to be more business-like in using case studies!

Conclusion

Samuel Huntington's (1993) 'clash of civilizations' is a grand metaphor for understanding the limits of diplomacy. Even while the thesis was severely critiqued, it continues to resonate in many ways, least of all in the fact that this thesis, like other understandings, marginalizes diplomacy. Fouad Ajami (1993) suggested one way out of this conceptual jail, albeit in a critique of Huntington. He notes that Huntington's thesis is like that of the Marlowe character in a Joseph Conrad novella who understands foreign words and images in the only language he knows: English. Ajami's point is that we can only get around the difficulty of misunderstanding if we allow ourselves to believe for an instance that we are hearing words we do not understand. How can Huntington speak for the civilizational other, he asks, when he does not understand what they are saying? That task would begin with diaries and the stories we need to collect, which for our diplomat anthropologist might begin to lay bare unknown Weltanschauung, or world views.

For the practitioner diplomat, this chapter offers a guide to being aware that they practice their craft in a world in which traditional forms of persuasion may not work. First, digital diplomacy must recognize that those to be persuaded are not just state actors but also societal actors with the ability to network domestically and internationally. Second, digital diplomacy must be alert to new meanings in information-rich and mediated environments. Third, the tools for learning to be an effective ediplomat are anthropological – participant observation, listening, and case study analysis. This is because **change management** in digital diplomacy cannot take interests, identities, and instruments as given. A well-prepared diplomat must know the processes for understanding new meanings and new cultures arising out of multisited cultural networks.

This chapter traces new world views to metapower processes that arise from interactive and communicative environments in digital diplomacy. Metapower provides an identity to the variety of actors engaged in global diplomacy, and the changing meanings of the issues they discuss. Thus, when states, international organizations, civil society groups, media and citizens and global businesses discuss security, economic and human rights issues, we cannot assume that the meaning of the issues and the interests of the actors discussing these issues is set in advance. Quite often, these meanings arise as a result of diplomatic interactions. Metapower provides a point of entry for understanding digital diplomacy.

Notes

1 Later, Buzan and Little (2000, 350) note: "Increases in interaction capacity driven by profound developments in both physical and social technologies were another key element in the transformation from the ancient and classical era to the modern one."
2 I developed the concept of metapower in the context of interactions over information networks (Singh 2002) and subsequently diplomatic conduct (Singh 2008).
3 Berger and Luckmann (1966) write that once meanings gets well-accepted – objectified or reified – we often cannot discern the processes that led to the formation of meaning.
4 Sociological understandings of power can be traced back to Weber and Durkheim and elaborated in current contexts through Foucault and Bourdieu.
5 There are intellectual antecedents to the term *metapower*. Metapower conceptualizations share with Baumgartner, Buckley and Burns (1975) the sociological understanding of what they also term metapower to note that relationships among international actors enable organizational rules and world orders. However, these understandings do not involve the ascription of new meanings.
6 Underhill (2006, 4–5) also emphasizes the role of political interactions in global social transformations.
7 Ruggie (1993, 155) notes: "In no sense could the medieval trade fairs have become substitutes for the institutions of feudal rule. Yet the fairs contributed significantly to the demise of feudal authority relations."
8 Gianni Vattimo's (1993, 214) notes on technology and postmodernity are instructive: "What *concerns* us in the postmodern age is a transformation of (the notion of) Being as such – and technology, properly conceived, is the key to that transformation."

9 Of course, US government agencies have also manipulated meanings. In his resignation letter to the US Secretary of State, career diplomat John Brady Kiesling wrote in the context of the US war on Iraq:

> The sacrifice of global interests to domestic politics and to bureaucratic self-interest is nothing new, and it is certainly not a uniquely American problem. Still, we have not seen such systematic distortion of intelligence, such systematic manipulation of American opinion, since the war in Vietnam.
>
> US "Diplomat's Letter of Resignation"
> *The New York Times* February 27, 2003. Accessed April 19, 2014. www.nytimes.com/2003/02/27/international/27WEB-TNAT.html

10 For example, diplomatic case histories are available through the Kennedy School of Government, the Institute for the Study of Diplomacy at Georgetown University (www.guisd.org/), and the Center on Public Diplomacy at the University of Southern California.
11 See previous footnote.
12 See USC Center for Public Diplomacy. "Research." Accessed April 19, 2014. http://uscpublicdiplomacy.org/research.

CONCLUSION

The future of digital diplomacy

Marcus Holmes

This volume has theorized and empirically demonstrated the very active, and continually evolving, phenomenon of **digital diplomacy** as a form of **change management** in world politics. By bringing together established scholars and seasoned practitioners of diplomacy, the volume has shed light on a form of diplomacy that is increasingly playing a major role in political outcomes. Two themes, in particular, stand out. First, at the policy level, social media affects the ways that diplomats and other leaders do their jobs. From data-gathering to negotiation, digital tools shape both the minutiae day-to-day practices of practitioners as well as the realm of possibility for future practices. Put another way, new digital tools allow diplomats to revaluate what will be possible to predict, and respond to, in the future. Second, at the institutional level, diverse organizations from foreign ministries to NGOs and international organizations are being reshaped and reimagined due to the revolution in digital technologies.

Each of the contributions have highlighted the different aspects of these two dimensions and have found areas where they converge. The **International Criminal Court** (ICC), as an international organization, is using digital technology to manage both the day-to-day aspects of **international change** through the prosecution of war criminals while simultaneously using digital technology to enhance its online presence, and convey its achievements, in order to promote its legitimacy. Major powers such as the United States, Japan and EU countries are suing social media platforms in China in order to promote their own activities, as a form of **public diplomacy**, as well as to open a dialogue with Chinese citizens. In other cases, states such as Australia may have fallen behind the curve with respect to such activities and are now on the other side of the "digital divide," vis-à-vis other allies, such as the United States.

Rather than summarize the findings and contributions from the individual chapters on these two dimensions, the aim of this chapter is to highlight a research agenda for digital diplomacy moving forward and to assess what the contributions mean for policymaking. The contributions in this volume have self-reflectively placed their perspectives within bigger debates about the role of diplomacy in international politics and the traditional paradigms of international-relations theory. As digital diplomacy emerges as its own area of study, however, new questions that transcend traditional IR questions will begin to emerge. Thinking through what those questions are likely to be, and how scholars can go about answering them, is a crucial exercise in determining the future of the study of digital diplomacy. Furthermore, we have approached the study of digital diplomacy from both academic and practitioner perspectives, drawing from a diverse cadre of authors to provide their insights on the nature of digital diplomacy. It is therefore useful to evaluate, in the end, what we have learned about digital diplomacy in terms of making actionable policy recommendations.

Digital diplomacy: Many answers, but new questions

As is often the case, this volume has raised as many questions as it has answered. In particular, the contributions have raised three sets of questions about digital diplomacy that will likely drive future research.

First, for the most part the contributions in this volume have focused on the salutary effects of digital diplomacy. Whether in managing change, serving as a tool of public diplomacy, limiting **secrecy**, enhancing legitimacy or creating **metapower**, the implicit normative valence of these activities is positive. Digital diplomacy as a form of change management is, after all, an exercise of politics and consequently less salutary dimensions are present as well. Terrorist groups, unsavoury organizations, and other non-state actors with dubious intent use digital technologies to manage changes in the international environment and promote their own messages as well. How do these less salutary instances of digital "diplomacy", understood broadly, interact with the more salutary dimensions? One under theorized area of diplomacy, which has gained more attention recently, is the use of diplomacy for symbolic violence (on symbolic violence in IR, see Bigo 2011). Symbolic violence refers to the use of insults, intimidation, truth-twisting comments and so forth to hurt the reputation or status of another actor without resorting to physical violence. Such types of violence *may* be ubiquitous with digital diplomacy since the relative costs of issuing this type of violence, versus physical violence, are quite low, though the conditions under which states or other actors issue them remain to be understood. Recent events in Ukraine, for example, anecdotally suggest that such forms of violence may be relatively common in times of crisis.[1]

Second, many of the contributions have highlighted distinctions between digital diplomacy and other more traditional forms, such as face-to-face or cable wire diplomacy. I have posited that there are functions, such as large-scale data accumulation and public information dissemination, that digital tools and social media can aid states in accomplishing. What these new tools lack, however, is some of the information richness of traditional diplomacy, such as face-to-face interactions, which may promote intention understanding and deception detection. In a world where states are making assessments of intentions, in order to manage change based on big data analysis, it remains a question what states can actually learn about the intentions of others with the data that is available to them. Relatedly, the rise of new communication channels, such as information and communications technology, raise important questions regarding how interpersonal trust operates in a world of social media. Can states convey trustworthiness through social media? Do the targets of social media feel that they can test the messages being received? There may be domains where immense amounts of data, analyzed through sophisticated digital tools, can lead to important insights of whether international actors are headed. There are likely others, however, where traditional personal diplomacy or an old-fashioned telephone call, is the better prescription. Elucidating the precise role for digital technologies relative to other forms of diplomacy will be a worthwhile endeavour, particularly in crafting policy-relevant recommendations.

Finally, the contributions in this volume have pointed toward different ways of understanding the *causal* and *constitutive* roles that digital technologies may play in diplomacy. Gaining a better understanding of foreign publics, projecting an image of the self to other states, enhancing legitimacy through more intensive communication and information dissemination and so forth imply important relationships between key variables in international politics, such as the form of diplomacy undertaken and variation in received state images. But the precise causal relationship is often difficult to articulate because digital technologies have become ubiquitous. Alec Ross famously indicated that one of the goals for the US State Department with respect to e-diplomacy was to "bake it in to everything we do at State" (Hanson 2012c; Hanson 2012e). To the extent that this has already happened it becomes difficult to disentangle the causal effects of a particular digital technology, of digital diplomacy strategy, with other approaches since "digital is omnipresent" (Savage, Ruppert and Law 2010). To the extent that digital has become constitutive of the daily practices of foreign ministries, it is difficult to then isolate digital diplomacy as a causal variable.

Dealing with the questions identified above and the problem of digital now constituting (to various extents) much of what states, institutions and organizations do in international politics requires developing a digital diplomacy research agenda. It is to that topic that we will now turn.

A digital diplomacy research agenda

J. P. Singh's contribution highlights an important aspect of digital diplomacy that will be increasingly salient moving forward: what ways in which we study digital diplomacy may be affected by the nature of the field. Singh highlights the usefulness of field notes, ethnography, elite interviews and case studies through which scholars can better understand the effects of digital diplomacy in political outcomes.

Ethnographic field notes will allow scholars to understand the uses of digital tools in the day-to-day activities of the diplomat. This empirical method resonates with Holmes' theoretical account of digital diplomacy as international change management, particularly in the endogenous incremental shifting that occurs through daily practice. Observing these practices will better enable scholars to specify precisely what is being managed, how, and crucially, at what level of effectiveness.

Similarly, elite interviews with practitioners who are either the source or target of digital diplomacy initiatives will be useful in assessing the perception of those strategies at the highest levels of government. After all, if digital diplomacy affects state decision-making and the foreign-policy process, it will be important to identify the extent to which digital efforts penetrate leaders at the highest levels of government.

Singh also identifies case studies as being particularly useful for understanding the dynamics of digital diplomacy. This view resonates with the contributors to this volume who have explored the effects of digital diplomacy with careful analysis of important cases, such as China, Australia, the United States, International Criminal Court and so forth. These arguably fall under the category of what Gerring calls "typical cases", those which are "typical examples of some cross-case relationship" (Gerring 2007, 89). In the case of this volume, the typical cross-case relationship is that between the choice of strategy to use digital tools, relative to other strategic choices, and the outcomes that stem from those decisions. By definition typical cases are supposed to be representative of a much larger set of cases in the universe of cases available for study.

As a first foray in to the study of digital diplomacy, the use of typical cases, such as with relatively powerful states that are likely to be engaged in public diplomacy and are compelled to manage change in the international system, this is a justifiable methodological decision. Moving forward, however, it will be useful to study instances of digital diplomacy from a plurality of perspectives. Diverse cases, those where there is a full range of variation on the variables of interest, such as cases where digital diplomacy is *not* pursued will be useful in establishing the conditions under which states and other actors strategically decide to engage in digital diplomacy (Gerring 2007). Extreme cases, those where there are instances of states exhibiting very unusual values of particular variables (Gerring 2007), perhaps using digital diplomacy to such a degree that it is indistinguishable from other non-digital practices, would be interesting to investigate. Most importantly, variation in the type of actor using (or not using) digital diplomacy strategies will be necessary to link the interaction between actor type and conditions for digital diplomacy use. As alluded to earlier, terrorist organizations can use digital diplomacy just as humanitarian NGOs can. Small states in sub-Saharan Africa employ digital diplomacy strategies just as states in the European Union do. Understanding when and under what conditions it makes sense for each of these different actor types to engage in digital diplomacy is crucial.

In addition, case studies of the use of digital diplomacy in states where national governments have taken steps to limit online access will be useful in providing scope conditions of many of the contributions in this volume. Sotiriu's chapter points to many of these issues of internet freedom. As Dhruva Jaishankar notes,

> Whereas the organic, even anarchic, nature of the Web's initial development enabled unprecedented new opportunities, it also confronted policymakers with new challenges – both real and perceived. Many national governments – both liberal and illiberal – now struggle to deal with security threats, social turmoil, and illicit activities that are ostensibly enabled or facilitated by online activity. And so they regularly resort to placing selective or indiscriminate restrictions on the public's ability to access and use the Internet without fear of repercussion.
>
> (Jaishankar 2014, 1)

States that actively restrict Internet content limit the ability for other actors, be they states, groups or individuals, to engage diplomatically with them in the digital landscape. Understanding the dynamics of what occurs in these instances, and how digital diplomacy is limited under such conditions, will be worthwhile, particularly as more states face the challenges that Jaishankar identifies.

Last, while case studies are useful for tracing causal pathways within and between cases, controlling for variables and other confounds is a difficult problem. It is often difficult in a case study to identify what it is precisely that a particular message sent through Twitter, or an image placed on Facebook, or data gathered through a web-crawler is able to *do* in a complex and messy international environment. Even more challenging, the study of digital diplomacy often confronts the well-known levels of analysis problem where it is difficult to aggregate the experiences of individuals or groups upward to state decision-making. While elite interviews, field notes and so forth might provide insight into the latter problem, by identifying what precisely went into the decision-making process at the highest levels of government, the problem of isolating the effects of a particular digital message or piece of data gleaned from a social media website remains a critical problem.

Experiments conducted in controlled environments, either in the field, among decision-makers and publics who have input into the action of the actor being investigated or in the laboratory may be valuable here. Experiments allow researchers to assess the internal validity of a theory by controlling, to a certain extent, the number of confounds, the participants selected for the experiment and the ways in which variables are manipulated. With respect to responses to a particular Twitter message, for example, a laboratory experiment might provide the same message through Twitter in one condition and the newspaper or television or Facebook, etc. in another condition. This would allow the researcher to identify a more precise understanding of the role of Twitter relative to other media. By assessing personality, demographic, ideological and other indicators in pretest surveys, researchers will also be able to determine if there are important personal or group characteristics that might affect the ways in which particular messages, or messages through particular media, are received.

Ultimately, the future of digital diplomacy research should be problem-driven and methodologically diverse. As is the case with most subjects in the social sciences, the questions one asks and the problems that one confronts ultimately should determine the methodological strategy for answering questions and solving problems. This volume has theorized digital diplomacy and provided a first foray into understanding the effects of digital diplomacy empirically. More theorization and rigorous empirical investigation will ultimately provide us with a nuanced understanding of both the nature of digital diplomacy and the conditions under which outcomes are affected by the use of it strategically in international politics.

Recommendations for policymakers

We conclude the volume with several recommendations for policymakers based on the preceding analysis by our contributors. First, while *digital diplomacy is likely here to stay, so are traditional forms of diplomacy*. Many of the contributions highlight the important role that digital diplomacy plays in managing international change, but it becomes clear that traditional diplomacy, be it in the personal face-to-face meeting, summits, concert, secrecy and so forth, continues to have its place. Digital diplomacy is particularly useful, as Holmes argues, in managing change of the incremental endogenous variety, where small changes in the international system are difficult to pick up on and analyze without technology tools devoted to that practice. Inherent in this perspective is that digital diplomacy cannot replace the "personal touch" when it comes to other forms of change, such as exogenous crisis and situations where careful analysis of state intentions is required.

Similarly Corrie has identified ways that digital diplomacy supports the mission of the International Criminal Court, both in terms of managing change on the ground in casework as well as enhancing its legitimacy, though there are also functions that digital technology presumably cannot replace, such as securing support at the highest levels for the organization from non-states parties. Last, Bjola and Jiang highlight the digital public diplomacy strategies of EU, US and Japanese embassies in China, many of which have been ostensibly successful in engendering a particular view that those embassies wish to convey, but digital initiatives are but one tool among a much larger set of public diplomacy tools that may be required to project a particular image abroad.

Along these lines, *the costs of digital diplomacy need to be considered alongside benefits*. While many studies have highlighted the relatively low costs of using digital technology to reach large numbers of individuals and groups, such connections necessarily may raise some costs, such as those associated with mistakes. As the UK Foreign Minister William J. Hague put it in a recent tweet, "#Twitter is a great way of making our staff nervous by communicating directly."[2] The nervousness likely stems from concern over the cost of an errant tweet or other social media message that could easily create misperceptions at best, and create a political scandal at worse. Put another way, as with many communication technologies, digital social media tools also have learning curves which may be required to scale before policymakers are comfortable with the risks of engaging in digital diplomacy.

On the other hand, one of the more profound implications of digital diplomacy, particularly as it relates to recent debates regarding Wikileaks, the Snowden affair, and the NSA is the role of **openness** and secrecy in diplomacy. Wichowski's contribution, among others, suggests that policymakers need to *rethink openness and secrecy* in the conduct of diplomacy. One reason is quite practical: the digital world is an accessible one where, as recent events illustrate, little can be assumed to be safe from exposure. As Wichowski points out, policymakers can either strategize to keep their secrets safe or embrace an ethos of openness that rejects many of the pressures for secrecy, which allows states to *increase* national security rather than decrease it, going against the grain of traditional wisdom.

With respect to data collecting and analysis, a key question for policymakers will be determining *what big data means for their particular functional unit*. The promises of big data have been vast, and there are many reasons to be excited about the ability to visualise trends in large amount of data gathered through social media in order to find connections in the numbers that previously would have been difficult, or impossible, to uncover. For example, increased access to data from a variety of social media sources theoretically allows for tracking of the evolution of international crises, from its nascent stages to the end result of the crisis. Ongoing conflicts in the South China Sea, between Iran–Israel or Russia–Ukraine would be particularly amenable to monitoring through big data analysis since these conflicts are occurring at multiple levels of analysis, from the highest levels of state decision-making to popular media and culture. Monitoring this evolution at lower levels may well serve to provide insight into decision-making at higher levels.[3]

Foreign ministries and state departments need to maintain a strategy with big data that recalls an important truism in the social sciences: analysis is not the same as policymaking. Big data has a place, but it requires thinking clearly about what data, and cannot inform with respect to policy. Or, as Erin Simpson recently argued, "the information revolution is too important to be left to engineers alone" (Simpson 2014, para. 13). Data-gathering, visualization and analysis all requires sophisticated engineering tools, but the policymaking and diplomacy that stems from it will require sophisticated approaches to understanding what the data means.

Conclusion

Ultimately, the study of digital diplomacy is in its relative infancy, as is its use by policymakers. As scholars and practitioners continue to explore how these technologies can be used to manage various forms of international change, and as the technologies themselves continue to evolve, new questions and perspectives will be raised. What we do know is that if many policymakers are to be believed, the advent of social media is responsible for the most important innovation in diplomacy since the cable wire. The number of diplomats participating in online social networks is truly impressive. Ultimately, the utility of these practices in managing change will be reflected not in the numbers of diplomats using the tools but what the tools allow diplomats to *accomplish*. Outcomes, in other words, represent the future of digital diplomacy scholarship and will determine whether digital diplomacy lives up to its significant and exciting promise.

Notes

1 See, for example, Lucy Westcott. "NATO Diplomats Give Russians Geography Lessons on Twitter." *Newsweek,* August 28, 2014. www.newsweek.com/nato-diplomats-give-russians-geography-lessons-twitter-267400.
2 February 26, 2014 Tweet: https://twitter.com/WilliamJHague/statuses/438647305911406592
3 Similar strategies have been used in the past in order to construct national identity and social consciousness in such a way that it informs foreign policy decision-making Hopf 2002. Big data analysis may significantly increase the sources that can be drawn from and the insights gleaned from those sources.

GLOSSARY OF TERMS

Digital agenda-setting: The ability of social media to influence the salience of topics on the public agenda. Public diplomacy helps build a certain image of the country for foreign audiences by directing the latter's attention to certain topics, while downplaying others through well-selected news. Diplomats can thus construct an issue as salient and worthy of attention for their audience by repeatedly providing relevant information on that issue. Compared with traditional mass media, social media boasts a great advantage in "grabbing headlines" due to its reach, frequency, usability, immediacy and permanence. The nature of the bilateral relationship between countries influences the way in which social media is being used for diplomatic purposes. For example, due to painful historical memories of World War II, Japan prefers a cautious agenda-setting strategy, free of political or controversial topics, for its digital communications in China.

Digital conversation-generating: Social media, with its interactive features, has the potential to generate a quasi-continuous dialogue between diplomats and foreign publics. Two-way conversations allow diplomats to readjust the focus of their agenda, reduce misinformation and enhance mutual understanding. The conversation process involves a repetitive circuit of information-providing, receiving comments and reposts, providing feedback, readjusting information and making new comments. The strength of the conversation is influenced by feedbacks and the level of influence of the response group. In the absence of feedback from the target audience, the repetitive process stops after a one-shot conversation. The higher the status and recommunication capability of social media users, the stronger the conversation-generating process.

Digital diplomacy: Digital diplomacy broadly refers to use of the Internet and information communication technologies (ICTs), from video conferencing to social media platforms, to help state and non-state actors to manage international change. Digital diplomacy often encompasses at least three main components. First, it refers to the ways in which actors engage with outside audiences in order to project a particular message or image (the public-diplomacy component). Second, it refers to the ways in which foreign ministries and other agencies, both public and private, structure and organize information resources for their diplomats and other constituents (the information-accessibility component). Third, it refers to the ways in which actors acquire data on the ground in order to monitor subtle endogenous changes in political structures and public opinion (the data-analysis component).

Digital presence-expansion: Information dissemination has always been a central task in public diplomacy. Traditionally, diplomatic presence in the public sphere has been realized through mass communication, cultural exchanges or educational programs. The emergence of social media has extended the scope of diplomatic presence over space and time via tweets, posts and visual narratives. Presence expansion is measured via the levels of repost layers. The stronger the impact of a message, the greater the number of repost layers. Two or more repost layers suggest the influence of the message reaches beyond the immediate group of followers to a wider range. It is in this way that public diplomacy is able to expand its presence on social media.

Diplohacking: Diplohacking is a concept that combines the specific know-how and skill sets of diplomats, social entrepreneurs, tech developers and designers, along with that of journalists, academics, NGOs and businesses to 'hack' traditional diplomatic problems in start-up style groups. A Diplohack aims at tackling problems of global concern for the benefit of citizens worldwide, through co-creation (ideation and design process/hackathon/ideathon). At a Diplohack, one will *do* something rather than just talk; she will add value, co-create and find solutions. These solutions can be digital, but don't need to be, and can also result in high-level concepts, new networks or other innovations.

Diplomacy as change management: Diplomacy as change management is a theoretical approach to diplomacy which seeks to explain how diplomats reconcile structural pressures for maintaining the status quo versus promoting change. Different sources of change require different diplomatic tools in order to be effectively managed. Incremental change is characterized by subtle and minute variations in quotidian practice that may be difficult to detect due to the vast amounts of data and information generated from daily political life that needs to be analyzed. Exogenous shocks are more easily detected, when they occur, but managing them requires a challenge on the "demand side": major changes to the international political structure demands significant attention to reputations, negotiations, shared understandings and relationship construction. Digital diplomacy represents the former set of activities – the gathering and analyzing of data from foreign publics that accrues through listening to discourse on the ground. As a new technological development, digital diplomacy has the potential to revolutionize the practice of diplomacy by changing how diplomats engage in information management, public diplomacy, strategy planning, international negotiations or even crisis management.

E-court system: Electronic management system used at the International Criminal Court to collect, store and provide access to all orders, decisions and judgments of the Court, the filings of the participants, and evidence submitted by the participants, as well as transcripts of the proceedings. The e-court system is a collection of systems, including TRIM (Total Record Information Management), a software produced by Hewlett Packard, to store all filings, decisions, etc.; Ringtail, an evidence storage and management tool produced by FTI Consulting; and Transcend, an application produced by Legal Craft, to manage and store transcripts from hearings and trials. The Registry is the organ of the Court that is responsible for the e-court system.

'Have not' foreign service: Simply, a have-not foreign service is a ministry that has yet to awaken to the digital age. A culture of resistance to change, innovation and technology is pervasive, and often embodied in its minister and/or government. Anything 'new' – such as digital diplomacy, is often regarded with disdain. In 'have not' ministries, ambassadors and diplomats are forbidden to Tweet or chat with foreign publics for fear of saying the wrong thing, of impinging upon historic, careful and intricate traditional diplomatic strategies, ossified relationships and anachronistic playbooks.

Information hyperpower: Somewhat exclusively, this term relates to the United States of America who, from the 1940s onwards, sought to capitalize on its nascent position of global information and communications hegemony to establish and uphold a preponderance of information power. In doing so, the Americans would enjoy an information edge over rival great power states. Subsequently, information dominance became a key strategic aspect of US foreign policy.

International change: International change refers broadly to the ways in which the international system is fundamentally dynamic. There are at least two forms of change that are of interest to diplomats and other actors engaged in the practice of digital diplomacy: exogenous and endogenous. *Exogenous change* refers to the salient moments of major transformation in the system, which may include changes in the polarity of the system (i.e. the end of the Cold War), state birth, state death, the development of new transformative international organizations and treaties, and so forth. *Endogenous change* refers to subtle day-to-day minute occurrences in the international system, such as small-level protests, episodes of symbolic violence through social media, the use of social media tools by individual citizens and so forth that may seen inconsequential in any one instance but nevertheless ultimately result in important changes. Exogenous change is often referred to in terms of transformation of the structure of the international nation-state system while endogenous change is typically referred to in terms of daily practices of individuals and groups.

International Criminal Court: The ICC is the first and only permanent and independent international criminal court. It was created by a treaty called the Rome Statute, which went into effect on July 1, 2002. The ICC is charged with prosecuting "the most serious crimes of concern to the international community as a whole," namely genocide, crimes against humanity, and war crimes, and may at some future point have jurisdiction to prosecute the crime of aggression. It prosecutes individuals, and does not deal with disputes between States. The Court is based in The Hague, the Netherlands. It has three main organs: the Office of the Prosecutor, the Chambers (judges), and the Registry (support organ for the Court). As of August 8, 2014, 122 countries are parties to the Rome Statute, and they convene as the Assembly of States Parties to, *inter alia*, elect the Court's judges, Prosecutor and Deputy Prosecutor, to set the Court's budget, and to amend the Rome Statute.

Intrapreneurship: Short for *intra*corporate entre*preneur*, a term that describes the act of behaving like an entrepreneur while working within a large organization, taking new ideas and turning them in to profitable realities. The term, coined by Gifford Pinchot, is often used to analyze the role of innovation within institutions and enterprise (Pinchot and Pellman 1999). Empowered employment intrapreneurship include the skills of opportunity perception, teamwork, analyzing, stakeholder management, outside the box thinking, capacity building, personal initiative, planning, resource acquisition, project execution as well as some degree of risk-taking. In order to maximize outreach and impact, the diplomatic craft needs to foster internal cultures of intrapreneurship and collaboration to be able to connect with and understand its surroundings.

Leakers: Persons who share sensitive or classified information with the media or with the public en masse. Their identity may or may not be revealed, as exposure comes along with professional and legal risks for the leaker (Eliason 2006, 423). For this reason, many leakers release their secret information via media outlets whose reporters may have experience in protecting the identity of their sources (432). Leakers are occasionally permitted, and likely even encouraged, by government wishing to steer the public narrative (Davidson 2011, 75). But in cases where leaks prove damaging to government credibility, leakers have been tried and imprisoned.

Legitimacy crisis: An entity's loss of legitimacy due to degrading perceptions about the entity's validity and worth by significant related actors. It can be caused, for example, by an entity's failings or perceptions thereof. It can lead to loss of political, financial and/or logistical support from key partners, and consequent reduced ability, authority and/or power of the entity. The International Criminal Court is currently facing a legitimacy crisis in the eyes of many significant states parties and others whose collaboration and cooperation is necessary for the Court to do its work. This legitimacy crisis is caused by, *inter alia*, largely erroneous perceptions that it unfairly targets Africans, imposes Western notions of "justice" on non-Western societies, is inefficient and ineffective and conducts one-sided investigations and prosecutions. This legitimacy crisis has led states and other parties to refuse to cooperate with the Court, even when legally obligated to do so, and to threaten to withdraw from the Court entirely.

Luddite holdouts: This label is often affixed to ministries of foreign affairs that are steeped in a culture of resistance to change, particularly in terms of information and communication technology. It is a rather boorish term that compares certain ministries that have yet to develop digital diplomacy operations to nineteenth-century English textile artisans who protested, often violently so, to new technologies such as spinning frames and power looms introduced during the industrial revolution.

Metapower: The *process* of metapower illustrates transformations in identities and interests as a result of international interactions. In highly interactive environments, such as in the digital sphere, multiple perspectives and actors with varied identities negotiate their understandings of issues, in turn giving rise to new meanings. By contrast, in a noninteractive environment, meanings are affixed through authority rather than interaction. Metapower is antecedent to instrumental power, or power as *resource*, understood as the ability of X to constrain or enhance the ability of Y to do certain things. Metapower explains the meaning the identities of X & Y (what it means to be a nation state, for example) and those of their actions. New meanings introduced in global politics through the interactions of varied actors include issues such as securitization, human security, global services economy, forms of violence and cultural rights.

Nation branding: The process by which a national image may be created, promoted, monitored and managed in order to enhance the attractiveness of the nation (Fan 2010, 6). Scholars maintain that in a globalized economy nations must differentiate themselves one from another in order to successfully compete over a shrinking pool of available resources (Aronczyk 2008, 42). This differentiation is achieved by developing a unique national image. A nation's image is understood to be a cognitive mechanism similar to stereotypes. Thus, altering a nation's image is understood to be a lengthy and complex process involving governments, media and people (Kotler and Gertner 2002, 251). Successfully branding a nation calls for close cooperation between all parties taking part in the process, including policymakers, governmental ministries, marketing agencies and private corporations (Papadopoulos and Heslop 2002, 306). As a tool of image management, nation branding is nevertheless limited by the necessity of the promoted national image to hold true to reality. Reputation is therefore a form of feedback from audiences regarding the credibility of the nation's promoted image (Fan 2010, 5).

Network diplomacy: Diplomacy conducted through building sustained connections between governments, corporations, NGOs and individuals and from having the "knowledge and skills to harness that power to achieve a common purpose," where the actor "with the most connections will be regarded as the central player, able to set the global agenda and unlock innovation and sustainable growth" (Slaughter 2009, para. 4). It involves both internal and external networks. Actors must "nurture their own internal networks," and, where they "amass a great deal of useful information in a multitude of areas," must find ways to "facilitate the exchange of information across agencies and hierarchies." At the same time, actors must build and maintain "broader networks outside of" themselves, including to foreign governments, civil society, and the public at large (Metzl 2001). The International Criminal Court engages in network diplomacy: it fosters internal communication and knowledge-sharing among its three organs, the participants in its court proceedings, and other internal actors, to facilitate efficient and effective investigations and prosecutions; and it builds and maintains a diverse external network of supportive states, NGOs, intergovernmental organizations and the public, who are necessary for the Court to successfully perform its work. Ultimately, these networks provide the Court with both legitimacy and power. Digital diplomacy is one of the ways that the Court engages in network diplomacy to manage its endogenous ever-evolving casework, and to manage exogenous perceptions of its legitimacy and garner the external support crucial for its success.

New public diplomacy: Changes that occurred in the conceptualization and practice of public diplomacy following the proliferation and rapid adoption of social media platforms at the beginning of the twenty-first century. The new public diplomacy was born out of the need to contend with a transformed media ecology characterized by a fragmentation of audiences to networks of selective exposure (Hayden 2012, 3). New public diplomacy calls on foreign ministries to incorporate social media platforms into the practice of public diplomacy while utilizing its advantages, mainly through two way communication between diplomats and audiences (Metzgar 2012, 6). Two way communication separates new public diplomacy from twentieth-century public diplomacy which was based on a one way flow of information and limited interaction between communicator and recipient (Pamment 2013, 3). Following the adoption of social media platforms by diplomats, the goal of public diplomacy is transformed from the transmission of information to the building and leveraging of relationship with foreign publics. This may be achieved by engaging with and listening to foreign publics. Thus, new public diplomacy is characterized by dialogue, collaboration and inclusiveness.

Openness/open government: The policy and practice of making government-run activities and government-produced information accessible to the public. Based on the notion that in democratic states, the government "represents, and is paid for, by citizens," thus citizens have a right to know about governments activities (Bannister and Connolly 2012, 2). Open government includes the notion that information produced by the government should be treated as a national asset (O'Reilly 2011, 12). Challenges exist for governments in balancing the public's right to know and governments' needs to preserve the secrecy of certain kinds of information, such as that relating to national security, infrastructure vulnerabilities, and citizens personally identifiable information (Roberts 2004, 73).

Policy change: With policy defined as "whatever governments choose to do or not to do" (Dye 2008, 2), policy change consists of any shift to the *status quo* policy of a government. Policy changes can be characterized by the extent to which they represent a departure from the status quo, as per Hall's scheme of first-, second- and third-order changes (1993). First-order changes signify the smallest departure from the status quo, defined as routine adjustments to the settings of existing policy instruments (the devices or means employed by governments to implement policy decisions, e.g. regulation, tax credits or education campaigns). Second-order changes represent a larger departure from the status quo and occur when a government changes the policy instrument(s) employed but does not alter the goals to which these instruments are directed (e.g. switching from the use of regulation to tax credits to reduce an industry's greenhouse-gas emissions). Finally, third-order changes represent the largest departure from the status quo policy and occur when the normative and ontological worldview of policymakers change. In these cases, policy paradigms (entrenched beliefs, values and ideas) and policy styles (enduring patterns of problem solving, or 'ways of working') in a given policymaking setting are the object of change (Howlett and Ramesh 2003). The recognition of climate change as a socio-economic problem that should be addressed by government action would represent a third-order change in the case of a government that previously did not recognize or act to remedy climate change as a policy problem.

Policy-oriented learning: The process by which policymakers refine or adjust their operations so that they more efficiently and effectively reach policy goals. In Hall's (1993) theory of policy change, policy-oriented learning enables first- and second-order changes but not more substantive third-order changes. That is, policy-oriented learning induces changes to the settings of policy instruments, or to the mix of policy instruments employed in addressing a particular policy issue, but not to the goals to which those instruments are employed, or the worldview within which the policymakers employing these instruments operate (Sabatier 1988; Sabatier and Jenkins-Smith, 1993).

Public diplomacy: Form of diplomatic engagement that aims at understanding, informing and influencing the attitudes of foreign publics for the purpose of advancing the interests and extending the values of a particular state (Sharp 2005, 106; Pamment 2013, 8). PD can be specific (e.g. directed at a particular public in a particular country) or diffuse (e.g. directed more generally at publics around the world). PD includes daily communications, to explain the context of domestic and foreign policy decisions; strategic communication, to develop a set of simple themes in support of a policy initiative; and relationship-building with key individuals over many years through scholarships, exchanges, training, seminars, conferences and access to media channels (Nye 2008, 102). The 'tough-minded' school of public diplomacy insists the main purpose of PD is to maximize influence on the attitudes of foreign audiences. Objectivity and truth are considered important tools of persuasion but they are not extolled as great virtues in themselves. The 'tender-minded' school argues, in exchange, the main objective of public diplomacy is the establishment of a climate of mutual understanding. Truth, therefore, is considered essential, much more than a persuasion tactic (Bjola and Kornprobst, 156).

Secrecy: The practice and culture within governments withholding information. Described as the "intentional concealment of information by individuals or groups (Simmel 1906; Bok 1989 in Maret and Goldman 2009, xv), and a form of calculated information control and concealment (Tefft 1980, 1992). Secrecy in government as a practice is associated with the idea of compulsory or mandatory information concealment, "reinforced by the prospect of sanctions for disclosure" (Friedrich 1972, 176). A culture of secrecy can also be thought of as a "second world" within government (Simmel 1906), in which the default action with respect to information is to withhold or conceal. Secrecy as a mode of information regulation within government co-exists with mechanisms that encourage transparency within some aspects of government operations (Maretand Goldman 2009).

Selfie diplomacy: The use of social networking sites (e.g. Facebook, Twitter) by foreign ministries in order to conduct nation branding activities. As a tool of image management, selfie diplomacy enables nations to reach large audiences without the mediation of local institutions. Moreover, it enables nations to publish content regarding their concrete actions in the global arena thus ensuring that a nation's promoted image holds true with reality. By operating at both the ministry and embassy levels, selfie diplomacy enables nations to tailor nation branding campaigns to the unique characteristics of local audiences such as culture, values and previous perception of foreign countries. By engaging with and listening to local audiences, nations may use selfie diplomacy in order to evaluate the effectiveness of their nation-branding campaigns. As a theoretical concept, selfie diplomacy suggests that the analysis of nations' social media channels enables the characterization of the image being promoted by a certain country while also evaluating the extent to which this image has been accepted by audiences.

Smart power (SP): Concept first described by Joseph Nye as the ability to combine hard and soft power resources into effective strategies. Academically, SP should be seen mostly as a practice of power conversion, the first step of which is understanding the full range of power resources and the problems of combining them effectively in various contexts (Nye 2013, 565). Outside academic circles, SP has also been seen as using the full range of new tools to protect national interests and leverage influence abroad – including through public diplomacy and social media sites in order to reach out to both friends and adversaries, to bolster old alliances and forge new ones (Filiatrault 2012).

Twiplomacy: Online form of public diplomacy through the use of Twitter by diplomats, politicians, foreign affairs departments and other public figures and stakeholders. Twiplomacy is meant to increase efficiency, inclusiveness, and engagement, through targeted tweets @ ("at") specific people/users, dissemination of official stances, engagement with stakeholders and members of the audience and/or direct connection through individual "following" and direct and private messaging. Twiplomacy is seen not as solving the world problems, or to have a conversation, but as increasing the audience of a country's messaging and bridging the gap between diplomats and citizens, since public users of the social platform can be followed by anyone, anywhere in the world.

Virtual embassy (VE): Online presence of a state that previously closed down its physical diplomatic mission in another country, thus severing diplomatic ties between the two countries. Examples of this can be seen through the VEs of the United States in Iran, where the former has not had a real-life diplomatic mission for several decades; and Israel for the Gulf Cooperation Council (GCC) countries where the Jewish State has not been allowed to open direct communication lines, or set up permanent missions. VEs can allow states to facilitate at least a one-way mode of conversing, usually with the dissenting minority voices of citizens where physical permanent missions no longer exist, and these conversations usually include maintaining some form of economic, political and cultural engagement with those citizens. Some of the VEs already set up have been used also as additional platforms for propaganda dissemination, through links to press releases and other pages about constitutional history, or rights and freedoms, with little to no support for real interactions. Finally, VEs also provide consular information and guidelines for citizens in need of such support.

Wikileaks: The November 2011 mass release of classified US government diplomatic information by Chelsea Manning, aided by the WikiLeaks organization and its founder, Julian Assange. The WikiLeaks organization had released hundreds of thousands of documents since its founding in 2006, but following the global shockwaves following the leak of the US diplomatic cables in 2011, the term "Wikileaks" became associated with that incident as much as than the organization itself (Hood 2011, 635). The November 2011 leak alerted diplomats to the complications of digital information sharing – while still valued for fostering greater collaboration and transparency, Wikileaks also created an air of nervousness among diplomats, some of whom vowed to scale back technology use (Cull 2011, 6). The popular support for Wikileaks has been tied to a backlash against a 'habit of secretiveness' in the US (Page and Spence, 2011).

BIBLIOGRAPHY

Articles and books

Adler, E. 1991. "Cognitive Evolution: A Dynamic Approach for the Study of International Relations and Their Progress." In *Progress in Postwar International Relations,* edited by E. Adler and B. Crawford, 43–88. New York: Columbia University Press.

Adler, E., and V. Pouliot (2011). *International Practices.* Cambridge: Cambridge University Press.

Agichtein, E., Castillo, C., Donato, D., Gionis, A. and Mishne, G. 2008. "Finding High Quality Content in Social Media."In Proceedings of the 2008 International Conference on Web Search and Data Mining, edited by M. Najork, 183–194. New York: ACM.

Ajami, F. 1993. "The Summoning: 'But They Said, We Will not Hearken'." *Foreign Affairs* 72(4): 2–9.

An, X. 2011. *EU in China: Herman Van Rompuy's Diplomacy on Weibo.* Accessed March 18, 2013. http://media.people.com.cn/GB/22114/150608/150616/17202343.html.

Andersson, J. 2009. "Q&A re Pirate Politics." Accessed October 13, 2009. http://liquidculture.wordpress.com/2009/10/13/qa-re-pirate-politics/.

Anholt, S. 2005. "Anholt Nation Brands Index: How Does the World See America?" *Journal of Advertising Research* 45(3): 296–304.

Anholt, S. and J. Hilderth. 2005. "Let Freedom and Cash Registers Ring: America as a Brand." *Place Branding* 1(2): 1–4.

Anonymized DFAIT official. (2012). *DM working dinner: open_policy@DFAIT* (Internal report). Ottawa: Department of Foreign Affairs and International Trade Canada.

Arias-Hernandez, R., T. M. Green, and B. Fisher. 2012. "From Cognitive Amplifiers to Cognitive Prostheses: Understandings of the Material Basis of Cognition in Visual Analytics." *Interdisciplinary Science Reviews* 37(1): 4–18.

Aronczyk, M. 2008. "'Living the Brand': Nationality, Globality, and the Identity Strategies of Nation Branding Consultants." *International Journal of Communication* 2: 41–65.

———. 2013. *Branding the Nation: The Global Business of National Identity.* Oxford: Oxford University Press.

Åström Gröndahl, J. 2014. *Diplomat idag, Röster om en ny verklighet.* Stockholm: Atlantis.

Bannister, F., and R. Connolly. 2012. "The Trouble with Transparency: A Critical Review of Openness in E-government." *Policy & Internet* 3(1). Accessed on December 18, 2014. http://onlinelibrary.wiley.com/doi/10.2202/1944-2866.1076/pdf.

Barnett, M., and R. Duvall, eds. 2005. *Power in Global Governance*. Cambridge, UK: Cambridge University Press.

Barton, C. 2012. "Twitter Diplomacy."Accessed September 5, 2014. www.nzherald.co.nz/business/news/article.cfm?c_id=3&objectid=10828967.

Baumgartner, T., W. Buckley, and T. Burns. 1975. "Relational Control: The Human Structuring of Cooperation and Conflict." *Journal of Conflict Resolution* 19: 419–440.

BBC. 2012, May 28. China's Weibo Microblog Introduces User Contracts. Accessed April 17, 2014. www.bbc.co.uk/news/technology-18208446.

BBC Home. 2014. "Chinese New Year." Accessed April 26, 2014. www.bbc.co.uk/schools/events/chinesenewyear/.

BBC World Service Poll. 2007. *World View of US Role Goes From Bad to Worse*. Accessed June 2, 2014. http://news.bbc.co.uk/2/shared/bsp/hi/pdfs/23_01_07_us_poll.pdf.

BBC World Service Poll. 2013. *The United States*. Accessed May 27, 2014. www.worldpublicopinion.org/pipa/2013%20Country%20Rating%20Poll.pdf.

Bengtsson, S. 2011. "Virtual Nation Branding: The Swedish Embassy in Second Life." *Journal For Virtual Worlds Research* 4(2). Accessed December 8, 2014. https://journals.tdl.org/jvwr/index.php/jvwr/article/view/2111/5547.

Bennett, S. 2013. "Social Media Overload – How Much Information Do We Process Each Day?" Accessed December 18, 2014. www.mediabistro.com/alltwitter/social-media-overload_b47316.

Berger, P. L., and T. Luckmann. 1966. *The Social Construction of Reality*. Garden City, NY: Doubleday.

Berridge, G. 2004. *Diplomatic Classics: Selected Texts from Commynes to Vattel: Studies in Diplomacy and International Relations*. Houndmills, UK: Palgrave Macmillan.

Beyer, J. 2014. "The Emergency of a Freedom of Information Movement: Anonymous, Wikileaks, and the Pirate Party and Iceland." *Journal of Computer-Mediated Communication* 19(2), 2: 141–154.

Bigo, D. 2011. "Pierre Bourdieu and International Relations: Power of Practices, Practices of Power." *International Political Sociology* 5(3): 225–258.

Bildt, C. 2013. *Statement of Foreign Policy 2013*. Accessed September 20, 2014. www.government.se/content/1/c6/20/90/55/6b351368.pdf.

———. 2014. "Talk to TedXSalonStockholm." Accessed September 20, 2014. https://www.youtube.com/watch?v=zldG_bhhNU8.

Bird, D., M. Ling, and K. Haynes. 2012. "Flooding Facebook: The Use of Social Media during the Queensland and Victorian Floods." *The Australian Journal of Emergency Management* 27(1), 27–33.

Bishop, D. 2014. "Interview: Ambassador Laurence Pope on the State Department, the Foreign Service, and Public Diplomacy in the 21st Century." *Public Diplomacy Council*. Accessed January 5, 2015. http://www.publicdiplomacycouncil.org/commentaries/03-05-14/interview-ambassador-laurence-pope-state-department-foreign-service-and-public.

Bjola, C. 2013. "Understanding Enmity and Friendship in World Politics: The Case for a Diplomatic Approach." *The Hague Journal of Diplomacy* 8, 1–20.

Bjola, C., and M. Kornprobst. 2013. *Understanding International Diplomacy: Theory, Practice and Ethics*. New York: Taylor & Francis.

Bok, S. (1989). *Secrets: on the ethics of concealment and revelation*. Vintage Books: New York.

Bolewski, W. 2007. *Diplomacy and International Law in Globalized Relations*. New York: Springer.

Booth, K., and N. Wheeler. 2008. *Security Dilemma: Fear, Cooperation, and Trust in World w*. London: Palgrave Macmillan.

Bourdieu, P. 1977. *Equisse d'une theorie de la pratique*. Cambridge: Cambridge University Press.

Brand, S., Kelly, K. & Dyson, G. 2011. "An Edge conversation in Munich." *Edge@dld*. Accessed December 10, 2014. http://edge.org/conversation/edge-dld-an-edge-conversation-in-munich.

Bronk, C., and S. Smith. 2012. "How Data Visualization Can Change Diplomacy." *Foreign Service Journal* March: 11–15.

Bush, G.H.W., and B. Scowcroft. 1999. *A World Transformed*. New York: Vintage Books.

Bull, H. 1997. *The Anarchical Society: A Study of Order in World Politics*. 2nd ed. Houndmills, UK: Macmillan.

Burns, A., and Eltham, B. 2009. "Twitter Free Iran: An Evaluation of Twitter's Role in Public Diplomacy and Information Operations in Iran's 2009 Election Crisis." *Record of the Communications Policy & Research Forum*: 298–310.

Burson-Marsteller, 2013. *Twiplomacy 2013: How World Leaders Connect on Twitter*. Accessed December 12, 2014. www.burson-marsteller.com/what-we-do/our-thinking/twiplomacy 2013/.

Buzan, B. 2004. *From International to World Society? English School Theory and the Structure of Globalization*. Cambridge, UK: Cambridge University Press.

Buzan, B., and R. Little. 2000. *International Systems in World History: Remaking the Study of International Relations*. Oxford, UK: Oxford University Press.

Callières, M. F. de (1716) 1963. *On the Manner of Negotiating with Princes; on the Uses of Diplomacy; the Choice of Ministers and Envoys; and the Personal Qualities Necessary for Success in Missions Abroad*. Notre Dame, IN: University of Notre Dame Press.

Capoccia, G., and R. D. Kelemen. 2011. "The Study of Critical Junctures: Theory, Narrative, and Counterfactuals in Historical Institutionalism." *World Politics* 59(3): 341–369.

Carnegie, D. 1936. *How to Win Friends and Influence People*. London: Vermilion.

Chatterjee, C. 2007. *International Law and Diplomacy*. London: Routledge.

"China Blocks Skype: Other Websites the Country Has Blocked." 2010. *Telegraph*, December 30. Accessed April 14, 2014. www.telegraph.co.uk/technology/internet/8231459/China-blocks-Skype-other-websites-the-country-has-blocked.html.

"China Completes Leadership Transition with Growing Maturity of Power Transfer Mechanism." 2013. *Xinhua Net*, March 17. Accessed April 24, 2014. http://news.xinhuanet.com/english/china/2013-03/17/c_124467482.htm.

Clark-Dickson, P. 2013. "OTT Messaging Traffic Will Be Twice the Volume of P2P SMS Traffic by End-2013." *Informatandm*. Accessed December 18, 2014. www.informa.com/Media-centre/Press-releases--news/Latest-News/OTT-messaging-traffic-will-be-twice-volume-of-P2P-SMS-traffic-this-year/Clase 2014 http://blog.swedenabroad.se/uk/.

Clase. 2012. Blog. Accessed August 29, 2014. http://blog.swedenabroad.se/uk/2012/09/28/modern-diplomacy-in-a-digital-age/.

Clinton, H. 2012. "The Art of Smart Power." *New Statesman*, July 18. Accessed April 17, 2014. www.newstatesman.com/politics/politics/2012/07/hillary-clinton-art-smart-power.

Cohen, R. 1998. "Putting Diplomatic Studies on the Map." *Diplomatic Studies Program Newsletter*: 1. Leicester: Centre for the Study of Diplomacy.

Corrie, K. 2013. *Victims' Participation at the ICC: Purpose, Early Developments and Lessons*. AMICC. Accessed August 8, 2014. http://amicc.org/docs/Victims_Participation.pdf.

Constantinou, C. M. 2013. "Between Statecraft and Humanism: Diplomacy and Its Forms of Knowledge." *International Studies Review* 15(2): 141–162.

Conti, L. 2011. *Il canale digital della diplomazia*. Accessed May 30, 2012. www.ilsole24ore.com/art/tecnologie/2011-07-21/canale-digitale-diplomazia-182239.shtml?uuid=AaD1g6pD.

Cooper, H. 2014. "Pentagon finds Washington Navy Yard killings could have been prevented." *The New York Times*. Accessed December 10, 2014. www.nytimes.com/2014/03/19/us/navy-yard-rampage-could-have-been-prevented-pentagon-review-says.html.

Copeland, D. 2009. *Guerrilla Diplomacy: Rethinking International Relations*. London: Lynne Rienner.

Cornago, N. 2013. *Plural Diplomacies: Normative Predicaments and Functional Imperatives*. Boston: Brill.

Couldry, N. 2012. *Media, Society, World: Social Theory and Digital Media Practice*. Cambridge: Polity.

Cowan, J, and A. Arsenault. 2008. "Moving from Monologue to Dialogue to Collaboration: Three Layers of Public Diplomacy." *The ANNALS of the American Academy of Political and Social Science* 616(1): 10–30.

Cox, R. 2013. "Shaheen to Obama: 'Over-Classification' in Government Costs Taxpayers Money." *The Hill*. Accessed May 30, 2014. http://itk.thehill.com/blogs/floor-action/senate/302629-shaheen-to-obama-over-classification-in-government-costs-taxpayers-money.

Coyne, C. J., and C. T. Leeson. 2009. "Media as a Mechanism of Institutional Change and Reinforcement." *Kyklos* 62(1): 1–14. Accessed September 20, 2014. www.peterleeson.com/media_and_inst_change.pdf.

Cull, N. J. 2011. "Wikileaks, Public Diplomacy 2.0, and the State of Digital Public Diplomacy. *Place Branding and Public Diplomacy*, 7(1): 1–8.

———. 2013. "The Long Road to Public Diplomacy 2.0: The Internet in US Public Diplomacy." *International Studies Review* 15(1): 123–139.

Currier, C. 2013. "Charting Obama's Crackdown on National Security Leaks." *ProPublica*. Accessed July 30, 2014. www.propublica.org/special/sealing-loose-lips-charting-obamas-crackdown-on-national-security-leaks.

Davidson, M. 2008. "Cultural Relations: Building Networks to Face Twenty-First-Century Challenges." In *Engagement: Public Diplomacy in a Globalised World*, 76–89. London: Foreign and Commonwealth Office. Accessed September 20, 2014. http://uscpublicdiplomacy.org/sites/uscpublicdiplomacy.org/files/useruploads/u26739/Engagement_FCO.pdf.

Davidson, S. 2011. "Leaks, Leakers and Journalists: Adding Historical Context to the Age of Wikileaks." *Hastings Communication & Entertainment Law Journal*, 27.

Denstadli, J. M., T. E. Julsrud, and R. J. Hjorthol. 2012. "Videoconferencing as a Mode of Communication: A Comparative Study of the Use of Videoconferencing and Face-to-Face Meetings." *Journal of Business and Technical Communication* 26(1): 65–91.

Department of Foreign Affairs and Trade. 2010. Annual Report 2009–2010, viewed December 8, 2014, www.dfat.gov.au/dept/annual_reports/09_10/performance/1/1.1.html

Department of Foreign Affairs and International Trade Canada. (2012). *Open Policy Development* (Unpublished Internal Document). Ottawa: Government of Canada.

Department of Foreign Affairs and International Trade Canada. 2013a. *Departmental Performance Report 2012–13*. Accessed March 18, 2014. www.international.gc.ca/department-ministere/plans/dpr-rmr/dpr_rmr_1213.aspx?lang=eng.

Department of Foreign Affairs and International Trade Canada. 2013b. *Report on Plans and Priorities* 2013–14. Accessed March 17, 2014. www.international.gc.ca/department-ministere/plans/rpp/rpp_1314.aspx?lang=eng.

Der Derian, J. 1987. *On Diplomacy: A Genealogy of Western Estrangement*. Oxford: B. Blackwell.

Deruda, A. 2012. *Diplomazia Digitale: La politica estera e i social media.* Milan: Apogeo.
Diamond, J. 1987. "Soft Sciences Are Often Harder Than Hard Sciences." *Discover,* August. Accessed January 14, 2015. www.jareddiamond.org/Jared_Diamond/Further_Reading_files/Diamond%201987_1.pdf.
Dill, J., R. Earnshaw, D. Kasik, J. Vince, and P. C. Wong. 2012. *Expanding the Frontiers of Visual Analytics and Visualization.* New York: Springer.
DiNucci, D. 1999. "Fragmented Future." *Print* 53(4): 32.
DiPLO. 2013a. *Background: e-Diplomacy.* Accessed August 11, 2013. www.diplomacy.edu/e-diplomacy/background%20info.
DiPLO. 2013b. *History and Approach.* Accessed August 9, 2013. www.diplomacy.edu/aboutus/history.
Diplohack. 2014. Accessed August 28, 2014. www.diplohack.org/.
Dizard, W. P. 2001. *Digital Diplomacy: U.S. Foreign Policy in the Information Age.* Westport, CT: Praeger.
Doidge, N. 2007. *The Brain That Changes Itself: Stories of Personal Triumph from the Frontiers of Brain Science.* New York: Penguin.
Douglas, M. 2003. *Purity and Danger: An Analysis of Concepts of Pollution and Taboo.* London: Routledge.
Drury, I. 2013. "Downloaded onto Lady Gaga CDs and Transferred to a Memory Stick: The Staggeringly Simple Theft of 250,000 Top Secret Documents." *The Daily Mail.* Accessed December 18, 2014. www.dailymail.co.uk/news/article-1333982/WikiLeaks-US-Army-soldier-Bradley-Manning-prime-suspect-leaks-case.html.
Duvall, Raymond, and Arjun Chowdhury. "Practices of Theory." In *International Practices,* edited by Emanuel Adler and Vincent Pouliot, 335–54. Cambridge University Press, 2011.
Dye, T. R. 2008. *Understanding Public Policy.* 12th ed. Upper Saddle River, NJ: Pearson/Prentice Hall.
Egardt, P. 2011. *Utrikesförvaltning i världsklass (SOU 2011:21).* Stockholm: Statens Offentliga Utredningar. Accessed September 12, 2014. www.regeringen.se/sb/d/108/a/162533.
Egashiru, S. 2013. *Globalism and Regional Economy.* London: Routledge.
Ekman, P. 2009. *Telling Lies: Clues to Deceit in the Marketplace, Politics, and Marriage.* New York: Norton.
Ekman, P., and M. O'Sullivan. 1991. "Who Can Catch a Liar?" *American Psychologist* 46(9): 913.
Eleta, I., and J. Golbeck. 2012. "Bridging Languages in Social Networks: How Multilingual Users of Twitter Connect Language Communities." *Proceedings of the American Society for Information Science and Technology* 49(1): 1–4.
Eliason, R. 2006. "Leakers, Bloggers, and Fourth Estate Inmates: The Misguided Pursuit of a Reporter's Privilege." *Cardozo Arts & Entertainment Law Journal,* 24.
Ellsberg, D. 2013. "Snowden Made the Right Call When He Fled the U.S." *The Washington Post,* Accessed December 18, 2014. www.washingtonpost.com/opinions/daniel-ellsberg-nsa-leaker-snowden-made-the-right-call/2013/07/07/0b46d96c-e5b7-11e2-aef3-339619eab080_story.html.
EPIC. 2013. "Electronic Privacy Information Center v. DHS – SOP 303." Accessed December 18, 2014. https://epic.org/foia/EPICVDHS-SOP303-Order.pdf.
Fagan, K. 2011. "Man Shot to Death by BART Officer Identified." *SFGate.* Accessed December 18, 2014. www.sfgate.com/crime/article/Man-shot-to-death-by-BART-officer-identified-2355477.php.
Fan, Y. 2010. "Branding the Nation: Towards a Better Understanding." *Place Branding and Public Diplomacy,* 6(2): 97–103.

Fang, I. E. 1997. *A History of Mass Communication: Six Information Revolutions*. Boston: Focal Press.
Farber, D. 2013. "Google Search Scratches Its Brain 500 Million Times a Day." *CNET*, Accessed December 18, 2014. www.cnet.com/news/google-search-scratches-its-brain-500-million-times-a-day/.
Farrell, H. and Finnemore, M. 2013. "The end of hypocrisy: American foreign policy in the age of leaks." *Foreign Affairs*. Accessed December 18, 2014. www.foreignaffairs.com/articles/140155/henry-farrell-and-martha-finnemore/the-end-of-hypocrisy.
Fearon, J. D. 1994. "Domestic Political Audiences and the Escalation of International Disputes." *American Political Science Review*: 577–592.
Fearon, J. D. 1995. "Rationalist Explanations for War." *International Organization* 49: 379–414.
Filiatrault, R. 2012. *The Rise of Twiplomacy: What Canada Can Learn from Hillary Clinton*. Accessed September 7, 2014. www.ottawacitizen.com/news/rise+Twiplomacy+What+Canada+learn+from+Hillary+Clinton/7209415/story.html.
Finnemore, M., and K. Sikkink. 1998. "International Norm Dynamics and Political Change." *International Organization* 52(4): 887–917.
Fisher, A. 2013. "Diplomats – Get Into Data." USC Center on Public Diplomacy. Accessed January 6, 2015. http://uscpublicdiplomacy.org/blog/diplomats%E2%80%94get-data.
Fitchard, K. 2013. "Ericsson: Global Smartphone Penetration Will Reach 60% in 2019." *Gigaom*, Accessed December 18, 2014. https://gigaom.com/2013/11/11/ericsson-global-smartphone-penetration-will-reach-60-in-2019/.
Fletcher, T. 2012. Blog: The Naked Diplomat. http://blogs.fco.gov.uk/tomfletcher/2012/10/02/the-naked-diplomat/).
Foreign and Commonwealth Office. 2012. Executive Summary. Accessed December 5, 2014. http://blogs.fco.gov.uk/digitaldiplomacy/digital-strategy/executive-summary/.
Foreign and Commonwealth Office. (2011). *Digital Excellence: Review of Digital Working Final Report* (Unpublished Internal Document). London: HM Government.
Foreign and Commonwealth Office. (2012). *The Foreign and Commonwealth Office Digital Strategy*. London: HM Government. Retrieved from https://www.gov.uk/government/uploads/system/uploads/attachment_data/file/39629/AB_12-11-14_Digital_strategy.pdf.
Foreign and Commonwealth Office. 2013a. *Annual Report and Accounts 2012–13*. London: H. M. Government. Accessed May 7, 2013. https://www.gov.uk/government/uploads/system/uploads/attachment_data/file/210136/HC_32_v0_2.pdf.
Foreign and Commonwealth Office. 2013b. *Mid Year Report to Parliament: 1 April to 30 September 2013*. London: H.M. Government.
Foreign and Commonwealth Office. (2013c). FCO Social Media Policy. Retrieved March 27, 2014, from http://blogs.fco.gov.uk/digitaldiplomacy/social-media-policy/.
Foreign and Commonwealth Office. 2014. *Working for FCO*. Accessed March 18, 2014. https://www.gov.uk/government/organisations/foreign-commonwealth-office/about/recruitment.
Frank, R. H. 1988. *Passions Within Reason: The Strategic Role of the Emotions*. New York: Norton.
Franke, T., 2011. *Social Media: The Frontline of Cyberdefence?* Accessed May 30, 2012. www.nato.int/docu/review/2011/Social_Medias/cyberdefense-social-media/EN/index.htm.
Freeland, C., 2012a. "Blending Governance and Twitter." *New York Times*, April 5. Accessed September 17, 2012. www.nytimes.com/2012/04/06/us/06iht-letter06.html?_r=1.
———. 2012b. "Statecraft via Twitter." *Reuters*, April 5. Accessed May 30, 2012. http://blogs.reuters.com/chrystia-freeland/2012/04/05/statecraft-via-twitter/.

Freeman, C. W. 1997. *Arts of Power: Statecraft and Diplomacy.* Washington, DC: United States Institute of Peace Press.

Freire, P. 2000 (1976). *The Pedagogy of the Oppressed.* New York: Herder & Herder.

Friedrich, C. J. 1972. *The Pathology of Politics: Violence, Betrayal, Corruption, Secrecy and Propaganda.* London: Harper & Row.

Fullerton, J. A., A. Kendrick, K. Chan, M. Hamilton, and G. Kerr. 2007. "Attitudes Towards American Brand and Brand America." *Place Branding and Public Diplomacy* 3(3): 205–212.

Fung, B. 2012. "Digital Diplomacy: Why It's So Tough for Embassies to Get Social Media Right?" *The Atlantic,* October 17. Accessed August 7, 2013. http://www.theatlantic.com/international/archive/2012/10/digital-diplomacy-why-its-so-tough-for-embassies-to-get-social-media-right/263744/.

"G-20Summit: A Billion Dollar Waste of Time." (2010). *Maclean's,* June 17. Accessed November 10, 2014. www.macleans.ca/news/canada/why-host-a-billion-dollar-photo-op-the-real-work-is-done-elsewhere/.

Garfield, S. 2013. *To the Letter: A Celebration of the Lost Art of Letter Writing.* New York: Gotham Books.

Geertz, C. 1973. *The Interpretation of Cultures: Selected Essays.* Vol. 5019. New York: Basic Books.

Gerring, J. 2007. *Case Study Research: Principles and Practices.* Cambridge: Cambridge University Press.

Gerstein, J. 2013. "Samantha Power defends Obama Syria stance." Accessed December 10, 2014. www.politico.com/story/2013/11/women-rule-event-samantha-power-100124.html.

Geybullayeva, A. 2012. "Nagorno Karabakh 2.0: How New Media and Track Two Diplomacy Initiatives are Fostering Change." *Journal of Muslim Minority Affairs* 32(2): 176–185.

Ghannam, J. 2011. *Social Media in the Arab World: Leading up to the Uprisings of 2011.* Center for International Media Assistance/National Endowment for Democracy. Accessed April 2, 2014. http://cima.ned.org/sites/default/files/CIMA-Arab_Social_Media-Report%20-%2010-25-11.pdf.

Giddens, A. 1984. *The Constitution of Society: Outline of the Theory of Structuration.* Berkeley: University of California Press.

Goffman, E. 1959. *The Presentation of Self in Everyday Life.* New York: Penguin.

Google. 2014. *Google Annual Search Statistics.* AccessedDecember 18, 2014. www.statisticbrain.com/google-searches/.

Granger, L. 2013. "Billions of Users and Tweets per Minute: Social Media in 2013 by the Numbers." *Memeburn,* December 30. Accessed December 18, 2014. http://memeburn.com/2013/12/billions-of-users-and-tweets-per-minute-social-media-in-2013-by-the-numbers/.

Griffiths, E. 2013. "Tony Abbott Seeks to Explain Baddies Versus Baddies Comment on Situation in Syria." *ABC News.* Accessed August 18, 2013. www.abc.net.au/news/2013–09–02/abbott-seeks-to-explain-baddies-v-baddies-comment/4929118.

Grübler, A. 1998. *Technology and Global Change.* Cambridge, UK: Cambridge University Press.

Gudjonsson, H. 2005. "Nation Branding." *Place Branding,* 1(3): 283–298.

Guttman, N. 2009. "Once labeled an AIPAC Spy, Larry Franklin Tells His Story." *The Forward,* July 10. Accessed December 18, 2014. http://forward.com/articles/108778/once-labeled-an-aipac-spy-larry-franklin-tells-his/.

Gustin, S., 2011. "Digital Diplomacy." *Time,* September 2. Accessed May 7, 2012. www.time.com/time/specials/packages/article/0,28804,2091589_2091591_2091592,00.html.

Hall, P. A. 1993. "Policy Paradigms, Social Learning, and the State: The Case of Economic Policymaking in Britain." *Comparative Politics* 25(3): 275–296.

Hall, P. A., and R.C.R. Taylor. 1996. "Political Science and the Three New Institutionalisms." *Political Studies* 44(5): 936–957.

Hall, R. B. 1999. *National Collective Identity: Social Constructs and International Systems.* New York: Columbia University Press.

Hall, T., and K. Yarhi-Milo. 2012. "The Personal Touch: Leaders' Impressions, Costly Signaling, and Assessments of Sincerity in International Affairs." *International Studies Quarterly* 56(3): 560–573.

Hallams, E. 2011. "From Crusader to Exemplar: Bush, Obama and the Reinvigoration of America's Soft Power." *European Journal of American Studies* 6(1) Spring: 1–21.

Hanson, F. 2010. *A Digital DFAT: Joining the 21st Century.* Sydney, Australia: Lowy Institute for International Policy.

———. 2012a. "Being E-aware Is Diplomacy 101." *The Australian*, March 28, p. 9.

———. 2012b. *Revolution@ State: The Spread of Ediplomacy.* Sydney, Australia: Lowy Institute for International Policy.

———. 2012c. "Baked in and Wired: eDiplomacy@State." *Brookings Institute Foreign Policy Paper Series, number 30 of 32* October: 1–41.

———. 2012d. "Ediplomacy: The Revolution Continues." *The Interpreter*, October 29. Accessed August 9, 2013. www.lowyinterpreter.org/post/2012/10/29/Ediplomacy-The-revolution-continues.aspx.

———. 2012e. "Alec Ross on the Future of Ediplomacy." *Brookings Up Front.* Accessed January 5, 2015. http://www.brookings.edu/blogs/up-front/posts/2012/04/12-ediplomacy-future-ross-hanson.

Hassett, M. 2011. "Social Media, Social Change." *CNN*, January 26. Accessed April 24, 2014. http://newsstream.blogs.cnn.com/2011/01/26/social-media-social-change/.

Hayden, C. 2012. "Social Media at State: Power, Practice and Conceptual Limits for US Public Diplomacy?" *Global Media Journal* Fall: 1–15.

———. 2013. "Engaging Technologies: A Comparative Study of U.S. and Venezuelan Strategies of Influence and Public Diplomacy." *International Journal of Communication* 7: 1–25.

Heibeck, T., and A. Pentland. 2010. *Honest Signals: How They Shape Our World.* Cambridge, MA: MIT Press.

Heine, J. 2006. *On the Manner of Practising the New Diplomacy.* Center for International Governance Innovation. Accessed August 8, 2014. www.cigi.org/sites/default/files/Paper11_Jorge_Heine.pdf.

Himelfarb, S. 2014. "Can Big Data Stop Wars Before They Happen?" *Foreign Policy Argument.* Accessed January 6, 2015. http://foreignpolicy.com/2014/04/25/can-big-data-stop-wars-before-they-happen/.

Hocking, B. 2008. "Reconfiguring Public Diplomacy: From Competition to Collaboration." In *Engagement: Public Diplomacy in a Globalised World*, 62–75. London: Foreign and Commonwealth Office. Accessed September 10, 2014. http://uscpublicdiplomacy.org/sites/uscpublicdiplomacy.org/files/useruploads/u26739/Engagement_FCO.pdf.

Hocking, B., J. Melissen, S. Riordan, and P. Sharp. 2012. *Futures for Diplomacy: Integrative Diplomacy for the 21st Century.* Netherlands Institute of International Relations: Clingendael. Accessed October 22, 2014. www.clingendael.nl/publications/2012/20121017_research_melissen.pdf.

Hoffman, D. 2002. "Beyond Public Diplomacy." *Foreign Affairs*: 83–95.

Holmes, M. 2013. "The Force of Face-to-Face Diplomacy: Mirror Neurons and the Problem of Intentions." *International Organization* 67(4): 829–861.

Holmes, M. forthcoming. Believing This and Alieving That: Theorizing Affect and Intuitions in International Politics. *International Studies Quarterly.*

Hood, C. 2011. "From FOI World to Wikileaks World: A New Chapter in the Transparency Story?" *Governance* 24(4): 635–638.

Hopf, T. 2002. *Social Construction of International Politics: Identities & Foreign Policies, Moscow, 1955 and 1999.* Ithaca, NY: Cornell University Press.

———. 2010. "The Logic of Habit in International Relations." *European Journal of International Relations* 16(4): 539–561.

Howard, P. N., A. Duffy, D. Freelon, M. Hussain, W. Mari, M. Mazaid. 2011. *Opening Closed Regimes: What Was the Role of Social Media During the Arab Spring?* Project on Information Technology and Political Islam. Accessed April 29, 2014. http://pitpi.org/wp-content/uploads/2013/02/2011_Howard-Duffy-Freelon-Hussain-Mari-Mazaid_pITPI.pdf.

Howlett, M., and M. Ramesh. 2003. *Studying Public Policy: Policy Cycles and Policy Subsystems.* Toronto: Oxford University Press.

Hughes, S. 2013. "Digital Diplomacy: Here to Stay and Worth the Risk?" *BBC Academy*, May 24. Accessed August 7, 2014. www.bbc.co.uk/blogs/blogcollegeofjournalism/posts/Digital-diplomacy-here-to-stay-and-worth-the-risk.

Huijgh, E. 2013. "Public Diplomacy's Domestic Dimension in the European Union." In *European Public Diplomacy: Soft Power at Work*, edited by M. K. Davis and J. Melissen, 57–84. London: Palgrave Macmillan.

Huntington, S. P. 1993. "The Clash of Civilizations?" *Foreign Affairs* Summer: 22–49.

Ikenberry, G. J. 2001. *After Victory: Institutions, Strategic Restraint, and the Rebuilding of Order After Major Wars.* Princeton, NJ: Princeton University Press.

International Criminal Court (ICC). 2004. *Prosecutor Receives Referral of the Situation in the Democratic Republic of Congo.* Accessed August 8, 2014. www.icc-cpi.int/en_menus/icc/press%20and%20media/press%20releases/2004/Pages/prosecutor%20receives%20referral%20of%20the%20situation%20in%20the%20democratic%20republic%20of%20congo.aspx.

———. 2005. *Integrated Strategy for External Relations, Public Information and Outreach.* Accessed August 8, 2014. www.icc-cpi.int/NR/rdonlyres/425E80BA-1EBC-4423-85C6-D4F2B93C7506/185049/ICCPIDSWBOR0307070402_IS_En.pdf.

———. 2010a. Case Matrix Brochure. Accessed August 8, 2014. www.legal-tools.org/fileadmin/user_upload/Case_Matrix-ENG-FRA-2010-Print.pdf.

———. 2010b. Legal Tools Project Brochure. Accessed August 8, 2014. www.legal-tools.org/fileadmin/user_upload/Legal_Tools_Brochure_ENG_FRA_V.2010.pdf.

———. 2010c. *Report of the Court on the Public Information Strategy.* Accessed August 8, 2014. www.icc-cpi.int/iccdocs/asp_docs/ASP9/ICC-ASP-9-29-ENG.pdf.

———. 2014a. "ICC Weekly Update #196." Accessed August 8, 2014. www.icc-cpi.int/iccdocs/PIDS/wu/ED196_ENG.pdf.

———. 2014b"ICC Weekly Update #197." Accessed August 8, 2014. www.icc-cpi.int/iccdocs/PIDS/wu/ED197_ENG.pdf.

———. 2014c. "Prosecutions." Accessed August 8, 2014. www.icc-cpi.int/en_menus/icc/structure%20of%20the%20court/office%20of%20the%20prosecutor/prosecutions/Pages/prosecutions.aspx.

———. 2014d. "Trial in the Ruto and Sang [Ruto's Co-Defendant] Case: Relevant Information and Materials." Accessed August 8, 2014. www.icc-cpi.int/en_menus/icc/situations%20and%20cases/situations/situation%20icc%200109/related%20cases/icc01090111/Pages/ruto-sang.aspx.

———. 2014e. "Unified Technical Protocol for the Provision of evidence, witness and Victims Information in Electronic Form." Accessed August 8, 2014. www.icc-cpi.int/iccdocs/doc/doc1437590.pdf.

———. 2014f. "What Are the ICC Legal Tools?" Accessed August 8, 2014. www.legal-tools.org/en/what-are-the-icc-legal-tools/.

International Telecommunications Union. 2013. *Trends in Telecommunications Reform: Transnational Aspects of Regulation in a Networked Society*. Geneva: ITU.

Internet World Stats. 2013. "Usage and Population Statistics 2013." Internet Growth Statistics. Accessed July 19, 2014. www.internetworldstats.com/emarketing.htm.

Internet World Stats. 2014. "Internet World Stats: 2014." Accessed December 18, 2014. www.internetworldstats.com/stats.htm.

IPCI. 2014. Accessed September 3, 2014. www.ipci2014.org/en.

Jain, R., and L. H. Winner. 2013. "Country Reputation and Performance: The Role of Public Relations and News Media." *Place Branding and Public Diplomacy* 9(2): 109–123.

Jaishankar, D. 2014. "Rebooting Digital Diplomacy." *Brussels Forum*. Accessed January 5, 2015. http://brussels.gmfus.org/files/2014/03/BF14Views_12_Jaishankar.pdf.

Jamieson, A. 2013. "NSA leaker Edward Snowden: 'Mission's already accomplished.'" NBC News. Accessed December 10, 2014. http://usnews.nbcnews.com/_news/2013/12/24/22029559-nsa-leaker-edward-snowden-missions-already-accomplished?lite.

Jiang, X. 2013. *U.S. Internet Diplomacy on China*, Thesis, Aalborg University and University of International Relations. Accessed August 8, 2014. http://projekter.aau.dk/projekter/files/76941438/U.S._Internet_Diplomacy_on_China_Xiaoying_Jiang.pdf.

Jervis, R. 1989. *The Logic of the Images in International Relations*. New York: Columbia University Press.

Johnston, D. 2006. "Pentagon Analyst Gets 12 Years for Disclosing Data." *The New York Times*, January 20. Accessed on December 18, 2014. www.nytimes.com/2006/01/20/politics/20cnd-franklin.html.

Jönsson, C., and M. Hall. 2005. *Essence of Diplomacy*. London: Palgrave Macmillan.

Kahneman, D. 2011. *Thinking, Fast and Slow*. New York: Farrar, Straus & Giroux.

Kaneva, N. 2011. "Nation Branding: Toward an Agenda for Critical Research." *International Journal of Communication* 5: 117–141.

Karim, K. H. 1998. *From Ethnic Media to Global Media: Transnational Communication Networks Among Diasporic Communities*. Ottawa: Canadian Heritage.

Kaufmann, J. 1998. *The Diplomacy of International Relations: Selected Writings*. London: Kluwer Law International.

Kay, John. 2010. *Obliquity: Why Our Goals Are Best Achieved Indirectly*. London: Profile Books.

Kerry, J. 2013. "Digital Diplomacy: Adapting Our Diplomatic Engagement." Dipnote: U.S. Department of State Official Blog. Accessed September 14, 2014. http://blogs.state.gov/stories/2013/05/06/digital-diplomacy-adapting-our-diplomatic-engagement 2013.

Khatib, L., W. Dutton, and M. Thelwall. 2011. "Public Diplomacy 2.0: An Exploratory Case Study of the US Digital Outreach Team." *CDDRL Working Papers* January 6. Accessed April 17, 2014. http://iis-db.stanford.edu/pubs/23084/No.120-_Public_Diplomacy_2.0.pdf.

Khazan, O. 2012. "Diplomats on Twitter: Putin Follows No One." *Washington Post,* July 26.

Kissinger, H. 1994. *Diplomacy*. New York: Simon & Schuster.

Kleiner, J. 2010. *Diplomatic Practice: Between Tradition and Innovation*. Singapore: World Scientific.

Kodrich, K., and M. Laituri. 2011. "Making a Connection: Social Media's Key Role in the Haiti Earthquake." *Journal of Communication and Computer* 8: 624–627.

Kohut, A. 2010. Reviving America's Global Image. *Pew Research Center,* Mar 5. Accessed April 17, 2014. www.pewglobal.org/2010/03/05/reviving-americas-global-image/.

Kornprobst, M. 2008. *Irredentism in European Politics: Argumentation, Compromise and Norms.* Cambridge: Cambridge University Press.

Kotler, P., and D. Gertner. 2002. "Country as Brand, Product, and beyond: A Place Marketing and Brand Management Perspective." *Brand Management* 9(4–5): 249–261.

Kremenyuk, V. A. 2002. *International Negotiation: Analysis, Approaches, Issues.* 2nd ed. San Francisco: Jossey-Bass.

Kremer, J.-F., and B. Muller. 2014. "SAM: A Framework to Understand Emerging Challenges to States in an Interconnected World." *Cyberspace and International Relations* 41–58.

Kurbalija, J. 1999. *Knowledge and Diplomacy.* Msida, Malta: DiploProjects.

Lazakidou, A. A., ed. 2012. *Virtual Communities, Social Networks and Collaboration.* Vol. 15. New York: Springer. Accessed April 29, 2014. www.springerlink.com/index/10.1007/978-1-4614-3634-8.

Lazer, D. M., R. Kennedy, G. King, and A. Vespignani. 2014. "The Parable of Google Flu: Traps in Big Data Analysis." *Science* 343(6176): 1203–1205.

Leger, D. 2013. "NSA contractor: 'I know I have done nothing wrong.'" *USA TODAY.* Accessed December 18, 2014. www.usatoday.com/story/news/nation/2013/06/09/edward-snowden-guardian-interview/2405873/.

Leguey-Feilleux, J. R. 2008. *The Dynamics of Diplomacy.* Boulder, CO: Lynne Rienner.

Leonard, A. 2014. "Evgeny Morozov's New Yorker put-down of the Maker movement misses the point." *Salon.* Accessed December 18, 2014. www.salon.com/2014/01/07/meet_the_anti_maker_evgeny_morozov/.

Leonard, M. 2002. "Diplomacy by Other Means." *Foreign Policy* 132: 48–56.

Levy, S. 2013. "Zuckerberg Explains Internet.org, Facebook's Plan to Get the World Online." *Wired.co.uk* Accessed July 26, 2014. www.wired.co.uk/news/archive/2013-08/27/mark-zuckerberg-internet-org.

Li, X., and J. Wang. 2010. "Web Based Public Diplomacy." *Journal of International Communication* 16(1): 7–22.

Langhorne, R. 2004. "Current Developments in Diplomacy: Who Are the Diplomats Now?" In *Diplomacy,* edited by C. Jönsson and R. Langhorne, 331–342. London: Sage.

Lichtenstein, J., 2010. *Digital Diplomacy.* Accessed October 15, 2011. www.nytimes.com/2010/07/18/magazine/18web2–0-t.html?src=tptw&pagewanted=all.

Lodge, C. 2002. "Success and Failure: The Brand Stories of Two Countries." *Brand Management* 9(4–5): 372–384.

MacLeod, C. 2011. "Social Media Pressure China for Answer in Rail Crash." Accessed April 24, 2014. http://usatoday30.usatoday.com/news/world/2011-07-27-china-train-crash-outrage_n.htm.

March, J. G., and J. P. Olsen. 1998. "The Institutional Dynamics of International Political Orders." *International Organization* 52(4): 943–969.

Marcus, G. E. 1995. "Ethnography in/of the world system: the emergence of Multi-Sited Ethnography." *Annual Review of Anthropology* 95–117.

Marcus, G., and E. Davis. 2014. "Eight (No, Nine!) Problems With Big Data." *The New York Times.* Accessed September 14, 2014. www.nytimes.com/2014/04/07/opinion/eight-no-nine-problems-with-big-data.html.

Marks, J. 2014. "Social Media Makes the State Department Nimbler." Accessed September 14, 2014. www.nextgov.com/emerging-tech/2014/02/social-media-makes-state-department-nimbler/78998/.

Maret, S. and Goldman, J. 2009 *Government secrecy: classic and contemporary readings.* Libraries Unlimited: Westport, CT.

Mazzone, J. and Rehman, S. 2011. "The household diary study: mail use and attitudes FY2011." The United States Postal Service. Accessed December 10, 2014. http://about.usps.com/studying-americans-mail-use/household-diary/2011/fullreport-pdf/usps-hds-fy11.pdf.

McCombs, M., and A. Reynolds. 2002. "News Influence on Our Pictures of the World." In *Media Effects: Advances in Theory and Research*, J. Bryant and D. Zillmann, Mahwah, NJ: Erlbaum.

McLuhan, M. 1994. *Understanding Media: The Extensions of Man.* London: MIT Press.

Medcalf, R. 2013. "The Diplomatic Tweet." *American Review.* Accessed August 4, 2014. http://americanreviewmag.com/opinions/The-diplomatic-tweet.

Melissen, J. 1999. *Innovation in Diplomatic Practice: Studies in Diplomacy.* New York: St. Martin's Press.

———. 2005. *The New Public Diplomacy: Soft Power in International Relations.* Basingstoke, UK: Palgrave Macmillan.

———. 2007. The New Public Diplomacy: Soft Power in International Relations, Palgrave Macmillan.

———. 2011. "Beyond the New Public Diplomacy." *Clingendael Paper* 3: 1–34.

———. 2013. "Public Diplomacy." In *The Oxford Handbook of Modern Diplomacy*, 436–452. Oxford: Oxford University Press.

Mergel, I. 2013. *Social Media in the Public Sector: A Guide to Participation, Collaboration, and Transparency in the Networked World.* San Francisco: Jossey-Bass.

Metzgar, E. T. 2012. " Is it the Medium or the Message? Social Media, American Public Relations & Iran." *Global Media Journal* 1(2): 1–16.

Metzl, J. 2001. "Network Diplomacy." *Georgetown Journal of International Affairs*, Winter/Spring. Accessed August 8, 2014. http://carnegieendowment.org/2001/04/01/network-diplomacy.

Michelson, M., and C. A. Knoblock. 2008. "Creating Relational Data from Unstructured and Ungrammatical Data Sources." *Journal of Artificial Intelligence Research* 31: 543–590.

Miller, C. 2013. "US Ambassador to Ukraine Geoffrey Pyatt Discusses E-diplomacy in First 'Twitterview' with Kyiv Post." Accessed September 14, 2014. www.kyivpost.com/content/ukraine/us-ambassador-to-ukraine-discusses-e-diplomacy-in-twitterview-328895.html.

Mitzen, J. 2013. *Power in Concert: The Nineteenth-Century Origins of Global Governance.* Chicago: University of Chicago Press.

Modelski, G. 1990. "Is World-Politics Evolutionary Learning." *International Organization* 44(1): 1–24.

Mondak, J. J. 2010. *Personality and the Foundations of Political Behavior.* Cambridge: Cambridge University Press.

Morozov. E. 2014. "Making it: pick up a spot welder and join the revolution." *The New Yorker.* Accessed December 18, 2014. www.newyorker.com/magazine/2014/01/13/making-it-2.

Moynihan, D. 1998. *Secrecy: The American Experience.* Yale University Press: New Haven, CT.

Murphy, H. 2014. "Ominous text message sent to protesters in Kiev sends chills around the Internet." *The New York Times.* Accessed December 18, 2014. http://thelede.blogs.nytimes.com/2014/01/22/ominous-text-message-sent-to-protesters-in-kiev-sends-chills-around-the-internet/.

Natarajan, K. 2014. "Digital Public Diplomacy and a Strategic Narrative for India." *Strategic Analysis* 38(1): 91–106.

Neumann, I. B. 2012. *At Home with the Diplomats: Inside a European Foreign Ministry.* Ithaca, NY: Cornell University Press.

Nicolson, H. 1957. *The Evolution of the Diplomatic Method*. London: Cassell.

———. 1969 (1939). *Diplomacy*. 3rd ed. London: Oxford University Press.

Norton, Q. 2012. "How Anonymous picks targets, launches attacks, and takes powerful organizations down." *Wired*. Accessed December 18, 2014. www.wired.com/2012/07/ff_anonymous/all/.

Nossel, S. 2004. "Smart power." *Foreign Affairs*. Accessed December 18, 2014. www.foreignaffairs.com/articles/59716/suzanne-nossel/smart-power.

Nye, J. S., Jr., and W. A. Owens. 1996. "America's Information Edge." *Foreign Affairs* March/April: 20.

Nye, J. S. Jr. 1990. "Bound to Lead: The Changing Nature of American Power." *Foreign Affairs* 69: 176.

———. 2004. *Soft Power: The Means to Success in World Politics*. New York: PublicAffairs.

———. 2008. "Public diplomacy and soft power." *Annals of the American Academy of Political and Social Science* no. 616: 94–109.

———. 2013. Hard, Soft, and Smart Power. In *The Oxford Handbook of Modern Diplomacy*, 559–574. Oxford: Oxford University Press.

Nuland, V. 2011. *Press Statement*. Accessed April 10, 2014. www.state.gov/r/pa/prs/ps/2011/12/178343.htm.

Nye, Joseph S. 2008. "Public diplomacy and soft power." *Annals of the American Academy of Political and Social Science* no. 616: 94–109.

O'Reilly, T. 2011. "Government as a Platform." Accessed December 18, 2014. http://chimera.labs.oreilly.com/books/1234000000774/ch02.html.

Otte, T. G. 2013. *The Foreign Office Mind: The Making of British Foreign Policy, 1865–1914*. New York.

Page, M., and J. E. Spence. 2011. "Open Secrets Questionably Arrived At: The Impact of Wikileaks on Diplomacy." *Defence Studies* 11(2): 234–243.

Pamment, J. 2013. *New Public Diplomacy in the 21st Century : A Comparative Study of Policy and Practice*. Routledge New Diplomacy Studies. London: Routledge.

Papadopoulos, N. and L. Heslop. 2002. "Country Equity and Country Branding: Problems and Prospects." *Brand Management* 9(4–5): 294–314.

Paris, R. 2013. "The Digital Diplomacy Revolution: Why Is Canada Lagging Behind?" *Policy Paper, Canadian Defence & Foreign Affairs Institute*: 1–17.

Park, S. J., and Y. S. Lim. 2014. "Information Networks and Social Media Use in Public Diplomacy: A Comparative Analysis of South Korea and Japan." *Asian Journal of Communication* 24(1): 79–98.

Parliament of the Commonwealth of Australia, Joint Standing Committee on Foreign Affairs, Defence and Trade. 2012. *Australia's Overseas Representation – Punching Below Our Weight? Inquiry of the Foreign Affairs Sub-Committee*, 1–158. Canberra: Government Printer.

People magazine. 1974. "Edgar Mitchell's strange voyage." Accessed December 10, 2014. www.people.com/people/archive/article/0,,20063934,00.html.

Pettigrew, A. M. 1990. "Longitudinal Field Research on Change: Theory and Practice." *Organization Science* 1(3): 267–292.

Pew Research Global Attitudes Project. 2013. *Chapter 1. Attitudes Toward the United States*. Accessed May 15, 2014. www.pewglobal.org/2013/07/18/chapter-1-attitudes-toward-the-united-states/.

Pfanner, E. 2009. "Four convicted in Sweden in Internet piracy case." *The New York Times*. Accessed December 18, 2014. www.nytimes.com/2009/04/18/business/global/18pirate.html.

Pinchot, G., and R. Pellman. 1999. *Intrapreneuring in Action: A Handbook for Business Innovation*. San Francisco: Berrett-Koehler.

Piratbyran. 2007. "The bureau of piracy: activities 2007." Accessed December 10, 2014.

Pogge, T. 2007. *Freedom from Poverty as a Human Right: Who Owes What to the Poor?* New York: Oxford University Press.
Potter, E. 2002. *Cyber-Diplomacy: Managing Foreign Policy in the Twenty-First Century.* Montreal: McGill-Queen's University Press.
Pouliot, V. (2010). *International Security in Practice.* Cambridge: Cambridge University Press.
Prantl, J. 2005. "Informal Groups of States and the UN Security Council." *International Organization* 59(3): 559–592.
Presenting Sweden. 2014. Accessed August 29, 2014. https://presentingsweden.si.se/.
Priest, D. and Arkin, W. 2010. "National security, inc." *The Washington Post.* Accessed December 18, 2014. http://projects.washingtonpost.com/top-secret-america/articles/national-security-inc/.
Qin, X., Li, Z., and Mina, R. 2011. "Embassies in China Launch Weibo Account." Accessed March 25, 2013. www.infzm.com/content/57090.
Quelch, J. A., and K. E. Jocz. 2009. "Can Brand Obama Rescue Brand America?" *Brown Journal of World Affairs* 16(1): 163–178.
Raddatz, M. 2009. *Hillary Clinton's New Approach to Diplomacy. ABC News,* February 20. Accessed April 7, 2014. http://abcnews.go.com/Politics/International/story?id=6921007.
Radicati, S. and Buckley, T. 2012. *eDiscovery Market 2012-2016: executive summary.* Accessed December 18, 2014. www.radicati.com/wp/wp-content/uploads/2012/10/eDiscovery-Market-2012-2016-Executive-Summary.pdf.
Ramsay, A. 2006. "Is Diplomacy Dead?" *Contemporary Review* 288, Autumn: 273–289.
Rawson, E.A.G. 2007. "Let Freedom and Cash Registers Ring: America as a Brand." *Place Branding and Public Diplomacy* 3(3): 213–221.
Rathbun, B. C. 2014. *Diplomacy's Value: Creating Security in 1920s Europe and the Contemporary Middle East.* Ithaca, NY: Cornell University Press.
Regeringskansliet. 2014. Accessed September 2, 2014. www.government.se/sb/d/18138.
Reynolds, D. 2007. *Summits: Six Meetings That Shaped the Twentieth Century.* New York: Basic Books.
Richardson, D. 2012. "Submission No. 28: Inquiry into Australia's Overseas Representation." *Department of Foreign Affairs and Trade* 1–48. Canberra: Government Printer.
Ringmar, E. 2014. "The Search for Dialogue as a Hindrance to Understanding: Practices as Inter-Paradigmatic Research Program." *International Theory* 6(1): 1–27.
Ritter, K., 2012. *Twitter Diplomacy New Face of Foreign Relations.* Accessed September 17, 2012. www.msnbc.msn.com/id/43185212/ns/technology_and_science-tech_and_gadgets/t/twitter-diplomacy-new-face-foreign-relations/.
Roberts, A. 2004. "National security and open government." *Georgetown Public Policy Review,* Vol. 9.2, pp. 69-85, Spring 2004.
Rogers, Simon. (2013, July 10). The Boston Bombing: How journalists used Twitter to tell the story. [Web log post]. Accessed September 16, 2014. https://blog.twitter.com/2013/the-boston-bombing-how-journalists-used-twitter- to-tell-the-storyx.
Rosenau, J. N. 1997. *Along the Domestic-Foreign Frontier: Exploring Governance in a Turbulent World.* Cambridge: Cambridge University Press.
Ross, A. 2013. "Alec Ross on '21st Century Statecraft' Diplomacy." *Bloomberg,* March 14. Accessed September 10, 2014. www.bloomberg.com/video/alec-ross-on-21st-century-statecraft-diplomacy-DCpmSXs9RRyvCzFMQE4p5Q.html.
———. 2014. "Can Social Media Change the Face of Diplomacy?" *Bloomberg,* July 30. September 11, 2014. www.bloomberg.com/video/can-social-media-change-the-face-of-diplomacy-DIX_CFtLTQSe~52dp4kBEw.html.
Ross, D. 2007. *Statecraft: And How to Restore America's Standing in the World.* New York: Farrar, Straus & Giroux.

Robertson, G. 2012. *Crimes Against Humanity: The Struggle for Global Justice.* New York: The New Press.
RT News. 2013. "Pirate Bay continues to expand despite mounting anti-piracy movement." Accessed December 18, 2014. http://rt.com/news/pirate-bay-downloads-piracy-lobby-999/.
Ruggie, J. G. 1993. "Territoriality and Beyond: Problematizing Modernity in International Relations." *International Organization* 47(1): 139–174.
Russom, P. 2011. "Big Data Analytics." *TDWI Best Practices Report, Fourth Quarter.* Accessed September 14, 2014. http://tdwi.org/research/2011/09/~/media/TDWI/TDWI/Research/BPR/2011/TDWI_BPReport_Q411_Big_Data_Analytics_Web/TDWI_BPReport_Q411_Big%20Data_ExecSummary.ashx.
Sabatier, P. A. 1988. "An Advocacy Coalition Framework of Policy Change and the Role of Policy-Oriented Learning Therein." *Policy Sciences* 21(2–3), 129–168.
Sabatier, P. A., and H. C. Jenkins-Smith. 1993. *Policy Change and Learning: An Advocacy Coalition Approach.* Boulder, CO: Westview Press.
Sandre, A. 2013. *Twitter for Diplomats.* Geneva: DiploFoundation and Istituto Diplomatico.
Sarotte, E. 2009. *1989: The Struggle to Create Post-Cold War Europe.* Princeton, NJ: Princeton University Press.
Satow, E. M., and N. Bland. 1957. *A Guide to Diplomatic Practice.* 4th ed. London: Longmans.
Savage, M., E. Ruppert, and J. Law 2010. *Digital Devices: Nine Theses.* Manchester: University of Manchester.
Savelyev, A., S. Xu, K. Janowicz, C. Mülligann, J. Thatcher, and W. Luo. 2011. *Volunteered Geographic Services: Developing a Linked Data Driven Location-Based Service.* Cambridge: Cambridge University Press.
Schiff, B. 2013. "Diplomacy and the International Criminal Court." In *The Oxford Handbook of Modern Diplomacy,* edited by A. Cooper *et al.* 745–762. Oxford: Oxford University Press.
Schmid, R. 2011. U.S. Postal Service survey reveals personal letters at record low. *The Huffington Post.* Accessed December 18, 2014. www.huffingtonpost.com/2011/10/03/postal-service-annual-survey-personal-letters_n_992432.html.
Scholte, Jan Aart. 2008. "From Government to Governance." In *Global governance and diplomacy: worlds apart?,* edited by Andrew Fenton Cooper, Brian Hocking and William Maley, Basingstoke; New York: Palgrave Macmillan: 39–62.
Schultz, K. A. 2001. *Democracy and Coercive Diplomacy.* Cambridge: Cambridge University Press.
Seib, P. M. 2012. *Real-time Diplomacy: Politics and Power in the Social Media Era.* New York: Palgrave Macmillan.
Simpson, E. 2014. "The Peril and Promise of Big Data." *Foreign Policy Argument.* Accessed January 6, 2015. http://foreignpolicy.com/2014/05/15/the-peril-and-promise-of-big-data/.
Sharp, P. 2003. "Herbert Butterfield, the English School and the Civilizing Virtues of Diplomacy." *International Affairs* 79(4): 855–878.
———. 2004. "For Diplomacy: Representation and the Study of International Relations." In *Diplomacy,* edited by C. Jönsson and R. Langhorne, 208–209. London: Sage.
———. 2005. *Revolutionary States, Outlaw Regimes and the Techniques of Public Diplomacy.* Edited by Jan Melissen, *The new public diplomacy: soft power in international relations.* Basingstoke [UK] ; New York: Palgrave Macmillan.
———. 2009. *Diplomatic Theory of International Relations.* Cambridge: Cambridge University Press.
Shearer, A., F. Hanson, and A. Oliver. 2011. "Submission to the Joint Standing Committee on Foreign Affairs, Defence and Trade Inquiry into Australia's Overseas

Representation." *Lowy Institute*. Accessed August 7, 2013. www.lowyinstitute.org/files/inquiry_into_australias_overseas_representation.pdf.

Shirky, C. 2011. "The Political Power of Social Media." *Foreign Affairs* 90(1): 28–41.

Shirky, C., and M. Gladwell. 2011. "From Innovation to Revolution: Do Social Media Make Protests Possible?" *Foreign Affairs*. Accessed April 23, 2013. www.foreignaffairs.com/articles/67325/malcolm-gladwell-and-clay-shirky/from-innovation-to-revolution.

Sifry, M., and A. Rasiej. 2009. "P2P2G: The Rise of E-diplomacy." *Politico*. Accessed September 14, 2014. www.politico.com/news/stories/0609/23310.html.

Silver, S. and S. Hill. 2002. "Marketing: Selling Brand America." *Journal of Business Strategy* 23(4): 10–15.

Simmel, G. (1906). "The sociology of secrecy and secret societies." *American Journal of Sociology*, 11, 4: 441-498.

Sina. 2012. "Report on Foreign Government Weibo Account." November 2. Accessed March 13, 2013. http://city.sina.com.cn/focus/t/20121102/173933606.html.

Sina. 2014. "Nasdaq IPO Prospectus 2014." Accessed April 25, 2014. http://tech.qq.com/a/20140315/001658.htm.

Singh. J. P. 2002. "Introduction: Information Technologies and the Changing Scope of Power and Governance." *Information Technologies and Global Politics: The Changing Scope of Power and Governance*, edited by J. N. Rosenau and J. P. Singh, 1–38. Albany: State University of New York Press.

Singh, J. P. 2008. *Negotiation and the Global Information Economy*. Cambridge, UK: Cambridge University Press.

Singh. J. P. 2010. "Security Implications of Multilateral Approaches to Negotiating Internet Governance," In *Ungoverned Spaces: Alternatives to State Sovereignty in an Era of Soft Sovereignty*. A. Clunan and H. Trinkunas, 232–254. Stanford, CA: Stanford University Press.

Skuba, C. 2002. "Branding America." *Georgetown Journal of International Affairs* 3(2): 105–114.

Slaughter, A. 2009. "America's Edge: Power in the Networked Century., *Foreign Affairs* 88 (January/February). Accessed August 8, 2014. www.foreignaffairs.com/articles/63722/anne-marie-slaughter/americas-edge.

———. 2011. "A New Theory for the Foreign-Policy Frontier: Collaborative Power." *The Atlantic*, November 30. Accessed August 8, 2014. www.theatlantic.com/international/archive/2011/11/a-new-theory-for-the-foreign-policy-frontier-collaborative-por/249260/.

Smith, A. 2011. "Americans and text messaging." Pew Internet & American Life Project. Accessed December 18, 2014. www.pewinternet.org/2011/09/19/americans-and-text-messaging/.

Smith, S. 2012. "Australia No E-diplomacy Slouch." *The Interpreter*. Accessed August 9, 2013. www.lowyinterpreter.org/post/2012/06/06/reader-riposte-australia-no-e-diplomacy-slouch.aspx.

Snow, N., and P. M. Taylor. 2008. *Routledge Handbook of Public Diplomacy*. London: Taylor & Francis.

Soltani, A. and Schlosser, A. 2011. Letter from American Civil Liberties Union of Northern California to the BART Chief of Police. Accessed December 18, 2014. https://www.aclunc.org/sites/default/files/asset_upload_file335_10381.pdf.

Stanley, A. 1984. "Spy vs. spy saga." *TIME*. Accessed December 18, 2014. http://content.time.com/time/magazine/article/0,9171,923689,00.html.

Stein, J. G. 2011. *Diplomacy in the Digital Age: Essays in Honour of Ambassador Allan Gotlieb*. Plattsburgh, NY: McClelland & Stewart.

Stockholm Internet Forum. 2013. Accessed August 20, 2014. www.stockholminternetforum.se/.

Sunlight Foundation. 2013. "US spy leaker Edward Snowden 'missing.'" Accessed December 3, 2013. http://churnalism.sunlightfoundation.com/. . ./8bec853dde325869bb1d9971fe7.

Swartz, O. 2009. "The Pirate Bay guilty: jail for file-sharing foursome." *Wired*. Accessed December 18, 2014. www.wired.com/2009/04/pirateverdict/.

Swedish Institute. 2011. "Curators of Sweden 2011." Accessed September 1, 2014. http://curatorsofsweden.com/.

Swedish Institute. 2014. Accessed September 1, 2014. www.swedenabroad.com/Pages/StandardPage.aspx?id=69869&epslanguage=en-GB.

Szondi, G. 2008. *Public Diplomacy and Nation Branding: Conceptual Similarities and Differences*. Netherlands Institute of International Relations: Clingendael/. Accessed May 23, 2014. www.clingendael.nl/sites/default/files/20081022_pap_in_dip_nation_branding.pdf.

Tefft, S. 1980. *Secrecy: A Cross-Cultural Perspective*. New York, NY: Human Sciences Press.

Tefft, S. 1992. The Dialectics of Secret Society Power in States. Humanities Press International: Atlantic Highlands, NJ.

Thelen, K. 1999. "Historical Institutionalism in Comparative Politics." *Annual Review of Political Science* 2(1): 369–404.

Tilly, C. 1992. *Coercion, Capital, and European States, AD 990–1992*. Rev. pbk. ed. Cambridge, MA: Blackwell.

Tracy, M. 2012. "Ambassador Oren on Why He Joined Twitter." *Tablet*, May 30. Accessed April 30, 2013. www.tabletmag.com/scroll/101023/ambassadororen-on-why-he-joined-twitter.

Tucker, P. 2014. *The Naked Future: What Happens in a World That Anticipates Your Every Move?* New York: Penguin.

Twiplomacy. 2014 *Twiplomacy Study 2014*. Switzerland: Twiploamcy.

Underhill, G.R.D. 2006. "Introduction: Conceptualizing the Changing Global Order." In *Political Economy and the Changing Global Order*, 3rd ed., edited by R. Stubbs and G.R.D. Underhill, 3–23. Oxford: Oxford University Press.

United Nations Development Program. 1994. *Human Development Report 1994*. New York: Oxford University Press.

United Nations General Assembly, Human Rights Council 2012Resolution L13, the Promotion, Protection and Enjoyment of Human Rights on the Internet. Accessed September 3, 2014. http://ap.ohchr.org/documents/E/HRC/d_res_dec/A_HRC_20_L13.doc.

United States Department of State. 2010. Quadrennial Diplomacy and Development Review. Accessed December 10, 2014. www.state.gov/documents/organization/153109.pdf.

UPI. 1971. "1971 year in review: the Pentagon Papers." Accessed December 18, 2014. www.upi.com/Archives/Audio/Events-of-1971/The-Pentagon-Papers/.

US Department of State. 2011. "IRM's Office of eDiplomacy." Accessed August 3, 2013. www.state.gov/m/irm/ediplomacy/.

US Department of State. 2013. "21st Century Statecraft." Accessed December 10, 2013. www.state.gov/statecraft/overview/index.htm.

US Department of State. 2013. "12 FAM 540 Sensitive but unclassified information (SBU)." Accessed December 10, 2014. www.state.gov/documents/organization/88404.pdf.

Uysal, N., J. Schroeder, and M. Taylor. 2012. "Social Media and Soft Power: Positioning Turkey's Image on Twitter." *Middle East Journal of Culture and Communication* 5(3): 338–359.

Van Buren, P. 2012. "Obama's war on whistleblowers." *Mother Jones*. Accessed December 18, 2014. www.motherjones.com/politics/2012/06/obamas-whistleblowers-stuxnet-leaks-drones.

van Ham, P. .2001. "The Rise of the Brand State." *Foreign Affairs* 80(5): 2–6.

———. 2008. "Place Branding: The State of the Art." *The ANNALS of the American Academy of Political and Social Sciences* 616(1): 126–149.

Vattimo, I. 1993. "Postmodernity, Technology, Ontology." In *Technology in the Western Political Tradition*, edited by A. M. Meltzer, J. Weinberger, and M. R. Zinman. Ithaca, NY: Cornell University Press.

"Virtual Relations." 2012. *The Economist*, Sep 22 2012. Accessed January 5, 2015. http://www.economist.com/node/21563284.

Wainfan, L., and P. K. Davis. 2004. *Challenges in Virtual Collaboration: Videoconferencing, Audioconferencing, and Computer-Mediated Communications*. Santa Monica, CA: RAND Corporation.

Waltz, K. N. 1979. *Theory of International Politics*. New York: McGraw-Hill.

Wang, J. 2006. "National Reputation and International Relations in the Global Era: Public Diplomacy Revisited." *Public Relations Review* 32(2): 91–96.

Watson, A. 1984. *Diplomacy: The Dialogue Between States*. London: Methuen.

Web Index. 2012. Accessed September 5, 2014. http://thewebindex.org/.

Weber, L. 2011. *Everywhere: Comprehensive Digital Business Strategy for the Social Media Era*. Hoboken, NJ: Wiley.

Welch, D. A. 2005. *Painful Choices: A Theory of Foreign Policy Change*. Princeton, NJ: Princeton University Press.

Wendt, A. 1992. "Anarchy Is What States Make of It: The Social Construction of Power Politics." *International Organization* 46(2): 391–425.

———. 1999. *Social Theory of International Politics*. Cambridge: Cambridge University Press.

———. 2001. "What Is International Relations For? Notes Toward a Postcritical View." In *Critical Theory and World Politics*, edited by R. W. Jones, 205–224. Boulder, CO: Lynne Rienner.

Wheeler, N. J. 2008. "'To Put Oneself into the Other Fellow's Place': John Herz, the Security Dilemma and the Nuclear Age." *International Relations* 22(4): 493–509.

———. 2013. "Investigating Diplomatic Transformations." *International Affairs* 89(2): 477–496.

White House. 1995. "Executive Order 12958-Classified National Security Information." Accessed December 18, 2014. www.fas.org/sgp/clinton/eo12958.html.

White House. 2009. "Remarks by President Obama on a New Beginning." Accessed May 20, 2014. www.whitehouse.gov/the_press_office/Remarks-by-the-President-at-Cairo-University-6-04-09. www.whitehouse.gov/the_press_office/Remarks-by-the-President-at-Cairo-University-6-04-09.

White House. 2013. "Liberty and security in a changing world: report and recommendations of the President's Review Group on Intelligence and Communications Technologies." Accessed December 10, 2014. www.whitehouse.gov/sites/default/files/docs/2013-12-12_rg_final_report.pdf.

Whole Earth. 1969. *The Whole Earth Catalog*. Accessed December 18, 2014. www.wholeearth.com/issue-electronic-edition.php?iss=1070.

Wichowski, A. 2013a. "Social Diplomacy or How Diplomats Learned to Stop Worrying and Love the Tweet." *Foreign Affairs*, April 5. Accessed September 14, 2014. www.foreignaffairs.com/articles/139134/alexis-wichowski/social-diplomacy.

———. 2013b. "What Government Can and Should Learn from Hacker Culture." *The Atlantic*, October 25. Accessed December 18, 2014. www.theatlantic.com/politics/archive/2013/10/what-government-can-and-should-learn-from-hacker-culture/280675/.

Widmaier, W. W., M. Blyth, and L. Seabrooke. 2007. "Exogenous shocks or Endogenous Constructions? The Meanings of Wars and Crises." *International Studies Quarterly* 51(4): 747–759.

Wight, M. 1966. "Why Is There No International Theory." In *Diplomatic Investigations: Essays in the Theory of International Politics*, edited by H. Butterfield, M. Wight, and H. Bull. London: Allen & Unwin.

Wilkenfeld, J., K. Young, V. Asal, and D. Quinn. 2003. "Mediating International Crises – Cross-national and Experimental Perspectives." *Journal of Conflict Resolution* 47(3): 279–301.

Wilson, E. J. 2008. "Hard Power, Soft Power, Smart Power." *Annals of the American Academy of Political and Social Science* 616: 110–124.

Woodroofe, T. 2012. "DFAT Isn't Ready for the Asian Century." *ABC News*, October 29. Accessed July 19, 2013. www.abc.net.au/unleashed/4339726.html.

Yarhi-Milo, K. 2013. "In the Eye of the Beholder: How Leaders and Intelligence Communities Assess the Intentions of Adversaries." *International Security* 38(1): 7–51.

Yarhi-Milo, K. 2014. *Knowing the Adversary: Leaders, Intelligence, and Assessment of Intentions in International Relations*. Princeton, NJ: Princeton University Press.

YouTube. 2014. Statistics. Accessed December 18, 2014. www.youtube.com/yt/press/statistics.html.

Zaharna, R. S. 2010. *Battles to Bridges: U.S. Strategic Communication and Public Diplomacy after 9/11*. London: Palgrave Macmillan.

Zelikow, P. D. and C. Rice. 1995. *Germany unified and Europe transformed: a study in statecraft: with a new preface*, Harvard University Press.

Zhang, J. Y. 2013. "A Strategic Issue Management (SIM) Approach to Social Media Use in Public Diplomacy." *American Behavioral Scientist* 57(9): 1312–1331.

Zhong, X., and J. Y. Lu. 2013. "Public diplomacy Meets Social Media: A Study of the US Embassy's Blogs and Micro-blogs." *Public Relations Review* 39(5): 542–548.

Court filings and transcripts

Prosecutor v. Banda and Jerbo, "Order on Translation of Witness Statements," August 16, 2011, ICC-02/05-03/09-199.

Prosecutor v. Banda and Jerbo, "Prosecution's Proposals on the Issue of Translation," August 8, 2011, ICC-02/05-03/09-192.

Prosecutor v. Bemba, "Decision on the Submission of an Updated, Consolidated Version of the In-depth Analysis Chart of Incriminatory Evidence," November 10, 2008, ICC-01/05-01/08-232.

Prosecutor v. Bemba, Transcript, June 17, 2013, ICC-01/05-01/08-T-324-ENG.

Prosecutor v. Jean-Pierre Bemba Gombo, Aimé Kilolo Musamba, Jean-Jacques Mangenda Kabongo, Fidèle Babala Wandu, and Narcisse Arido, "Prosecution Response to 'Defence Request for an In-Depth Analysis Chart'," January 24, 2014, ICC-01/05-01/13-125.

Prosecutor v. Jean-Pierre Bemba Gombo, Aimé Kilolo Musamba, Jean-Jacques Mangenda Kabongo, Fidèle Babala Wandu, and Narcisse Arido, "Decision on the 'Defence Request for an In-Depth Analysis Chart' Submitted by the Defence for Mr Jean-Pierre Bemba Gombo," January 28, 2014, ICC-01/05-01/13-134.

Prosecutor v. Muthaura and Kenyatta, "Order on the E-Court Protocol," June 19, 2012, ICC-01/09-02/11-438.

Prosecutor v. Muthaura and Kenyatta, "Registry submissions on the Generic E-court Protocol Pursuant to Order ICC-01/09-02/11-438," July 5, 2012, ICC-01/09-02/11-449.

Prosecutor v. Ruto, Kosgey and Sang, "Prosecution's Submission of Comprehensive In-Depth Analysis Chart of Evidence Included in the list of Evidence," August 1, 2011, ICC-01/09-01/11-241.

Prosecutor v. Ruto and Sang, Transcript, January 15, 2014, ICC-01/09-01/11-T-72-ENG.

Situation in the Republic of Kenya, "Corrigendum to Decision on the Defences' Requests for a Compliance Order in regard to Decision 'ICC-01/09–02/11–48'," July 12, 2011, ICC-01/09–02/11–167-Corr.

Legal documents

Regulations of the Court, adopted May 26, 2004.

Regulations of the Registry, adopted March 6, 2006.

Rome Statute of the International Criminal Court, preamble, opened for signature July 17, 1998, 2187 U.N.T.S. 90.

Rules of Procedure and Evidence, adopted September 9, 2002.

Videos

ICC. 2011. "International Criminal Court (ICC-CPI) – Institutional Video." Accessed August 8, 2014. www.youtube.com/watch?v=zfo7lMnR4O8&list=TLITxw64hyZg7o I8x7EjLYztcw1ENEwSqn.

ICC. 2013a. "Gbagbo Case: Appeals Chamber Confirms Decision Adjourning the Hearing on the Confirmation of Charges." Accessed August 8, 2014. www.youtube.com/watch?v=mb0t5wBdvyA&list=UU183T5VoMh5wISSdKPaMgRw.

ICC. 2013b. "Kenyatta Case: 'Ask the Court' Programme, 20 December 2013." Accessed August 8, 2014. www.youtube.com/watch?v=dkHThOlTdPc&list=PLz3-Py_E3klDHV-d73-CchOKe-0FDvXOw.

ICC. 2013c. "Statement of the Prosecutor of the ICC on the Occasion of Human Rights Day, 10 December 2013." Accessed August 8, 2014. www.youtube.com/watch?v=FjjU FauaQ1o&list=UU183T5VoMh5wISSdKPaMgRw&feature=c4-overview.

ICC. 2014a. "A Day with Defence Counsels." Accessed August 8, 2014. www.youtube.com/watch?v=JomqtGphHOE&list=UU183T5VoMh5wISSdKPaMgRw.

ICC. 2014b. "Ruto and Sang case/'In the Courtroom' Programme: Trial, Witness P-0356, 17–28 January 2014." Accessed August 8, 2014. www.youtube.com/watch?v=21uFw-u56 Tc&list=UU183T5VoMh5wISSdKPaMgRw&feature=c4-overview.

INDEX

African Union 151, 152
Anonymous 66

big data 24–8, 111, 125, 192, 206
Bildt, Carl 48–9
Boston marathon bombing 14, 62, 66
Burson-Marsteller 47–8

CaseMap 154, 155
"cognitive punch" 22
Cold War 16, 17, 22, 23, 30, 35, 95, 130, 131, 133, 188
Communities@State 39

data asphyxiation 24, 25
digital diplomacy 4, 33–5, 37–8, 40–3, 47, 49–51, 55, 71, 111, 128, 165, 181; agenda-setting 74, 76; conversation-generating 75, 84; institutional adaptation 5; policy change 113; policy innovation 5; presence expansion 75, 79; promises 41–6; realities 46–51; revolution 140; Stockholm Initiative 166
Diplohack 165, 177
diplomacy: change management 1–2, 20–4, 94, 104, 197, 200; crisis 23; innovation 175; network 145, 149; personal 13, 17, 23, 31, 201; selfie 89, 96–8; traditional 13, 29, 39, 111, 124, 172, 175, 204
Diplopedia 39

e-court system 152
ediplomacy 13–14, 35, 130, 137, 141, 201; see also digital diplomacy
emotion 17, 21, 28, 29, 85

face-to-face diplomacy 5, 15, 28, 31, 200–1

G-20 13
Goffman, Erving 17, 21, 28

information hyperpower 132, 134
International Criminal Court (ICC) 145
Internet communication technologies 13, 14, 15, 18, 24, 31

leakers 54; see also Wikileaks, Edward Snowden
liminality 22
logic of habit 17, 21–2, 23, 195

McFaul, Michael 43
metapower 181, 184, 189–90
Morozov, Evgheni 39–40

naked diplomacy 174
nation-branding 90–1, 169
neuroplasticity 21
norms 2, 5, 21–2, 54, 149, 161, 191, 194

openness 53, 66, 156, 165; see also secrecy

policy change 19, 73, 111, 112, 113, 114, 116, 118, 121, 124, 125 public diplomacy 4, 13, 20, 30, 36, 71, 115, 128, 168, 188; *see also* social media, nation-branding

Ringtail (ICC) 153–4
Ross, Alec 37–8, 42, 50

secrecy 52; *see also* openness
slacktivism 19, 49
smart power 35–6
Snowden, Edward 6, 14, 24–5, 38, 47, 52–4, 64, 70, 128, 193, 205
social media 73
soft power 35, 64, 172
State Department 14, 19, 20, 27, 37, 38–40, 42, 44, 46, 47, 50, 60, 73, 75, 88, 89, 92, 97–107, 192, 194, 201, 205

Transcend (ICC) 155, 156
trust 8, 17, 28, 29, 48, 50, 164, 165, 167, 171, 172, 201
twiplomacy 48

Ukrainian crisis 2014 22, 26, 29, 70, 120, 200, 205
United Nations 13, 14, 25, 67, 147, 170, 181; Security Council 146, 148, 151

virtual collaboration 15, 24, 29, 31, 35
virtual embassy 45–6, 143, 169

Web 2.0 36–7, 51
Weibo 71–2, 78, 80, 84–6
Wikileaks 54

Printed in Great Britain
by Amazon